Penis Politics

Penis Politics

A Memoir of Women, Men & Power

Karen Hinton

SARTORIS
LITERARY
GROUP

SARTORIS LITERARY GROUP
Metro-Jackson, Mississippi
www.sartorisliterary.com

*To our daughters who will be stronger women, and our sons
who will be fairer, kinder men;
& to mine in particular, Tali, Sarah, Erica and Zach.*

CONTENTS

Prologue
Speaking Up

Snuggled on the couch in my apartment overlooking the French Quarter in New Orleans in the spring of 2021, I listened in horror to Charlotte Bennett on *CBS Evening News* as she described New York Governor Andrew Cuomo's attempts to groom and seduce her. Bennett had been Cuomo's twenty-five-year-old executive assistant. She also is a survivor of sexual assault, as Cuomo was well aware.

With Bennett alone in his office during the workday, the Governor told her he was "lonely...tired" and wanted "to be touched."

"Do you believe he was propositioning you?" *CBS News* anchor Nora O'Donnell asked.

"Yes," Bennett said, loud and clear.

"For what?" O'Donnell asked for clarity.

"Sex," Bennett said loud and clear again.

At sixty-two, Cuomo didn't mind dating a woman her age, Bennett said. Had *she* dated an older man? Would *she* consider dating an older man?

Bennett did not go public for several months about the inappropriate conversations with the most powerful man in New York. She felt ashamed, for a time, because "people always put the onus on the women to shut that conversation down...and by answering (him) I was somehow engaging or enabling it, when in fact, I was terrified," she said.

"I was scared to imagine what would happen if I rejected him, so I disappeared instead. My time in public service ended because he was bored and lonely."

I understood what it meant to disappear.

Though I was far from New York and from my own time working for Andrew Cuomo, I immediately understood Bennett.

A week before Bennett first went public, the *New York Daily News* published a piece I wrote about the phenomenon of what I termed "penis politics," based on my four decades of experience working with powerful men. I defined penis politics as a man in a position of authority using gender to control and dominate. Men like this need women but rarely value them. This kind of man needs to feed his ego and hide his insecurities, often at the expense of the women who surround and support him. Penis politics, I wrote, is not always about sex but it's always about gender.

Andrew Cuomo and other powerful men in politics often create a public image as a champion of women's rights and equality. Behind closed doors, they use gender domination to assert their power over women. Andrew, who I had known since 1995, isn't the only practitioner of penis politics. He just happens to be a master of the art.

If Bennett's story resonated with me, Cuomo's reaction infuriated me. He followed the classic playbook of a man credibly accused of sexual harassment or abuse: He said women "misinterpreted" him, but as the facts against him mounted and proved any misinterpretation of his actions was no defense, he simply denied the truth and called the women liars. Finally, he went on the attack and claimed he was the victim. His denials and attacks on the women pushed me to recount my own history with Cuomo in a series of interviews after Bennett came forward.

Bennett coming forward personified the difference between Cuomo's eleven accusers and myself: I had experienced and observed different forms of sexual harassment and abuse during my life and career and the only time I spoke up, I lost two jobs.

After that, I decided to stay silent for over twenty years until I watched Bennett's interview when she had to relive her own past abuse on national television as I curled up on my couch in a fetal position.

His entire life, Andrew Cuomo always played right to the edge. It served him well for a long time, propelling him to Housing Secretary, New York Attorney General and Governor. He had his share of successes. Yet the more power he gained, the more daring—and reckless—he became.

When I was Andrew's press secretary at the U.S. Department of Housing and Urban Development, he told me a story about when he was in college and his father Mario Cuomo was New York Secretary of State. Andrew and a friend of his were standing next to his father's state car, waiting for Mario to finish up an event. The college-aged Andrew and his friend passed the time by comparing the attributes of breasts of women they knew: Who had large "titties," who had small ones, and the pros and cons of how to handle each. They were beside themselves with laughter. The window came down. Unknown to them, Mario was in the car already and heard every word. The laughter stopped. Mario Cuomo was fuming. "Don't ever talk that way again about women, whether I hear it or not," Mario lectured Andrew. No wink, wink, nod, nod from Mario Cuomo to his son. Andrew Cuomo told New Yorkers on the day he resigned, that "the lines" on behavior by men toward women had moved as he grew older. But Mario knew where the line was, even forty years earlier, and he tried to teach his son, one future Governor to another.

Andrew was a world class flirt at HUD. But what began as mostly (but not always) harmless flirting evolved to outright harassment and abuse by the time he was in his last term as Governor.

Yet this book is not about Andrew Cuomo, though he plays a role in it. The focus of the book is on women and how they deal with men who abuse their authority over women, as told through my experiences in mostly political environments. In politics, there's a toxic brew of ego, entitlement, power, testosterone and a "bro culture" that is especially difficult for women to navigate.

In rural Mississippi, I learned lessons in penis politics early in life from my interactions with high school coaches and principals, boyfriends, college professors, newspaper editors, lovers and politicians (including Bill Clinton, when he was still a future President). Along the way, I struggled to master strategies for dealing with men of power that many women will recognize from their own lives. While the details of their stories may vary from mine, what remains consistent are the ways in which misogyny, sex and discrimination shape how girls and women view themselves and their options, as well as the

iii

ways women often build a trusted coterie of girls and women around themselves simply to survive.

Several years ago, while serving as Mayor Bill de Blasio's press secretary, I told a group of young women working in NYC's City Hall that "you're damned if you speak up, damned if you shut up." But the women who came forward about Cuomo — and Harvey Weinstein and Bill Cosby and so many others since the dawn of the #MeToo movement — may have proven me wrong. When New York Attorney General Tish James released her investigation of the allegations made by Cuomo's accusers, she said, "I believe these eleven women."

I wish that the women of a generation ago—my women friends and I— had found enough courage to believe in ourselves and speak up in a world in which we would be believed.

At sixteen, my coterie of high school girlfriends and I stayed silent about a sexual assault on one of us by the school's head coach. Our silence, as much as the assault itself, changed the trajectory of all of our lives.

It took me a long time to learn that it's better to pay the cost of speaking up, loud and clear.

I ran outside to blow air inside the holes of doodlebug sand beds in the ground, repeating several times the phrase, "Doodlebug, doodlebug, your house is on fire" into each one. I tried to scare a doodlebug out of his sand house, taking a tiny stick or a piece of grass and twirling it inside his sand hole. Sometimes he climbed out of his itty-bitty sand bed, leaving a scribbly trail behind him. Was he a good or a bad bug? The trail was my tale.

"Doodlebug, doodlebug, your house is on fire!"

—A Mississippi children's rhyme sung to scare hidden doodlebugs from their holes.

Part 1
The Coterie

C h a p t e r 1

The Bookroom

Midnight was our secret place for serious meetings. That's why I knew to pay close attention to the tense clip in Janice's voice when she called that summer afternoon in 1974. She had to see us at the old, abandoned rail car in a growth of woods near our high school in Soso. I remember the day as one of those most important moments, burned into one's brain cells: it was July, the hottest, muggiest month of the year in Mississippi when a trip to a swimming pond couldn't wait. Except if Janice, my best friend, called for a meeting on the Midnight Train.

She needed to talk. Straight away.

"It's about Coach," she said.

We'd named Midnight Train after the Gladys Knight song we loved to sing as loud as possible out the open windows of Myrtle, a 1954 Lincoln Capri my momma had bought me for $1,500 from Preacher Brent not long after I got my driver's license earlier that summer. Myrtle was gray, but I later painted her yellow. The yellow screamed attention.

17

Midnight, though, was hidden. It was a passenger car, off its tracks and forgotten. Onboard the train that never moved, we often gathered at twilight, when a little light remained above the horizon. As the car darkened, we beamed our flashlights through the dust and told ghost stories or stayed outside on the grass and stared at her, with the fireflies surrounding it and the stars sparkling above.

We had discovered the rail car years before, near the tracks that carried the 3:14 p.m. train through Soso every day. Most days during the summers, when we were in junior high, we chased the 3:14 until it pulled away from sight down the tracks. We ran alongside that train until our legs and lungs burned to get in shape for the upcoming basketball season, sometimes with the idea of jumping onto one of the open freight cars to leave our small, rural town forever — or, at least, for the summer. It was easy to jump trains, we told our classmates, and we'd ride for free by hiding in a car.

Of course, we never jumped a train out of town. We only chased them, watching as they pulled into the distance, off to some far-flung place far away from tiny Soso.

I did as Janice asked and called Libby and Maggie. The four of us— sixteen years old and between our sophomore and junior years at West Jones High School—were best friends. We told each other everything about everything, sharing our deepest, darkest secrets. Like a lock on a door, we fastened ourselves to each other and thought only thieves, or worse, could release us. That's what I told Janice once. Our favorite English teacher, Mrs. Cook, took to calling us "the coterie." We didn't know the word's origins, and it seemed vaguely foreign, but we liked the way "coterie" sounded, and we liked sharing secrets.

"Janice wants to talk about Coach Waters, but I don't know what about," I said to Maggie on the drive to Midnight.

"I've told y'all a hundred times Coach has always been hot for her. Always has been," Maggie said. "I brought the lists, just in case we need them."

18

We kept a growing collection of our favorite curse words and a running list of individual questions about boys, sex and other topics, which one or all four of us showcased at our Midnight meetings. Was the boy under discussion sexy *and* handsome, or just sexy? Could he kiss? Did he wear braces? Would he try to touch our boobs? Did he always have a condom stuck in his jean's pocket? Should he be the one to have sex with one day, one night? None of us had had sex yet. Maggie had come closest, with a finger fuck.

When we arrived, Janice and Libby were inside Midnight, waiting for us. The old railway car had passenger seats intact but tattered and layered with dust. Yet it smelled like the wildflowers growing beside it. Janice was standing near one of the seats with her head down, a stream of tears covering her face.

Janice never cried. Ever. She wasn't a crier.

Even as her body trembled and her face reddened, Janice was still beautiful. She always had been when she was smiling, when she was angry, and now when she was crying. She dried her face on her tee-shirt and told us about what happened that afternoon in the bookroom. Janice worked for the school's front office during the summer, organizing the bookroom and taking breaks there to enjoy the solitude to sit and read.

"I heard the door slam shut and then lock behind me. The noise scared me. I'd been reading *Pride and Prejudice*, and I almost dropped it," Janice told us, as I swatted a dust mote hanging in the seats between us. "I turned around and saw Coach across the room, leaning against a bookshelf with his arms crossed," she said. "He smiled and walked towards me. He was lookin' straight at me."

Janice, though, wouldn't look straight at us. She continued to stare at the floor as she spoke, her voice a little shaky, yet the words poured out to tell her story as quickly as possible. "I wanted to run around him, but there was no way around the shelves. I guessed he was going to try to kiss me, and then he did."

Midnight turned silent. For once, we had nothing to say. I remember feeling so stunned it was almost an emptiness: of all the boys we talked about

19

kissing, we never expected Coach Waters to do something like this. He was nice to me, Maggie and Libby because we were close to Janice, but we took orders from him and complied. He was the coach who had been there the longest, the head coach of the athletic program. Everybody called him Coach, just Coach.

"The kiss shocked me. Then, he kissed me again. I ... I liked it," Janice said, quickly, shuddering, "but I knew he shouldn't have done it. Then he took the book from me and pressed my hand against his zipper."

Maggie grabbed my hand and squeezed it tight. She needed someone to hold onto; she knew bad news was coming. I wondered why Janice had liked his kiss. I wondered what it had felt like.

"He unzipped his pants and pulled out his ... thing. And then he put my sweaty hand on it. It was so hot and muggy in the room that—."

"His thing?" I screamed. "You mean he took your hand and put it on his cock?"

"Shutup, Karen," Libby demanded. "Don't say that word!"

Libby pronounced my name "Kay- run," like my momma did when she was cross with me.

This was the first time one of us had seen or touched a real penis. We had seen them in porn magazines (loaned to us by boys) during sleepover parties and our discreet gatherings in our abandoned railway car. Sitting on the torn seats, we scanned page after page of pictures packed with penises and pussies. Leaning into each other, we would scream, look at each other in shock, and then laugh loudly, crowing, kicking our legs and feet into the air.

"Don't say cock?" I said. "We say it all the time!" We rarely called it a penis. We used what seemed like dozens of other names for penis on our lists of forbidden words from music, books, movies, and the porn magazines. Was *cock* or *peter* a more descriptive word than *penis*? Did we want a magazine with *cunts* and *cocks* in it or just *vaginas* and *penises*? Was there a difference?

Whatever we called it, Janice said Coach's was hard.

"Janice, he should not have forced you to touch him anywhere. That's all

I'm sayin'," I declared.

Janice suddenly flopped her body down on the dusty, musty train seat and pulled herself into a fetal position. Libby stroked her shoulder, her hand, her head, trying to comfort her. Maggie and I looked at each other. We knew Janice had more to tell us.

"We can handle this, Janice," Libby said. "You don't have to. We can talk to Coach or tell his wife or even Principal Sawyer."

Janice immediately sat up, throwing Libby off her. "No! Don't tell anyone anything. Only you three can know. No one else."

"Why no one else?" I asked.

"Because! They'll think it's my fault! They will blame me," Janice hollered. She was hysterical, eyes bugged, body rigid.

"Yeah!" "Okay!" "Sure!" We all agreed, just to get her to calm down.

It was unclear to me what really had happened with Coach. I knew Janice even better than her sisters knew her, and I could tell she wasn't sharing everything. Did she scream at him to stop? Did she hit him? Did he hit her? Did they do something more than Janice was confiding? Why did she like his kiss? He wasn't that good-looking. He had a poochy stomach, a big nose and was shorter than me. But what did I know about looks?

"Look," I said, as these questions drifted through my mind. "We'll all have sex soon. We shouldn't be afraid to talk about a pecker."

In the face of my rambling about cocks, Maggie took charge. "We need a plan. Janice, you should call the school office in the morning and tell them you're sick and can't work in the bookroom for the rest of the summer. Plus, basketball practice starts soon. You'd need to quit, anyway. We'll meet at your house tomorrow morning to hear how the call goes. Libby will drive you back home tonight. You should rest, and we can talk more tomorrow."

Janice nodded her head, slowly; she was almost catatonic, as she leaned against Libby, arms folded. Her eyes were lidded, almost glazed. We huddled together and hugged each other, watching the sunset through Midnight's streaky windows.

21

On the drive home, I wondered about Janice and Coach. Janice wasn't pushy or hateful. Maybe that's why she didn't stop him? She was decisive and strong, but sometimes too nice.

"Maybe Janice let him have sex with her," Maggie said, as if she were reading my thoughts. "Maybe she didn't. It doesn't matter, though. He did something very fucked up." She paused. "Nothing will ever happen to Coach. Never. He won't be questioned or punished, much less arrested. Maybe a quick slap on the wrist from Principal Sawyer."

"Fuck Coach. He should get more than just a slap on the wrist, you know what I mean?" I asked. It seemed like the right thing to ask. I was angry at Coach, even a little at Janice for liking his kiss, for letting him do it. And I didn't know what to do with that anger. I didn't know where to direct it. I only knew that if I didn't direct it somewhere, it would hang around my neck forever.

The next morning, I was first to arrive at Janice's house, located in the middle of the woods near a pond surrounded by trees. Like my house, Janice's had no air conditioning, and we were suffering in the morning heat. Janice paced her bedroom, trying to cool herself with a fan bearing the face of Jesus she had taken from a church service.

"I hear Maggie's car," Janice said, as she picked up dirty clothes and shoes, threw them in the closet, and grabbed several clean towels from the bathroom. Janice hollered at Maggie and Libby as they walked into the house. "Let's go for a swim first."

She was buying time. The coterie stripped and dove into the pond naked. We were never shy about taking off our clothes. The first time we saw each other naked was in the basketball locker room, where we took showers after practice. When we were old enough to think about what we looked like, we compared what we had or didn't have. Maggie, Janice and I had no boobs. Libby had them, but she and I were super skinny and straight, without Janice's curvy build, her skin brown even in winter, her long legs and dark eyes. Maggie was curvy, too — but short.

Janice walked into the shallow end of the pond taking the towels to the small pier that stretched out to the deepest end. We followed, spreading the towels on the pier and laying naked in the sun after a short dip, listening silently for a few minutes to a battery radio and letting the warmth cradle then dry us off.

Janice spoke first. "I called the school. It's all set. No more bookroom."

"That's a relief," said Maggie.

Silence. Almost overwhelming silence.

"The sun feels so good after a swim," said Libby, whose soaring, lovely voice joined a Tommy James & the Shondells' song, "Crystal Blue Persuasion," playing on the radio.

"It does," Maggie agreed, "but the sun is arisin', and I'm now hot as hell."

Janice sighed and said, "Someone is cutting their grass nearby. I can't hear the lawnmower, but I can smell the grass. Can't you? I love that smell." She paused. "Jump in the pond to cool off, then let's go inside."

It was going to be a really hot day, we could tell. We covered ourselves with our towels and mimicked the bullfrogs' croaking as we headed for the house, racing to Janice's room. We sat on her bed, our hair dripping wet, still naked.

"You know we get special treatment from Coach because we're on the basketball team," Janice said, slowly, choosing her words, standing up in front of us. "How he always gives us passes when we're late for class. How he's always so nice to us." She took a deep breath, then her voice dropped almost too quiet to hear. "He scared me in the bookroom, though. I wanted him to kiss me. But then he dropped his pants and made me touch his thing and I wanted him to leave me alone. I yanked my hand away from him, but he tried to push my shoulders down and put my mouth on ... you know ..."

We sat with our eyes on her, our mouths open.

"I started crying, and then he stopped. He stood me up with his hands under my arms and pulled me close," said Janice, mimicking the bookroom scene like a game of charades. "His thing was up against my shorts, and he

23

whispered in my ear, 'Relax, Janice.' And then he said, 'Let me touch your pussy.'"

"Janice!" interrupted Libby. "That is so nasty. He said the word pussy?"

"Yes!" Janice cried. "He was so nasty! He put his hand down my shorts. I screamed at him to stop, but he didn't, and then he said, 'I love you. You're so beautiful. I've wanted you for so long. Please let me touch you.' Blah, blah, blah.'" She stopped, breathing as hard as she would in a train chase. "Part of me wanted to run away, part of me wanted him to kiss me, and part of me just wanted to make him happy."

"He's a fucking sick old man," I said. "Did you end it?"

Janice didn't answer my question. She sat down beside us.

Maggie looked at me and Libby, then back to Janice, confusion and concern in her eyes. "So," Maggie said, "What do you want us to do now?"

We were a coterie. We were sisters. It was up to us to figure out how to help each other.

"I don't know!" she screamed, jumping up from her bed. "Don't you know that I don't know what to do? How did it end? He asked me to lie down on the floor. I did. He pulled my shorts and panties down. Then, he put his thing into my thing."

"What? His thing into your thing? What does that mean? You mean sex? How did it feel?" asked Libby.

Maggie cut in. "Libby, hush."

Janice stared into space. No one moved or spoke.

Finally, she looked at the three of us and said firmly, with no tears, "I had to tell you. You're my best friends. But you can't tell anyone anything. Not anyone at school, even Principal Sawyer. Nobody, anywhere. If my parents find out, they'll punish me, and other people will think I'm a slut. What about Coach's wife? What will she say?"

We had agreed already to never speak about the kiss. We each took an even more solemn vow that we would never tell the rest of the story, either. Janice was calmer after talking it out and accepting our pledges of silence.

The next day I sprung my idea for revenge on Coach.

***

Coach reminded Janice and me of Gene Hackman in *The French Connection*. They looked a lot alike. We had seen the movie right after school broke for summer at the drive-in across the railroad tracks in Laurel, the closest city to Soso. Janice, Libby and Maggie hid in the trunk, so we only had to pay for one ticket. We snuck into the drive-in a lot on weekends.

In the movie, Hackman thought that being a detective gave him the power to choose between right and wrong. He could break the law or enforce it. We decided Hackman wasn't exactly handsome, though Janice said, "He has a sexy look." We couldn't describe the difference between handsome and sexy, at least not yet.

Coach had been our basketball coach from seventh to ninth grade. I could never remember his first or last name because we never used it. He always gave Janice extra attention. He liked her the best of all the girl basketball players, giving her more one-on-one time on the court, showing her the shots and how to play defense. Janice was becoming a very good basketball player and I was jealous, but not in a resentful way. Everyone, including me, said she was the prettiest girl in school, and she was often praised for her athletic skills, excellent grades, and sweet disposition. She also was a cheerleader, unbelievably.

I wanted to be just like her. Maggie and Libby did, too.

The day after we got the full story of the "bookroom kiss," as we would later and always refer to it, I laid out my revenge plan to the coterie. It revolved around our typing class. We'd already had one year of typing and dreaded having to take a second year when we returned to school in the fall. Boys only had to take one year. The typing teacher was a Black woman, Miss Curtis, who sounded like she had a sore throat all the time. She was a smart, demanding teacher and should have taught something other than typing, but that is what she got stuck with. We liked Miss Curtis, but we didn't like typing, and we were pissed that girls had to take more typing than boys.

"I don't understand why we have to take two typing classes when boys only have to take one," I said to Janice. "Coach should clear all of our late or absentee slips so we can miss typing class at least once a week. He can make that happen. That will be his payment for what he did, Janice. Since we can't tell anyone about it."

Janice agreed with the plan, but she didn't want to confront Coach with us. Maggie thought it was a stupid idea but hanging out in the gym dressing room on our missing-in-typing day was reason enough to torture Coach.

"I don't think it's a stupid idea," Libby said. "I don't think" were her first words after a two-hour discussion on the pros and cons of our revenge plan. Libby mostly liked our ideas. She didn't speak up often.

"Why not?" Maggie asked.

"Because it's all we can do. If we put holes in his car tires, it will make him mad. Meanwhile we get nothing." With the pink slips, we got something.

The next day, Maggie, Libby and I approached Coach near the Coke trailer, where I worked during summer school to sell snacks and Cokes during class breaks. The three of us motioned him into the trailer with the doors and the big serving window open. Class break had ended, and no one was around.

"Coach, we wanna tell you something," I told him. "We need to talk now."

"Okay, girls," Coach said. He smelled of Old Spice, a cologne worn by most forty-something Mississippi men. I wondered if Janice had noticed his smell in the bookroom.

We all stood in the trailer, looking at each other. I had told Libby and Maggie that I could deliver the demand because I wasn't afraid. At that moment, though, I was shaking all over. Worried I couldn't speak clearly, I blurted it all out at once: "Janice told us about the bookroom and how you pulled out your you-know-what in front of her and had sex."

Coach eyed us warily and shook his head back and forth like a windshield wiper. "Now, girls, that's not true."

Maggie laughed, then Libby shot back, "You think Janice is a liar? We don't." She sang it more than said it.

Coach spread his hands, palms up. "I'm a liar? Come on, girls. Janice was upset. I tried to help her, and she didn't understand I was just being kind. I would never …"

I interrupted him. "Understand? She didn't understand you had a you-know-what?"

Maggie jumped right in. "Here's the deal, Coach. We all have to take Miss Curtis' second typing class, but we already know how to type. Once a week, we will skip class, and you will write a pass for us to do something that sounds like we are helping the school. If you don't write the pass, we will tell on you. Also, you have to make sure we get an A from Miss Curtis." The demand for an A hadn't been part of the plan, but Maggie was on a roll.

Coach grew nervous and fidgety as Maggie spoke. His eyes darted down. Amazingly, he agreed. He didn't try to change our minds. He just wanted out of the Coke trailer. He pushed us hastily aside, exiting quickly. He was sweating. We were sweating, too. Then, it was over.

Libby said, "He's a sick fuck!" I grew to love those two words. Coach really was a sick fuck.

Janice cried more when she heard the news that he said she was lying. I wondered if her reaction meant she might still want to see him, or if her tears proved that she would be blamed if the news ever got out. We agreed it was best for her to ignore any future advances. The passes gave us the freedom to hang out in the gym with Janice, plan plots against our enemies, or organize parties with friends instead of typing class.

A few days after the bookroom kiss, we chased the 3:14 train, but with less effort and enthusiasm than in the past. Afterwards, lazing around in the rail car, I tried to liven up the conversation. "I've decided I want a guy with a small dick. It won't hurt as much. Of course, it's hard to tell until he takes his pants off and gets hard. If it gets bigger, then what do I do?"

Libby and Maggie snickered, but Janice stared out the window, watching bumblebees flit around Midnight and the flowers nearby.

The last few weeks of that summer, Janice lost interest in our conversations. She had stopped talking about *Pride and Prejudice* or any of her favorite books. She was losing interest in us. Her mind was taking her to other places, as though she was listening to a song or watching a movie or reading a book we could neither see nor hear.

Chapter 2
Last in Everything

Back in junior high, our home economics teacher told us that paychecks in Mississippi were a lot less than paychecks for people in the other forty-nine states. Our health teacher told us many Mississippians never saw a doctor often enough to care for their health. She also said we had too many fat people; we ate too much bad food made with lard, butter and sugar. Our history teacher said too many of our babies died at birth. Mississippi was first in poverty and last in education, he told us.

One day after school, I asked Daddy, didn't he think we should move from Mississippi to Alabama or Louisiana or even Florida so we wouldn't be last in everything?.

"We need to get a better reputation," I told him. "Because most people ..." Daddy cut me off.

"Life is a competition, Kat," he said, calling me by his chosen nickname for me. "You have to compete to be first. It's not about which state you live in," he continued as he sketched a building plan on what he called his architect's desk. He wasn't an architect, though. He was a commercial contractor with an eighth-grade education who taught himself how to engineer a building.

"Most people up North think we are dumb," I shot back, in my own eighth grade voice. With a pencil and a ruler, Daddy continued to sketch, draw, erase and sketch again, ignoring me.

"Well, I can't leave Mississippi now, anyway. I can't leave my friends," I conceded.

"Go help your momma cook dinner," he said without looking up.

"Momma thinks I'm last in cookin' too," I said loudly, stomping from his home office, near the garage.

By the time school started, Janice said everything had ended with Coach. We weren't sure she was telling the truth, but we accepted her answer. If anything had happened again and if she didn't tell us, it was a breach of the coterie compact.

The coterie compact had identified five types of males, always up for discussion: friends who were boys, boys we dated or boyfriends, coaches, principals and finally fathers. Brothers were a passing nuisance, and male teachers were few and far between.

Women did most of the teaching, and our principals were men, usually former coaches. All the types, boys or men, had one thing in common: criticizing and making fun of us. They rarely encouraged us to feel good about ourselves. Male coaches lost their tempers at games; principals and preachers demanded respect but seldom returned it, and fathers disappeared, ignored their daughters, or just didn't know how to talk to them.

"Karen, what is wrong with you tonight? You need to learn how to jump higher, honey," shouted somebody else's father, who was a member of my church, as I hustled down the basketball court during one game.

"*Shut the fuck up*," I thought as I walked past him after the game, smiling sweetly and waving at him nicely.

What the Soso coterie wanted more than anything was to be close to each other, washing the dust and dirt from each other's faces after our train chases, brushing the tangles out of our hair, sharing advice about boys and basketball, learning how to curse, grabbing a bottle of Coca-Cola and a Moon Pie from Mr. Shotts' grocery store after school before heading home or skinny-dipping in a pond during the seven steamy months of the year.

Janice was the book lover. I was obsessed with movies. Maggie and Libby sang. Actually, Libby sang more than she talked. At least once a week, the four of us wore jeans and the exact same shirt to West Jones High School, usually a purple and green one bought at TG&Y, the local general store. Some of our classmates speculated we were queer, but we didn't care. We encouraged the rumor by holding hands and blowing kisses to each other.

But most days, the train chase was all that mattered to Janice, Maggie, Libby and me in junior high.

Before we heard the whistle of the train, we walked along a bumpy, dirt road that led to the tracks. The spot was where students, older than we were, kissed in parked cars late at night on the weekends, even after Sunday night church services.

At fourteen, the coterie was less interested in kissing and more interested in running faster and scoring more basketball goals. The path beside the tracks was uneven, rocky, and in some spots covered with Bahia grass. We sometimes tripped or stumbled, turning ankles and stubbing toes. We also put our hair into ponytails to keep the breeze from the train cars from blowing strands into our faces. Except Libby, whose walnut brown hair was short and wavy around her head.

We never beat the train, but Janice usually beat the rest of us.

We also realized that no matter who won the race, we were girls and we were from Soso, Mississippi, population 434, which meant we were destined to be last in pretty much everything else.

Maggie, who rarely won the chase on her petite legs, said she didn't want

31

to hear the train sounds and swore we needed sounds in our minds to mask the noise. "Let's sing this to ourselves as we run: 'Don't stop runnin'. Faster. Don't stop runnin'. Faster. Don't stop runnin'. Faster.'"

We tried to keep up with the train and make the chase last as long as possible. Legs burning, we ran until our lungs collapsed. We still managed to pump barrels of laughter out of our chests as we let the chase end, the train moving out of sight.

"Goddamn, I'm going to faint," whined Maggie.

"I'm an Olympic champ!" screamed Libby, jumping up and down when she stopped.

"We won!" shouted Janice, waving her arms back and forth.

"No, I lost. I hate y'all," I said with my hands on my hips, breathing harder than them all.

When the train pulled away, we gave it the bird or screamed curse words from our list. One day we would leave Mississippi and be allowed to curse whenever and wherever we wanted. For now, curse words could only be uttered among the four of us.

"Fuck you, train! I'll beat you next time!" I boasted.

"Kiss my ass, engineer!" hollered Libby, who then suddenly dropped her shorts to pee.

"Go to hell, too!" said Janice. "Hell is right around that curve!"

***

Our town of Soso had one main road that wasn't so much a Main Street as it was a road that people used to drive to Laurel, the county seat, about ten miles away. It was said that before the town was founded, the postman who dropped by every so often would always respond "so-so" to a question about how he was feeling. That's how the town earned its name. That's pretty much how Soso is still doing today: so-so. More roads were dirt than paved. Families lived in modest houses or trailers, with a fair number of rundown shacks with large families of kids, cats and dogs. Their homes were flimsy; good enough to protect them from the sun and rain but not from the tornadoes that often twirled through Soso. Piney woods surrounded this area of Mississippi. The thick growth of trees kept us buffered from the outside world. Soso had been a bustling logging town way back when, but it was quiet now, especially for teenage girls.

If you wanted to do serious shopping, or go to a movie, you had to go to Laurel. Some people might have considered Laurel to be a small town but compared to Soso, it was lively. It had a traditional downtown with a movie theater—we pronounced it "thee-ATE-her"—which was very grand. The Arabian thee-ATE-her sat next to the Pinehurst Hotel, a majestic building with over a hundred rooms from Laurel's long gone lumber and oil heyday. Along the highway from Laurel to Soso, strip malls had begun to appear in the '70s, along with McDonald's and Hardee's. In turn, businesses began to disappear in the quaint, small downtown, either going out of business or moving to the strip mall.

Still, we always wanted to go to town, Laurel, to do something more than just pick peas in the garden and shell butterbeans on our porches in Soso.

While the houses in Jones County were mostly small, many of the families were big. Both of my parents came from families with nine children. Daddy had six brothers and three sisters, but one of the "sisters" was an illegitimate child of an actual sister. Few people knew that back then, though. Most of them were born in a dogtrot house in Soso, to a father who drank way too much. The father, Josh, and the mother, Jackie—my grandparents—died before I was born. My mother's parents lived two hours away in Louisville, near Philadelphia. They married when Mamaw was fourteen, and Papaw was eighteen.

Mamaw immediately got pregnant with twins, but they died at birth. Mamaw got pregnant again a year later and went on to give birth to seven more children over a twenty-year period. Mamaw and Papaw pumped out babies primarily to help them work on a tenant farm they worked. Papaw worked long hours every day picking cotton, and Mamaw joined him in between pregnancies. They and their children milked cows and churned butter

33

in the mornings. The kids walked to school, and my grandparents made their way to the field. Momma and her siblings joined them from a young age after school and on Saturdays. The man who owned the tenant farm paid Papaw five cents for a pound of cotton. The landowner got seventeen to twenty cents by the pound in 1935. Sometimes my papaw and mamaw had to take a loan from the landowner to pay for clothes and shoes. He also would provide food and other supplies until harvest time. They would pay him from the crops they raised that year. Sometimes he would keep over half of the money my grandparents earned from working the field.

Their life wasn't that different from their parents. Both sets of family—my momma's and my daddy's—were extremely poor. Very little of daily life in rural Mississippi had changed for poor whites and all Blacks between the start of the Civil War until the end of the Great Depression. I guessed my life was pretty good by comparison, and my parents had more time for their two children.

My daddy came to see a few of my basketball games in junior high. He was older than most parents at the games; he was forty-eight when my momma gave birth to me at thirty-one. She had my brother fourteen months later. She told me Daddy didn't want children until he had enough money to build our house, but he never told Momma he was ready to have children until one night he didn't pull out while making love.

When they were first married, Momma and Daddy lived in a small yellow office trailer parked on the twenty acres of piney woods he owned. They had a bunk bed in the office but no toilet. Momma would drive up to Mr. Shotts' grocery store to take a number two in his bathroom. The woods behind the trailer were good enough for number one. After Daddy finished jobs at construction sites, he saved excess concrete and other materials and stored them in his warehouse, at the bottom of a hill not far from the trailer. At the top of the hill, he slowly replaced the yellow trailer with our house, using the leftover building supplies and buying the things he needed with the money he had earned from his jobs. He was a saver, not a spender.

34

Daddy built the house with concrete walls, and Momma had the two babies, my brother and me. I hated the concrete. All my pictures or banners or news articles on my bedroom walls had to be hung with glue hooks, and the dankness of the Mississippi summers made the walls sweat. After a day of high humidity, the pictures and anything else glued to the walls fell to the floor. The only good thing about a concrete house was the protection it provided from hurricanes and tornadoes. We never worried about strong winds and heavy rains like most of our neighbors. I just worried about the heat.

Daddy only spent money for what we needed, not wanted. Our neighbor had an air conditioner, and I would run over to their house to stand in front of it. Daddy finally generated some relief for us during the windless days of summer with huge, homemade electrical fans made from four sheets of wood on the top, bottom, and sides, standing about four feet high. We sat them in different parts of the house to move the listless air around the rooms. My brother Robbie, a year younger than me, called it "less hotter air." When we were around six or seven, Robbie and I would sit in front of the cool fans and sing or yell into them, as the blades moved, making our voices quiver until Momma told us to hush.

At church, Daddy always wore a very fashionable hat. He had bought several for church and dances, though the dances had been part of his past. He looked like someone famous when he wore one of his two good suits, like a combination of Bing Crosby and Frank Sinatra. At work, he dressed in dark gray cotton pants and a shirt to match. When his construction site closed around 4 p.m., he headed out to the Soso farm where he fed the cows and two horses, worked in the garden or hay field, or just hung out talking to his three brothers who lived on or near the farm. He usually pulled up our dirt driveway to the house five hours later.

Daddy and his brothers smoked cigars, pipes, and cigarettes or chewed tobacco and snuff. I didn't like the smell or mess of tobacco. I hated to clean up the nasty remains, but I had decided to keep our concrete house spotless.

When my friends or my brother's friends walked into the house with mud or dirt on their shoes or feet, I grabbed the mop and cleaned up after them as they walked down the hallway and into the kitchen or the dining room or a bedroom.

"Karen, please stop," Momma whispered to me the first time I chased our friends with the mop. "You are making your friends feel bad. That's not nice. Clean up after they leave."

"No," my twelve-year-old self said. "I don't want dirt to ruin the floor. Why should anyone care if I follow them around with a mop? They don't have to do anything. I'm the only one workin'."

My cleaning compulsion and Daddy's tobacco habits led to a serious showdown in the summer of 1970. My brother and I went with our momma to her parent's home. Our papaw had passed the year before, and Momma wanted to check on Mamaw. We stayed for two weeks, leaving Daddy to himself. When we returned, the house on the hill was a disaster full of grunge and tobacco filth.

Daddy often chewed tobacco when he watched the nightly news or the *Dean Martin Show* in a rocking chair near the back door. He loved Dean Martin and Joey Heatherton, the sexy singer and dancer who often appeared on the show, so much so that he would wait until the very last second before forced to leave his rocking chair and spit out his tobacco juice onto the back porch. It really wasn't a porch, just dirt with a porch swing and a spot for the push lawn mower. I often told him to stop spitting on the ground, but for some reason he never did.

For two weeks, the spit and what I called the tobacco turds had collected on the floor from the rocking chair inside to the porch outside. He also didn't clean his shoes from his construction work or the farm, and dirt had dried on almost every floor. No one was there to mop up after he fell asleep or make the beds after he woke up. When I saw his tobacco juice, his shoe dirt and unkept bed, I ran to him and complained.

"Why did you mess up the house? Now I have to clean it."

"That's right," he said. "That's your job. That's why I have you around.

36

To clean up the house."

"That's not what a daddy is supposed to say," I said.

"Yes, it is. Now get the broom and the mop and get to work, young lady."

"I get to work all the time, old man," I said. My voice lowered on "old man" because I already knew I was going to be in big trouble.

"Kat, you want to bring me my leather strap?" Daddy asked. If Robbie and I were going to get a whipping, we had to bring the weapon to Momma and Daddy both. That was the rule.

Daddy didn't make that threat idly; I watched him use the leather strap on Robbie once, although I never got a whipping from Daddy. Momma, however, switched Robbie and me all the time with a small branch from a bush or tree. She switched us so good one time, she rubbed Vaseline all over our legs to try and remove the red stripes before Daddy returned home. She knew he'd be mad for beating us too hard.

I ran for my broom and mop to do my job, but I was spitting angry. Robbie laughed at me, and Momma gave me a quick kiss and ignored me. Robbie and I loved our daddy, even though we didn't really know much about him. I don't think Momma did, either. He was just the boss. He made all the decisions. He wasn't around a lot, either. Momma cooked, cleaned and shopped, earning her wifely salary from Daddy's checking account each week, from the same account that paid his construction workers and his secretary, a woman. Momma always wanted her job, but Daddy said no. He'd always hand Momma the wifely check on Friday afternoon, about the same as everybody else. When he did, Momma would ask, "That's it? Can I get $10 more?"

"No, that's it," he said, answering both questions with a cigar hanging from his mouth. He reduced the paycheck once when he bought some deer meat on his own, subtracting the cost from Momma's paycheck because, he said, the deer meat was groceries. It tasted terrific, but Daddy's cigars stank up the house. Momma stayed madder about the checks than the cigars.

Maybe it was the weekly paycheck for staying home and not having her own job or the tobacco turds or his long work hours that drove Momma and

Daddy apart. They didn't talk to each other much. They slept in separate bedrooms, Momma usually sleeping with either Robbie or me or both of us. Daddy slept alone on a twin bed with a large slab of wood under one mattress. Momma never left him, though. She loved him. They rarely argued in front of us, except for one fight. I only heard part of the argument. Daddy handed Momma a check for $500 and told her to leave the house.

"Here, take this and leave," he said.

She told him, "I'm not leaving you for $500. If you want to get rid of me, it will take a hell of a lot more money than that." Maybe that was why she switched us so often. Maybe she was really switching him.

The day Daddy died, Robbie and I were playing one-on-one basketball down the hill from the house, near Daddy's warehouse. By this time Robbie was thirteen, and I was fourteen. Robbie had grown taller and ran faster than me. He also was good at stealing the ball and scoring. He beat me that afternoon, for the first time. It was January 17, 1973, but not too cold to play ball outside in Mississippi. I didn't notice Daddy watching us play from the warehouse.

"You are a cheat! I hate you!" I hollered unfairly at Robbie. "You don't know how to play basketball. You just know how to cheat."

Robbie laughed and laughed and laughed, lying down on the ground, rolling in the dirt, and standing up to skip around the basketball goal. "I beat Karen! I beat Karen!" he crowed.

I looked up and saw Daddy as he leaned against his warehouse door, smoking a pipe and smiling about the fact I'd lost my first one-on-one to Robbie. "Why are you staring at me?" I screamed at Daddy. "Your son is a cheat! I'm not playing against him anymore!"

My daddy puffed on his pipe, grinning. "You just need to get better."

"I can't believe you just said that to me. Robbie is a cheat!" Tears flowed down my face, I was so upset I had lost. I never wanted to lose.

I ran fast up the hill to the house, screaming loud enough for the whole neighborhood to hear that I would not go to the farm with the two of them to help Daddy, something we often did when homework was done. "I'm staying with Momma! She loves me!"

I watched Daddy and Robbie drive away in Daddy's new truck, a 1972 gold El Camino, from the big windows in the dining room, then fell on my bed and cried. A few minutes later, I went to the bathroom and took a hot bath. I filled the tub to the top and floated underneath the water, looking up at the ceiling, thinking that my loss to Robbie marked the beginning of the end of my basketball career. I would have to study all the time. Oddly, I began thinking about my father being so old, at sixty-one. I thought about how he might die soon. I thought about what I would wear to his funeral.

While I was in the tub, I heard Momma talking on the phone, her voice getting louder and more upset, clearly agitated. I jumped out of the tub and grabbed a towel. Momma was leaning against the refrigerator in the kitchen with her hands on her face. She turned, looked at me, and spoke forcefully. I couldn't get a read on her emotions.

"We need to drive to the hospital. Red"— my father, nicknamed after his red hair and how his face and neck would get red after a long day's work on the farm —"is in the emergency room."

On the way to the hospital, I said, "We can't let Daddy go to the farm again and work. He works too hard. Can we tell him, Momma?"

"Yes, of course, we can," she said. "Everything is gonna be fine. Don't worry."

At the hospital, a nurse brought us into a room where Robbie was sitting on a stretcher. He was crying, his eyes squeezed tight, his lips purple and trembling. His face, red. He couldn't speak. Then Momma and I saw Daddy on another stretcher, a few feet away from Robbie. He looked dead, pale and unmoving, almost waxen. Our doctor from Soso, Dr. Matthews, told us he was, in fact, dead.

"Robbie drove him to the drugstore from the farm," he said to Momma. "Red looked like he was regaining his strength, and he seemed okay. I gave him a shot. That helped, and I told Robbie to drive him to the hospital in Laurel, and I would follow him directly."

Standing over Daddy as the doctor spoke, Momma glared at him for a few seconds before snapping, "Why in the hell would you ask his thirteen-year-old son to drive him to an emergency room ten miles from Soso?" She turned to Robbie and hugged him close, both sobbing.

As I cried, the doctor held me, and I accidentally let a piece of chewing gum fall from my mouth into his shirt sleeve. I didn't feel embarrassed. I didn't care about his stupid shirt. I no longer had my daddy. Killed by a stupid doctor.

I don't know how we got back home from the hospital. All I remembered was Mamaw, wiping my face with a warm rag while I was on the couch in the TV room, crying. She had been staying with us for several weeks. It was the first and only time Mamaw showed me love.

The neighborhood turned out to our house later that night and the next day. Everybody said Daddy was a great man, but I never heard anyone say that before he died. They talked about his building our church, Trinity Baptist Church, the Sears building in downtown Laurel, the Gardiner Green Shopping Center, and the firehouse. Everyone came over with casseroles and Tupperwares full of dumplings, butter beans, black-eyed peas, fried chicken, banana pudding, pies. Maggie, Libby and Janice came, too, sooner than anyone else. They sat with me in my bedroom, and they cried for me and with me.

Other people floated in and out of my bedroom, too, but the coterie stayed most of the night into the morning. They took turns coming and going. Momma was in the living room, greeting people, but then she disappeared into Daddy's bedroom. Maybe she thought he would be there.

Robbie took a bath, put on a white housecoat, sat on a piano bench, and didn't say much to anybody. I had never seen him in his white housecoat. Momma must have given it to him to wear since everyone from Soso came to pay respects. I never asked her why she put him in a white housecoat. His face was as white as the robe.

A few days after the funeral, Robbie told us the whole story:

"Driving to the farm, Daddy was laughing with me about Karen gettin'

40

so mad about our game at the house. He told me I needed to be nicer, that I was gettin' taller and stronger than Karen. That's what happens with boys and girls, he told me. Before we got to the barn he rubbed his chest and made a face. I asked him what was wrong, and he said, he was fine. After a few minutes, he seemed to be feelin' better.

"He drove into the barn, blew his horn, and the cows started running over from the back of the pasture. They knew it was feedin' time. I started throwing bales of hay into the truck. He was feedin' the horses.

"A few minutes later, I heard him screaming my name, 'Robbie. Robbie. Get over here.' I ran over. He was leaning on a rail and told me, 'Go get me some water from the Big House.' I ran up to the Big House (what we called the family house on the farm). When I got back, he said, 'Take me to the drugstore.' He drank the water and then ripped his shirt and his belt buckle off, so he could breathe and laid down on the ground. I was upset, but I knew I had to pick him up and get him in the truck. I did, and then I hightailed it to the drugstore."

The Soso drugstore is where Dr. Matthews worked two times a week to see patients. I couldn't picture Robbie lifting Daddy, 5' 8" and 230 pounds, up off the ground, into the truck, and driving over the bumpy dirt roads, knowing Daddy had had a heart attack. Maybe some inner panic button had been pressed to enable a thirteen-year-old to do what he couldn't have done otherwise.

"By the time we got to the drugstore, Daddy was spitting up blood. He sat in the truck while I got Dr. Matthews who then gave him a shot. He told me to drive Daddy to the emergency room. He said he would call ahead. I didn't think twice about it. I just did it."

It was then that Robbie had to stop talking to stop the tears. We waited.

"I grabbed his knee in the truck and told him it's gonna be alright. Daddy didn't say much after that. Bales of hay kept falling off the truck; I was driving so fast. Not long after we got on the highway, his head fell into my lap. I screamed, 'Daddy, what's wrong? You, okay?' He didn't say anything. I thought he might have died, then and there. That's when I decided to stop at

41

the Texaco station. The guys at the station said they would call for an ambulance." He looked up at me, his face puffy from the night's tears. He couldn't speak. I didn't know what to say. I was just shocked. Numb.

After the funeral, Momma immediately installed central air conditioning and black-topped the driveway to the house. Even though both had been on her to-do list for a long time, Daddy had refused to spend the money. He left Momma $50,000 – a good bit of money in 1973—and the house and the twenty acres, already paid for. The Social Security checks we received in the mail every month helped, too. I got a check until I graduated from college, and Momma for the rest of her life.

***

I missed a few junior high basketball games after that, but in a couple of weeks, I was back at it on the court. I didn't want anyone to think I was too sad or depressed about losing my daddy. I wanted them to know I was his daughter, and I was following in his footsteps, dominating whatever field I was standing on. I hit the court, steaming with energy. If I rebounded the ball from an opponent's missed shot, I dribbled hard and fast down the court, looking to score. If blocked by defense, I passed to someone ready to shoot. I needed to run and gun. Run and gun. No time to set a play, only to score.

Every night in bed I listened to the '70s song, "Green-Eyed Lady" on my record player. I liked the driving beat of the music, visualizing a run and gun move with my blue eyes closed. Caught in the groove at the end of the record, I jumped out of bed and started the 45 over, again and again. I wanted to make myself better at basketball, like my Daddy told me to do the day he died. My brother, Robbie, had a tougher time. He blamed himself for Daddy's death, and he no longer wanted to run and gun with me in basketball anymore. I kicked the shit out of my grief. He let it weigh heavy on him for a very long time.

For a while, I didn't stop thinking about Daddy. Walking up the hill from the school bus, I hoped he would be in his home office, next to the TV room in the house, drawing a new construction plan on his architect's desk. As each day passed, though, basketball, boys, books, movies and music took up my time and, by the summer of 1973, I didn't dwell on my dead daddy so much. I dwelled on me, Janice, Maggie and Libby. And on pushing myself harder and faster to catch a train out of Soso—to prove that I was my daddy's daughter, even though he had been dead wrong when he said my job was to clean the house. I wasn't going to bargain with my future husband over a paycheck, either.

C h a p t e r 3
A Black Panther

I wasn't the best at anything, but I did practice longer and harder after my daddy died. I got a lot of playing time my freshman year in school. The girls team had six players: two guards, two forwards, and two rovers. The following year we finally played with a smaller squad of five girls, full court, just like the boys. We'd fought for it, too, and more: We wanted the same amount of time as boys to practice during school. We wanted the same number of away games as the boys' team had. We wanted our wins announced on the PA system at school every morning after a game.

We demanded to be allowed to participate in the annual athletic banquet and win awards. Basketball made us stronger and more opinionated than most girls in our class, and it also made us value being part of a team. My sophomore year I worked on moving the ball as fast as I could, trying to avoid set plays and create opportunities to score on the run. It was my run and gun play.

44

Maggie said I reminded her of the Black actress Pam Grier from the movie *Foxy Brown.* "You're turning into Foxy Brown. You don't take shit from nobody."

During summer breaks, I always practiced and kept a log of how many shots I hit at each point on the circle. Almost every day of the week, I aimed shots from all angles of my dirt court. Next to a secret diary that I kept in my closet in a shoebox beneath a pair of worn-out basketball shoes was my "hits" book, where I kept the log of my shots.

"Seven hits out of ten shots on the left wing," read one mark. "Eight of out of ten from the center and seven out of ten bank shots," read another.

If no one from the coterie showed up to shoot with me, my momma would. Robbie had stopped playing ball with me. It reminded him of the day Daddy died. Momma scribbled on my score sheet for the hits book, and she always rewarded me with a banana split from the nearby Dairy Bar.

Coach Michaels was our high school coach. (Not be confused with "Coach" from the bookroom kiss who had been our junior high coach and had been promoted to head coach of our high school.) Before reporting for summer practice, the coterie often compared notes on our informal scrimmages to show Coach Michaels we had improved not just individually, but also as a team.

At practice and in games, he often screamed at us to slow it down and set a play, even though we almost always scored using our rapid-movement shots: my run and gun. Wendy, Janice's older sister, sometimes took the ball straight to the goal. During time-outs Coach Michaels demanded she follow his lead. We all stared at Coach Michaels and then glanced at each other, trying not to laugh. Wendy's average score was fourteen points a game—a pretty good average to justify a laugh at Coach Michaels.

He rarely laughed himself. He threw his chair down on the floor when we made mistakes during practices. Once during a game, he broke his big toe after kicking a chair. He paced both ends of the court, loudly expressing his disgust with our game. His red and purple neck veins looked like they were going to pop. When we won, he praised us as a team, but never hesitated to criticize our individual mistakes, win or lose. But when he complimented our moves, we glowed inside and out. A compliment meant a lot. We needed Coach Michael's approval to get playing time.

We also discovered from Janice that Wendy was having some kind of relationship with Coach Michaels. Wendy had confided in Janice, who then confided in the coterie, that Coach Michaels suggested after practice one day that he take the wheel of Wendy's used, light blue Mustang for a drive to talk about the upcoming games. The drives became more regular. One night, Wendy came home with her socks and basketball shoes off after a ride. Another time, she walked in barefoot with her panties stuffed in her purse. Janice told us Wendy would disobey Coach Michaels at times to show she had some control over their relationship.

As our junior year began, Coach Michaels raved about our summer performance during our first in-school basketball practice. "All of you look fit and are shooting much better. We're going to have a great season. Priority is always about school and your classes, but the game is very close behind. Not boys, you understand? Only winning the game."

"Yes!" we all screamed.

"I don't believe you," he answered. "No boys. All game."

"No boys! All game!" we repeated, yelling like we were at a football game.

Coach Michaels required that we not have a boyfriend, specifically not have sex, or what he called "romancing" with boys; that, aside from our studies, we must concentrate only on basketball. He once told Wendy that he could tell if one of us had had sex by the way we walked. He didn't explain the walk; he just said he could tell.

Janice whispered to Maggie, Libby and me, "He thinks he owns us."

It was our mommas who really owned us. They never missed a game, from elementary to high school. Mommas washed our basketball uniforms before every game, even though they disapproved of them. They thought the girl uniforms were too tight and short, exposing our thighs up to almost the top of our legs. The boys, meanwhile, had long, baggy shorts. Yet boys never

46

hesitated to expose their dicks and balls through their loose britches.

Freddie, who played on the boys' team, was a serial flasher who had a habit of spreading his legs while sitting on a gym bench or up in the stands during our practices. Maggie grew tired of seeing it. After finding a jockstrap on the floor near the gym's washing machine, she decided to whack it up against Freddie's head. Luckily, no coach was around.

"Damn, girl, get away from me. You're fuckin' crazy." Freddie was mad as hell; he grabbed the jock strap from her and hit Maggie with it. Of course, we had to protect our friend and teammate. Five of us surrounded him and put one of the jockstraps on his head, and Janice took a Polaroid from her purse and saved the photo for possible blackmail use later.

I got as close as I could to Freddie's face and whispered loud enough for the girls to hear, "We're here to beat your ass. Have no fear, Foxy Brown is here."

Maggie, Libby and Janice all hollered, "Oh yeah, girl."

It made me feel something new, being that close to a boy. Like I was in charge, for once in my life.

We were trying to figure out how to like boys, love them, or just tell them to go to hell and kiss our ass.

***

"Karen, stop and make a play!" Coach Michaels shouted so loudly the veins in his neck tightened once again, and his forehead revealed pronounced stretches. I already had scored sixteen points by halftime against one of our toughest opponents, the Mount Olive Pirates. A team of Black girls, Mount Olive had come off a winning season the year before. The Pirates never hesitated to push and shove during a game, especially when the referee wasn't focusing, which was most of the time. It was a strategy they intentionally and successfully implemented. Mount Olive girls were battling, not setting plays. They figured out their advantages and maximized them. Why didn't we do that? Girl players needed to be more aggressive and less girly. Basketball was becoming more and more physical.

Still, thanks to the run and gun play—which I deemed my strategy—we were five points ahead of Mount Olive.

Coach Michaels called a time-out and wanted us to run a "pick" play. The "pick" required one of us to block the opponent's guard so that a teammate could get free for a shot or for a pass to another player. Problem was, everyone knew about the pick. It worked occasionally, so it wasn't a complete failure. In my opinion, though, run and gun was the better choice. No one knew what a player would do with a run and gun—including, sometimes, the player herself.

"Why should we do a pick?" I protested to Coach Michaels. "Run and gun works for us. They'll beat us otherwise. This ain't no Southern tea party. This is real professional basketball. You score more and win. You score less and lose."

"Yes," Coach Michaels seethed, "I know how basketball works, Karen. Either you follow my direction, or you sit on the bench. What would you like to do?"

Being disrespectful to a coach was never allowed, but it was the 1970s. We listened to music and watched movies featuring tough women, not pussies. Pam Grier, Jane Fonda, Aretha Franklin, Janis Joplin—they never took any shit from men. Why should we?

"I'll sit and see how it rolls out," I said, defiantly. I took the bench.

Now, just about anyone sitting behind our bench could hear my conversation with Coach Michaels, and word spread quickly that I was sitting out the game. Even my momma came down and whispered in my ear, "Karen, I know why you're doing this, but you need to show respect for your coach. Get some sense."

"Momma, I got sense. And I'm using it."

Nearing the end of the game, Mount Olive was up by eight points. With the clock running down, Maggie took the lead and ran Coach Michaels's play while I watched from the bench. Maggie stood at the top point and four others lined up at the high and low spots on both sides of the square. Wendy had one of the two lower spots. With Maggie holding the ball, Wendy placed a pick on the girl guarding Maggie, and Maggie dribbled once to the right side. She almost passed the ball to the forward on the left, but hesitated and waited for Wendy to turn and run to the goal. Maggie passed. Wendy shot and scored. A Mount Olive guard got a foul, and Wendy scored one free throw. We were down by five when the buzzer rang to end the game.

The pick play was successful, but run and gun plays would have been faster and given us a chance to win. I said nothing to Coach Michaels as we left the court.

Libby, Janice and Maggie all teased me with agony from the moment I got on the bus, way to the back. "You have lost your mind! You just wanted to show off by staying out of the game," said Libby.

Maggie whined, "We would have won if you had ignored Coach Michaels. You could have done a few of his plays and then just gone ahead and done your own run and gun. Or whatever you call it."

"I made the right call," I said. "Why can't we just call plays ourselves or run and guns when we read the game? We should be able to make our own decisions as the challenges at hand present themselves."

"Challenges at hand, Southern tea parties," Janice said. "Very clever comments. I like 'em." She whoo-hooed and then the other ten or so girls at the back of the bus repeated her yell.

They stopped when Coach Michaels appeared. I sat with my arms crossed below my smirky face.

Standing in the aisle close to me, Coach Michaels told us that a black panther had been spotted some years ago in this part of Covington County, at the location of the Mount Olive school. I was curious: He didn't mention our recent loss. Not at all.

"Mr. Bantor, the janitor at West Jones back then, spotted the same black panther slithering around near our school and told the principal he could kill it with his shotgun," Coach Michaels began. "The sheriff then, Walt Collins, told him to try and, if he did shoot him, Mr. Bantor would get a nice reward from the county supervisors. Sheriff Collins thought people needed to be protected from the dangerous and mysterious black panthers. When Mr. Bantor went out to hunt the panther, he could hear it screechin' from far away." Coach Michaels tried to mimic a panther screech.

Several of the players screamed. I didn't.

"Mr. Bantor tracked the panther by following the sound of the screechin'. But, an hour later, the panther's calls had died down, and Mr. Bantor decided to rest by a tree for a while. He fell asleep at the base of the tree trunk."

I felt something brush the back of my neck, then felt Coach Michaels' hands pushing down on my right shoulder.

"'Bout midnight, Mr. Bantor opened his eyes and looked up. He saw the panther lookin' down at him from a large tree branch. It was pitch dark, but the clouds parted, and a full moon shed light onto the panther. He kept his eyes on the panther as it moved down the tree, branch by branch. Mr. Bantor shivered inside but tried to remain still and calm, hopin' the panther would walk away."

Everyone on the bus huddled around so they could catch every word. Squeezing my neck with a pinch, Coach Michaels made damn sure that I wouldn't move.

"Instead, the panther snarled and growled, softly at first. He showed his teeth. Mr. Bantor slowly moved his arm to lift his shotgun from the ground, but the panther quickly placed his paw on Mr. Bantor's arm. The panther turned his head close to Mr. Banton and whispered, 'A lot of panthers have been killed out here for years. Don't let it happen again. Tell that to your sheriff.'

"Mr. Bantor nodded his head yes. 'Don't worry, Mr. Panther. As long as you agree that you will never hurt none of us in the future. Please be fair. We just want to live peacefully.'

"'Yes,' said the panther. As the panther backed away into the woods, Mr. Bantor reached for his shotgun and took aim at the animal. Before he could pull the trigger, the panther lurched forward and clawed Mr. Bantor to death."

Coach Michaels released his hands from my neck. The bus was silent for a moment.

Maggie asked loudly, "Is this story true?"

"Can't be true. Coach Michaels, did you make this up?" asked Janice.

Libby said, "It's too scary. I won't be able to walk in the dark ever again."

Wendy had nothing to say. She looked like she was asleep.

Coach Michaels turned to walk to the front of the bus, then stopped and looked at me. "Karen, come by my office tomorrow during study hall."

The icy feel of Coach Michaels' fingers on my neck lingered, leaving me shivering like Mr. Bantor under the gaze of the panther.

***

When I showed up to Coach Michaels's office at the appointed time the next day, I knocked on his gym office door. The blinds had been lowered on the window so I couldn't see inside. I could, however, hear Wendy's voice. She was crying. I couldn't hear what she was saying. I could only hear the sobbing. I knocked again, and Coach Michaels opened the door a crack.

"Another time, Karen," he said, quickly dismissing me.

Whatever he had planned to say to me, or do, he apparently had other priorities at that moment.

I grew less worried about Coach Michaels complaining about my basketball strategy. I began following his orders ninety percent of the time at our games. But every now and then, I broke free and went for the run and gun, ignoring the sputtering outburst he sent in my direction. He knew I knew about Wendy, even though we never discussed it. Plus, he couldn't complain as long as I made the shot. And, I always made those shots, most always anyway.

Most importantly, my friends and I needed something to control and make our own—if only for a moment at a basketball game.

I suppose we also wanted to take the things that had happened to us, really Janice, and turn them around. We hadn't talked about the bookroom kiss for weeks, but one night that fall, as I was driving Janice home with the coterie from a home game, she asked if we wanted to go to Midnight to talk. We always wanted to go to Midnight to talk.

Once there, sitting on the ground outside the train car and running her hands up and down her forearms, as we ate some freshly-picked strawberries, she wanted to tell us she had seen Coach a few more times—twice in the bookroom again, and one time in the Coke trailer when no one was nearby. After each encounter, she said she felt sadder than the time before. The sex itself got a little better; it didn't hurt so much the second and third times. He was fast, though, and it didn't last long.

Coach gave her a few kisses on the mouth, then the breasts, a rub on the pussy before taking her panties off. She was glad that he was fast. He put his hands on the sides of her neck, and his thumbs moved across her throat. He fastened his eyes on her and after a couple of intense pushes inside, he came, and then said, "That's sweet, Janice."

"'That's sweet'? That's what he said? He's a dog. No—my dog is much better than he is," I told Janice.

She really wasn't listening to my nonsense; she wanted to do the talking.

"He always locks the door to the bookroom and the Coke trailer," she said. "He tries to make sure no one is around the trailer or close to the bookroom. He knows it's wrong. I know it's wrong. He's my head coach! It's at school! I'm so much younger! I want it to stop. I think, maybe the next time will be better. Maybe it will start to feel good, and I don't have to ... I wouldn't ... Anyway, he brought a small blanket last time that he put on the floor. I told him I didn't want to be with him. I asked him to leave me alone. He softened his voice and put his lips close to my mouth, and said, 'Janice, Janice, Janice. This is the way it should be. Don't make me stop.'"

"Janice, why don't you make him stop?" I asked.

"What if sex with someone else is never any better than sex with Coach? Who will marry me?" she asked in a voice that made her seem worse than sad, almost pitiful.

"Any man on the face of this earth, Janice," I said, pulling her close for a long time. Her hair was silky and smelled like the strawberries we had eaten. I buried my nose in the top of her head and gave her a peck.

Maggie and Libby watched.

***

Janice had fallen asleep on Maggie's bed during a typical tampon drama among the three of us. She was sleeping a lot since the bookroom kiss, through many of our daily dramas about not just tampons but also boys, basketball practice, homework, or our mommas. We had become a low priority for Janice.

Libby shook Janice awake. "Stop being a Pruitt, Janice," she said. We laughed, but Janice frowned at us. "That's not nice," she said.

The Pruitts lived in an old dogtrot shack, the one with an open hallway down the middle of the house, where the dogs could walk from front to back. The Pruitts were dirt poor, and they were white. A retired football coach drove my school bus and, if a kid acted up on the bus, Coach Hammond thought it was the ultimate and most acceptable put-down to call the kid a "Pruitt."

Coach Hammond had retired from being the best football coach he thought we had. The fact that the Pruitt kids rode the bus, too, never fazed him. It caught on, and calling someone a "Pruitt" became a kind of generalized insult in school.

The Pruitts had a large garden, bigger than ours on the farm, and sometimes my momma and I would go to their house and buy some peas and butterbeans from them. Momma did it to share some money with the Pruitts since we had plenty of peas and butterbeans. We didn't have a lot of money, but more than they had. The older ladies—the mother and her sister—always rocked on the porch and shelled the butterbeans during the middle of the day. They also sold sugarcane. We'd buy their sugarcane stalks, peel them, and suck on pieces of the stalk. It was hard work to peel the sugarcane, and the taste didn't last long, but the juice was very sweet, sweeter than honey. Sugarcane was a piece of the sun with a rainbow over it.

A very pretty Pruitt girl, the youngest girl in the family, wore the same dress every day on the bus. She was in our class, always passed her tests and made good grades. One day Coach Hammond told her, "Buy yourself a new dress, Pruitt girl" when she walked off his bus. She turned and looked at him with hate. I couldn't blame her for feeling angry. Janice told me the Pruitt girl could become an actress or a model or a schoolteacher, even.

"She's so slight but she is as pretty as an angel," Janice said.

"What does slight mean?" I asked.

"Insignificant."

"That's a terrible word," I said.

"That's the way she's treated."

***

On an unexpectedly blazing hot afternoon in early November, Tim, a boy Wendy had been dating, approached Janice in the parking lot and asked her to go to a movie with him.

"Why are you asking me?" Janice said. "Ask Wendy. She's your girlfriend."

"No, not anymore," Tim said. "Wendy doesn't want one boyfriend. She wants a lot. I don't think you're like that."

"You don't know what I'm like," Janice laughed.

"Then spend some time with me, and I'll find out."

Janice heard a car pulling up behind them and turned to see Wendy, in her Mustang, arriving to pick her up from school after cheerleading practice. The tires kicked dust in Janice's face as Wendy shouted at Tim through the car window. "What are you doing with my sister?"

Janice quickly jumped in. "Tim just wanted to know if he had left a baseball glove at the house."

"I can't find it," said Tim. "If you see it, Janice, let me know."

Before school ended our junior year, Janice gathered the coterie one more time in the abandoned railcar. She had some news, she said.

She often got her words out quickly, like I did once when I told Coach about the bookroom.

"I am going to marry Tim. I'm dropping out of school."

I felt nauseous.

The four of us stood in Midnight. For a moment, I felt the train moving on the tracks and grabbed the back of a seat to steady myself. Libby teared up.

"He's joining the Navy. I'm gonna go with him," said Janice, matter of factly.

Maggie was the first to recover from the shock of it all. "Are you nuts? Why are you doing this? Are you trying to get away from Coach?"

Janice smiled, expecting both the outburst and our ashen faces. She sat down on her Midnight seat. "All of you, sit down, too. Be quiet and let me explain. You know how we've always chased after these trains, trying to follow them out of town. I want to escape from here. I know y'all do, too. And Tim loves me, and I love him. I need to be with someone who loves me."

She didn't mention Coach. But we all felt his name thick in the air.

"Coach should be the one kicked out of West Jones," Libby said, spitting his name out loud and sobbing at the same time. "Not you!"

"That's not the way it works," Janice said, gently. "You know that. As long as I'm around, he'll keep following me. Wandering into empty rooms. I don't want that, I know that now. I really don't. But I can't stop it, either. I need someone else. Tim will protect me from him."

"Does Tim know about Coach?"

"No. No one knows, except you three. And no one will." Her voice hardened, a rumble of thunder not quite a threat.

"Tim won't protect you if the Navy floats him 3,000 miles away from you. Stay here with us. We can help you. Just don't go," I pleaded, brushing my knees up against Janice's leg. I'd never felt this desperate before, this helpless. Not with my coterie.

"Stop. I hate feeling bad," Janice said. "Everything that happened to me during the past year has just … it's been awful, and disgusting. I want to get away from this hateful place. I want to start over."

"What will you do?" I asked.

"I'll be a wife, and then I'll be a mother. That's all good," said Janice.

55

"Besides, I think we'll be on the Gulf Coast. It's really not that far away."

"You can wait to be a wife and a mother," Maggie insisted. "Finish school and go to college. Remember? That's what your daddy told us to do, that day in the jewelry store," said Maggie, trying to make a practical appeal to Janice. "Tim can wait for you while he's in the Navy."

A smile curled up on the corners of Janice's lips. "My daddy likes Tim. Momma, too. Wendy pushed Tim away. They think I'm lucky to have him."

"He's the lucky one, but I don't think he knows it. Are you sure he's not just punishing Wendy by seeing you?" I asked.

"C'mon, y'all. Tim is terrific. He is not getting back at Wendy by using me. I don't need to graduate from anything except living here."

We were silent, suddenly out of words and out of arguments. Maggie, Libby and I could tell we were losing her. It was really happening.

Libby tried again, one last time. "It's not just about you, Janice. *We* need you here. We've always figured out our problems together. We can't do it without you." We were all crying now, except for Janice. She hadn't been a crier until Coach.

Janice looked at each of us, like an adult would look at us, removed, distant and with pity, just like I looked at her not that long ago. She took a breath. "The times in this old, beat-up railway car with the three of you have always made me happy. I'll keep that happiness inside me wherever I end up going." Janice spread her arms around a train seat.

Janice's decision settled in with Maggie, Libby and me over the next few days. We would no longer be fastened together. Janice was taking a big piece of our hearts, a song Maggie always sang. We decided, though, that like Janis Joplin, we would be tough. We needed a special goodbye party to wash away the grief, and it couldn't just be a trip to McDonald's or the Dairy Queen. The Soso Big House was the perfect place for a spend-the-night celebration of our friendship.

The Big House had been occupied by Daddy and most of his brothers and sisters at some point in their lives. Daddy built the house for his family when he was twenty-two. By 1975, the house still had its original furniture and curtains, bought in the late 1920s. In two chifforobe dressers, upstairs, hung old dresses from the 1930s that my aunts wore to dance parties when they were young. Parts of the Big House were raggedy, but the couches had deep blue coverings, soft but sturdy. It was another house high on a hill in Soso with a field of grass as green as green can be in a Deep South spring. In summer, the grass got brown and browner from heat that burned the ground. Full of paintings of my great grandparents and grandparents who died before I was born, the Big House was my house for a short time while Momma and Daddy nursed his sister, Ruth, whose illegitimate daughter became his third sister, so to speak. Ruth had a stroke and died a year later.

After going to the Big House for family gatherings for years and living there, I concocted stories behind each of the portraits. They were not excellent paintings. I, however, imagined they were very expensive, and I stared at them or as long as I could to dream up horror tales after sneaking away from shucking corn on the Big House porch.

Janice said the Big House was where the Hinton ghosts lived; an invitation to spend the night was always irresistible. The night we gathered to say goodbye to Janice, I gave the coterie one more tour of terror that had evolved over time. I walked from one end of the living room to the other with my girlfriends, describing the paintings and the people in them. I had a well-developed stock of stories centered around my dead relatives.

"All the women in these pictures look sad, don't they? And the men look pissed off." I walked to the next painting in the living room, where we planned to sleep on the two couches and two sleeping bags we brought near a fireplace. "This woman, my great-grandmother, became a witch. She treated her children badly because her husband beat her. This woman here, my other great-grandmother, died in a pond when her husband pushed her out of a fishing boat. She couldn't swim."

Janice, Maggie and Libby always appreciated a good story and never argued about the degree of accuracy in my tales. Although the good-bye party was in the middle of May when the sun started spewing heat, we built a fire that night in one of the two fireplaces, and I told more stories about deaths in the house. The scariest was about a much older cousin, who had killed her husband accidentally. It was a new story after a shotgun had been mounted on the living room wall, and my Aunt Jean filled me in on why it had been hung.

"This shotgun was hers, and his," I said.

I paused, letting it all sink in as we looked at the shotgun.

"She wasn't sent to jail because everyone said it was an accident. But she must have meant to do it because his ghost returns to the Big House at different times of the year. It could be tonight. If he comes, we should be careful he doesn't take his shotgun from the wall and shoot us!"

"Is *she* dead?" Libby asked. "Could she come back to haunt the place, too?"

As old as we were, the story scared the shit out of us. I was a good storyteller.

"Let's get the hell out of here," demanded Janice. "Your stories are always about death. This is *not* the way I want to say goodbye."

We headed for a drive in Myrtle. Maggie and Libby sat on the front hood, just to feel the breeze from the movement and the heat from the engine. With Janice up front, I drove slowly to make sure the other two didn't fall off. No one wanted the radio on.

Windows down, Janice said, "You're driving the right speed. This way we can hear the frogs and the crickets and see the lightning bugs. Let's just not talk for a while so we can take it all in," she said, placing her head on the windowsill.

Soon after, we stopped the car on the side of an open field; Libby and Maggie begged to turn the radio back on, so we could hear the music.

"Damn, girl. Turn the radio on. It's too quiet!"

Walking into the field, we held hands.

"It's 'Crystal Blue Persuasion,'" said Janice. I could hear a smile in her voice, even in the dark. I knew her that well. I wondered how long I would know her like that and if we would change with her away from us. "This song always makes me feel brave," she said.

We had sung that song so many times in Janice's pond. Janice and I closed our mouths and shut our eyes so we could hear Maggie and Libby sing it once again. "So don't you give up now," they crooned in union. When the song ended, we looked at each other when Maggie whispered, echoing the lyrics of the song, "We'll never give up, will we?" Libby and I whispered, "Nope."

Listening to the miniature sound of the car radio a football field away, we embraced together for the last time, on a hayfield, with the moon, the lightning bugs, mosquitos, frogs, crickets and cow shit surrounding us.

Janice never answered Maggie's question.

Chapter 4
Let the Fucking Begin

After Janice left, it seemed we could never really find the energy to chase the train. We needed something new to do so we could get Janice off our minds.

My cousin Katri in Tupelo told me that Ole Miss had a summer girls' basketball camp for high school players, and Libby and I signed up. Maggie said she needed to stay home and help her momma. We convinced our parents to pay the fee for camp, which seemed to be the only requirement to get in. Not long after, Libby and I drove the four hours to Oxford for the start of basketball camp at Ole Miss. We did a quick campus tour, then spent the rest of our time playing ball. I had found heaven on Earth for a short time after Janice's departure, playing ball with a whole bunch of girls I had never met from across the state.

The first day of camp, the Ole Miss women's basketball coach spoke to the two hundred girls assembled in the gym. She told us that the first women's basketball team in Ole Miss history would officially hit the Rebel court in the fall. We all clapped and cheered. Finally, a women's team! She also told us about Title IX.

"What the fuck is Title IX?" Libby leaned over to ask me.

"I don't know. Maybe it's the chapter of a book," I said, shrugging my shoulders.

Turned out it was about one of our favorite topics: money. Title IX was not a chapter in a book, we learned, it was new law from 1972 that banned sex discrimination in sports. The coach told us that in 1971, U.S. Senator Birch Bayh of Indiana was keen on supporting women's employment and ending sex discrimination, including the Equal Rights Amendment, legislation that we had heard about but only a little. The ERA wasn't going anywhere, so Bayh took Title IX from the ERA and stuck it in an education bill.

She gave the campers a flyer that included an article about Bayh and Title IX. It quoted Bayh, who said, "We are all familiar with the stereotype that women are pretty things who go to college to find a husband, go on to graduate school because they want a more interesting husband, and finally marry, have children, and never work again."

Bayh delivered the bill to President Nixon. With a stroke of his pen, Nixon did more for girls and young women than Gloria Steinem.

Libby and I didn't know who Bayh was, but we knew we didn't want to be stereotypes.

Molly, a basketball player from Houston, Mississippi, became our friend at the Ole Miss camp. She wasn't a great basketball player, but she was a good storyteller, and she knew how to avoid pregnancy.

"Are you sure this is how it works?" I asked.

"I've never gotten pregnant, Karen, and I won't be, as long as I don't have sex on these days," she said, pointing to a calendar marked with red X's.

"Well, what if you get all turned on and can't resist, even though it's a red X night?"

"If he has a condom, he's gotta wear it. If he doesn't, then you don't have

61

sex. Do everything else, but don't let him put his dick in you."

"Sex doesn't sound very good. I'd rather watch movies with sex than actually have sex," I joked.

Back in Soso, we kept the calendar news to ourselves, except to Maggie, of course. I hoped the calendar plan would keep Maggie, Libby and me from getting pregnant. After all, we had big plans for the year ahead.

Janice was gone when senior year began, but Coach wasn't. We could see him in his office window as we walked from the school parking lot as graduates-to-be on yet another hot Monday morning in mid-August. West Jones looked the same but felt different without Janice—like everything around us was the same, but we were the ones who had changed.

"Coach is a fucking monster," Libby scowled.

"Let's hit the motherfucker over the head," I responded.

"I've got an idea," said Maggie, no emotion in her eyes.

***

A few days later, Maggie opened the closed door of Coach's office without bothering to knock. Maggie entered; Libby and I were right behind her. I turned and locked his door. Coach sat in his usual comfy chair with wheels, behind his steel-gray desk, eyeing us warily as we stepped right up to the edge of it. He started to speak, but the look on our faces made him stop. It made me feel more powerful than I'd ever remembered feeling before—true power, like the time I told Donny with a jockstrap on his head, "Have no fear, Foxy Brown is here."

The three of us stood over him as Maggie spelled it out, speaking slowly: "Janice is gone, and we are mad as hell about it. If we see you or we hear about you kissing, touching, having sex, or so much as looking wrong at another girl, like you did with Janice, this is what we are going to do: We will tell the principal. We will tell the other teachers. And we will tell your wife. We will never talk about Janice, but we will spread the word about you and your sick habits so far and so wide you will wish it was in the newspaper instead."

When Maggie told us her plan to confront Coach head on, we thought

Coach might scream at us or threaten us or maybe even get physical. Instead, he just looked down at his lap.

"I'm sick of this," he said, shaking his head.

At first, I wasn't sure if he was talking to us or his pecker.

"Okay, be sick, then. But beware, too," Libby said. It was the first time I had ever heard Libby with such venom in her voice.

We went to the gym dressing room and sat down, curled into little balls.

"I wish Janice could have heard y'all," I said.

"Me, too," said Maggie.

Libby said, "Me, too, too."

I was proud of Maggie for leading our run and gun on Coach. It had been my idea the year before to get revenge on him by blackmailing him for typing passes, but now that seemed silly in comparison to Maggie's revenge method. The three of us had learned a lot since then. Janice ran away, but we stayed. She felt that she needed to. We loved her, still, perhaps more in her absence than ever before.

Yet we needed to move on. Boys were starting to pay attention to us — I'd heard that Mitch, a football and basketball player, was into me. He was an inch taller. That was important because I was 5' 10", taller than most guys. Girls shouldn't be taller than their boyfriends. Dark hair, brown eyes, muscles. His friend Sam, who provided the porn magazines for our sleepover parties, had told me Mitch thought I was pretty. I was shocked, but we also figured Sam and his friends would ask us out at some point, since they knew we wanted porn.

"What do you think?" I asked the girls after I'd told them the big news.

"Mitch is cute," said Maggie. "Actually, he's even handsome."

"Yeah," I said, "but he has a funny walk."

"What do you mean, funny walk?"

"He bounces. He walks on his toes first and then bounces on his heels. It's a walk some athletes have," I said.

"Strange. I've never noticed it. Is there any reason the bounce will get on

63

your nerves? Last year you watched Mitch eat an ice cream cone and you said he looked ridiculous, wrappin' his tongue around it. Remember?" Maggie asked.

We always had made a habit of noticing odd behavior in boys that many girls and most parents would ignore or miss. We never ignored or missed odd behavior. Odd, strange behavior was important to recognize early in any dating plan, the coterie decided. The behavior could come back to haunt us.

"I mean, it's like he wanted girls to watch him lick the ice cream cone, so twirling his tongue around would be a trick to seduce them. It was stupid," I said.

"Karen, I don't think so. Mitch is so arrogant, he wouldn't think for a second about what you or any girl thought about him licking his ice cream cone," said Maggie, throwing both arms up in the air. "Sometimes you overthink things."

"Hmmmm," said Libby. "On a scale of one to ten, how much would lickin' ice cream matter now versus last year?"

"Libby, Maggie, enough. I'm desperate. I'm a senior, and I haven't had sex," I said. "I kissed Sam when I was a sophomore, but he had braces, and his kiss was no good, so I jumped out of his car. Dan also asked me out later that year, but I was too scared."

Maggie, in addition to the finger fuck, had given a guy she was dating, Bud, a blowjob, the previous year before Janice said goodbye. Libby and I were hanging out with Janice in Maggie's bedroom waiting for her to return from a night out with him. We wanted the latest and greatest info about any progress made on the sex front. We heard footsteps bounding up the stairs, and Maggie burst into the bedroom, breathing hard with her hands covering her face.

"Now what? We have too much drama in our lives," I blurted.

"I am so stupid. Why do I keep seeing him? He doesn't love me. He never says it. I say it, but he never does."

"Then tell him to break up with you, just like Janice says," I said pointing to Janice.

"He asked me to go for a drive. I knew what could happen, and it did. Y'all will be disgusted with me. He asked me, you know, to swallow his—oh, my God, I can't say it."

"Swallow what!" Libby screamed.

Maggie and I knew what she was trying to say.

"You didn't, right?" I asked.

"He scared me. I didn't know what to say. I didn't know what to do with it, so I spit it out the window."

"Holy shit," said Libby.

"Maggie," I said. "Please don't see him anymore. He's not good for you or to you. He's not your Robert Redford. Go find your Robert Redford," I said. In 1975 I was obsessed with Robert Redford.

"What the fuck are you talking about," Maggie screamed. "I am so tired of hearing about Robert fucking Redford."

"Maggie, you have to watch his movies again. Robert Redford wanted Natalie Wood to go to New Orleans with him and get married in *This Property Is Condemned*. And he married Barbra Streisand in *The Way We Were*."

"They're just movies, you idiot. Natalie Wood died when she got sick running in the rain, and Redford left Streisand when she got pregnant. His movies are not comforting."

"Yes, but *This Property is Condemned* is based on a play written by Tennessee Williams. We gotta go to New Orleans. Alva in the play goes." Alva was Natalie Wood's character.

"Who the hell is Tennessee Williams? Why is his name Tennessee, for goodness sake?"

Janice stepped in. "Let's stop talking about Tennessee and Redford. Let's talk about Bud and you. You fell in love with him. Now fall out," she said. Janice was talking as much about Coach as she was about Maggie's Bud.

"It's not that easy," said Maggie.

I tried to think up some solid advice to recover from my earlier silliness about Redford and his movies. "If we just move forward one day, we will forget backwards," I said.

Maggie looked at me and said, "Now what movie is that from?"

"It's not. I thought it up."

Maggie later had sex with him, but the love affair was over by senior year.

"Maggie, you are done. You should check 'sex with Bud' off the list of things to do. Who's next? Libby, what about Scott? He wants you, I can tell." Scott had been one of my neighbors until his family moved after building a new modern home closer to the small town of Soso. I had fixed them up.

"Maybe," answered Libby.

"So?" I asked.

"Go for it. Let the fucking begin!" Maggie hollered, throwing her arms into the air again and smiling big.

Mitch was a mystery, though. He reminded me of Barnabas Collins, a vampire on the TV show *Dark Shadows*. In junior high, I watched the re-runs every afternoon after the bus dropped me off at the house. I made myself a ham sandwich with mayo and a bowl of vanilla ice cream with chocolate syrup and placed the food on a blanket near our large Montgomery Ward television set.

The first words uttered on *Dark Shadows* offered girls keen insights into boys, and they were important enough for me to memorize. A woman's voice intoned: "There are no limits to the things some men will do. They sink to the bottomless depths of corruption. They will desecrate sacred ground and violate that which should remain sealed forever."

The scary music, intense words, and the appearance of vampires sucking blood out of the opposite sex and, in some instances, the same sex appealed to my then-fourteen-year-old curiosity. I needed to understand what it all meant. Were vampires real? Or were they symbols of bad people, like in books? Barry, a classmate who lived in Gitano, near Soso, thought so. He had read volumes about vampires and gave me vampire storyboards he wrote with drawings of vampires literally picking up girls and women and holding their entire bodies in his arms, their heads limp and their long hair touching the ground. The storyboard lines were hilarious and frightening at the same time.

"You are a beautiful girl," wrote Barry. "Let me suck your blood." Or "I love you, but I will kill you anyway."

I didn't think Mitch was a vampire, but he had asked me once about my period when he thought I was in a bad mood. "Stop asking me that," I demanded. "Are you a vampire?"

"No, but I could drink your blood."

After the coterie decision was made that I should date him, I was determined to be bold. I had already learned through basketball to speak out, not be shy. I am woman. Hear me roar. Hear me complain. Hear me fuck, I told myself.

The next day, I saw Mitch from a distance in the school hallway. When he saw me walking toward him, he suddenly stopped and lurched toward another girl. Definitely a move with the purpose of flirting with me and making me jealous. I continued my hall walk and passed him without a look before he pounced. "Karen, what happened to Janice? Why did she get married? She's too young."

"I agree. I wish she hadn't, but each person has to make his or her own decision," I said coolly.

"Well, can you make decisions?" Mitch asked.

"I make them all the time," I said, chin high. "You know there are limits to the things women will do, but they always rise to the top. They protect sacred ground, and never violate that which should remain sealed forever."

Mitch paused and placed his hand under my chin. "What the hell are you talkin' about?"

"You never watch *Dark Shadows*," I said, keening for dead vampires.

Still, Mitch was my best choice for making my senior year a memorable one in all of the ways that I wanted, and I volunteered to make signs for the cheerleading squad for our first football game of the 1975-76 season, when Mitch would be starting as running back. Libby and I met at her house, and we wrote on long rolls of wide paper, "Mustangs have muscle!" Then, drew a picture of a football player with muscles, riding a Mustang. It was a bad drawing. We had no talent.

Before the game, Libby and I took several other signs to the football field and were hanging them around the bleachers when Mitch came out of the football house with Sam. They waved and walked closer to the field.

"Libby! Karen! Come closer," Sam called.

"I think we're close enough," I retorted. I don't know why I said that. I would happily have gone closer. I just wanted to make it clear that I wasn't one of those preening girls who fawned over everything the football players said.

"Don't be shy and stand-offish," Mitch chuckled. He seemed more amused than pissed. "We know you girls like Jane Fonda."

"Why would you say that?" I snapped. "You don't know anything about Jane Fonda."

"Yeah, I do. And I know you, girl." He raised his eyebrows in a way that I did not want to find as attractive as I did. "Why don't we meet up after the game?"

"And where will we go? What will we do, Mitch?"

"I don't know," said Mitch slyly. "What do you want to do?"

"What I want to do changes minute to minute. So why don't we see how we feel after the game?"

"Sure. Maybe we can chase some trains."

"What do you know about chasing trains?" I asked. How this boy even knew to mention the chase was a concern to me. A boy took Janice away, and still we were letting them into our lives senior year. We couldn't let them into Midnight, too.

But Mitch just shrugged, grinning that same grin that gave nothing away. "Nothing. I'd rather be chasing you, anyway."

"See ya later," I responded, turning my back to Sam and Mitch. Libby had watched the whole thing in amusement and turned to me, trying to stifle her giggles.

I didn't know if he was the chosen one or not, but I was prepared to kiss Mitch, at least. He wouldn't lock me in the bookroom like Coach locked Janice. He knew I would beat the shit out of him.

From the football stands, Maggie, Libby and I started some of the cheers that we knew Janice loved, which pissed off the cheerleading squad. They knew our friend was gone; Janice had been a cheerleader, and this was the first football game without her. We thought the Mustangs might lose just because she wasn't there. She'd always made a difference, an instinct for the right cheers, the right jumps, the right dances, the right everything to drive the team to victory. In the sixth grade, she wore white gloves to show off her moves with a message. No one could take her place. And we didn't want anyone to, either.

Without Janice, the cheers got stupider and stupider. We wanted the old ones, from junior high. Our cheers were simple and direct, with no rhymes or funny lines. Go, Mustangs, go. Fight, Mustangs, fight. Repeat. That worked. All that mattered was to cheer the team to a first down or a touchdown.

At the start of the game, we joined hands with the other Mustang supporters and prayed to protect the players and win the damn game. The game began and it was really something watching Mitch out on that field, knowing that he wanted to meet up with me after. He suddenly seemed more powerful, faster, better than usual. I started to feel pride—over what, I didn't know, since Mitch damn sure wasn't mine, and I damn sure wasn't his. But I was protective, willing to draw him into my circle in a way I hadn't been expecting.

At one point, Mitch's daddy screamed out, "Son, get it together! You not runnin' fast enough! You bein' lazy! Get with it or I'm gonna make you sleep in the pigpen!" Everyone laughed when Mitch's dad spoke, and he enjoyed the attention. He also enjoyed his tobacco wad.

I returned fire. "Mitch, you're doin' great! Running faster than anyone! Use your muscles and your brain! You decide the plan!"

Right at that moment, I remembered what Mrs. Cook had told us in

English class, about an Eleanor Roosevelt quote: "Women are like teabags. We don't know our true strength until we are in hot water." Suddenly, I felt as if I was in hot water, steeping myself for a test I thought might be coming. I wanted and needed to be ready for it.

That night, Mitch caught a pass and faked off a defensive end, running for the goal. He ended up getting a first down. The Mustangs were down by five points, but Mitch caught yet another pass and stormed through the defensive line. He scored. Everyone, including his daddy, went crazy screaming his name. Then, Jack, another Mustang, kicked the ball over the goal, and our Mustangs won.

Everyone cheered, and several students and parents told me I had done a good job cheering Mitch on. "He must have heard you from the stands," said Mrs. Brent, Preacher Brent's wife, the preacher my momma bought Myrtle from.

I basked in the compliments. Watching Mitch on the field, I had gotten turned on, for the first time in my post-period life. He was the focus of everyone's attention, and I was the focus of his. He seemed so fluid that night, so competent. It made me want him. Bad.

I stood outside the football field house after the game, waiting for Mitch to appear. Libby and Maggie stood with me. But as time went on, the nervous seed in my stomach started to grow, whispering its doubts to me in the downtime. What if I really didn't know what I was doing? What if Mitch wanted a more attractive girl, a more experienced girl? What if he'd heard me cheering for him and he changed his mind about me? After several minutes passed, I told them I was going to leave; that I was too nervous and scared. I had temporarily lost my teabag. My water froze.

"Don't be a chicken," Maggie scolded. "He has to prove himself to you, too. Don't let him fool around tonight. Just like Janice said, 'Flirt first and then fuck.'"

"She didn't say that," I said.

"Yes she did," said Maggie.

"Uh-huh," said Libby.

In the middle of our flirt and fuck argument, Mitch and Sam walked out of the field house talking to each other, not even noticing us. I said hello as they walked closer. "Good job on the catch and run."

Mitch stopped, as if remembering my existence for the first time. "Oh, hey, Karen. Thanks for the compliment. You never compliment us."

"On special occasions I do. This is one."

He sucked in his lip, appraising me. I didn't want to overreact, but damn, he did look good like that. "Do we still have plans?" he asked.

"Sure. Where's your car?"

"Follow me," Mitch said.

Sam said, "You should follow him for the rest of your life."

"Are you smokin' pot?" I asked, cackling at him.

Mitch waved Sam off and walked me over to his car, opening the door for me. I jumped in. He had plenty of eight-tracks with music I loved: Jimi Hendrix, David Bowie, Rolling Stones, Queen, Heart, Beatles, Janis Joplin, Diana Ross, Chaka Khan, Guess Who, and more. I was impressed. Nothing stupid, and not all the same. Some of it included covers of blues songs by Mississippi musicians, like Muddy Waters and Robert Johnson.

"Who you like best, Mitch?" I asked.

"Jimi."

He popped a Hendrix eight track in and strummed his tummy, faking a guitar while he sang "Voodoo Child." Hendrix sang that making love caused no pain. No pain? I feared pain from sex just like I feared pain from giving birth. But I was ready. I thought.

"All right," I said. "You a voodoo child or a vampire or both?"

"I be whatever you want, girl," Mitch said. He was playing it cool, eyes straight ahead, trying not to pay me much mind.

"I don't know what I want yet." I winced—that was a dumb thing to say. My not-so-clever comment might encourage his suggestions for what I should want. I wasn't sure if I was ready to go there, just yet. It had only been a minute.

71

Mitch, though, didn't bite. "What do you like in music?"

"Probably same as you, but I also like the blues and some jazz." My stomach was fluttering like it was keeping time with the music. Every moment, every answer, felt loaded. Like some kind of test I hadn't studied for. Were my teabags smokin'?

Mitch scoffed. "You don't listen to the blues or jazz. You don't know nothing about it."

"I have a cousin from Texas who taught me all about it. The Mississippi Delta is the birth of the blues. Did you know that? And I saw the movie *Lady Sings the Blues* about Billie Holiday. She sang blues *and* jazz songs. Libby, Maggie, Janice and me saw it a year ago, right when it came out at the Arabian Theatre. It was terrific. We also bought the album and played Diana Ross a million times, singing Billie Holiday's songs."

As I spoke, Mitch scooted over to me, closer and closer. He leaned in to smell my perfume. I'd chosen it just for him that day before the game at TG&Y, the store where the coterie had bought the same shirts to wear to school as freshman. "Okay, girl. Sing one for me."

I leaned back, just a little. "I ain't gonna do that. You'll make fun of me."

"Come on, voodoo girl." Mitch touched the side of my face with his hand. It was surprisingly soft, for a boy. I liked it. I wanted him to keep it on my cheek a little longer. But after a stroke or two, he dropped it back into his lap.

I swallowed, hard. "Let's see what you think of this song." I sang a few lyrics, which included the title, "Lover Come Back," several times.

"That's a good one." Mitch laughed. "I'll always come back."

"Shut up. You're not my lover," I said. Why did I say that? "What's the name of the song?"

"I don't know."

"'Lover Come Back,' you idiot." Now I was calling him an idiot! Smooth moves, Karen.

"I'm not an idiot. I'm your lover," he said slowly. As if I was the idiot.

That put me even more on edge. "No, you're not. Not even close."

72

"What happened to Billie Holiday?" Mitch asked, shifting the conversation. Clearly he didn't like where that was going—into non-lover territory.

"She died from a drug overdose. Her voice was perfect, and she was beautiful."

"Blacks always overdose."

"No, they don't. White men gave her the drugs to take."

"So?"

"So, it's not about whether you're Black or white. Taking drugs or drinking too much can kill both. It's not a joke."

"I don't think it's funny," replied Mitch.

"Well, good, then," I said.

"Yep."

"Yep?"

"Yep."

Silence, then: "I heard about the party at Gloria's," said Mitch.

"What did you hear? Who did you hear it from?"

"I won't tell you who, but I will tell you what," he said.

"Okay. What?"

"Gloria's momma got sloppy drunk at her spend-the-night party, and one of you called Coach Michaels to pick you all up and drive you home. Gloria's momma has problems," he said.

"You still go out with Gloria?" I asked. What was I doing? No, this time I knew what I was doing. I was getting ready to take the plunge, and I didn't want to make that jump if Mitch was spending time with someone else.

"I might."

"Oh, so you have a thing with her?"

"What's a thing?"

"Like, do you like her?"

"Kind of. Kind of not."

"What do you like and what don't you like?"

"I want to talk about you, Karen Hinton."

"There's not much to say."

"How about something to do, then?"

"You want to do with me what you did with Gloria?" I asked.

"Are you talking about having sex?" Mitch asked.

"I'm not talking about sex. You're talking about sex." I paused. "Well? Did you have sex with her?"

"You talk too much," said Mitch.

"Yeah, I've been told that before."

We sat in his car with our arms crossed. He was mad, and I knew he wasn't going to kiss me. I was disappointed and thought myself stupid for talking too much and disagreeing with him. I just didn't know how to turn it off. I figured that if a boy knew me—if he knew me and then liked me—he would know what he was getting into, but apparently not.

Mitch cranked his car and drove me to mine at the other end of the football parking lot. "Let's try this again sometime. I'll call you," he said.

"Okay. Thanks for playing your music."

"Next time let's listen to the music, not talk about it," he responded.

I watched him drive off feeling that shadow brush of his lips on mine — a glimpse into where the night might have gone, had I let it. I said, aloud, "Lover come back" and promised myself that I wouldn't mention Gloria again. She wasn't my problem.

A week later, I wrote in my diary, the one I kept in my closet underneath the worn-out basketball shoes. I had been keeping the diary for a couple of years and treated it like I was talking to a person. Lacking a boy to confide in, I had named the diary, Brandon.

October 17, 1975—Dear Brandon, Libby told me she broke up with a guy whose tennis shoes were always holey. Sounds exactly just like me! CRAZY. It's great to be able to relate to other girls about things. Like it helped me a lot to know that Libby and I weren't the only stupid heads in the world. I bet there are thousands and thousands of girls like us and they just won't admit it! They should, it helps you when you talk things over with other girls.

I try not to be a fake. It's hard sometimes because you try not to impress people. I do not want to impress anybody. I just want to do right for myself. I miss Janice. If she were here, instead of married, she would tell me what to do. Maggie and Libby miss her, too. We haven't heard from her. We are better together when she is here.

Mitch is all I think about. Libby told me to hush last night. I know she's right I should just try not to think and talk about him. Easier said than done. I have even thought about having HIS BABY! I used to say I would NEVER have a baby because it would hurt. But I don't care now. Not if it's Mitch's.

I'm only seventeen and a whole life ahead of me. Here I am thinking about having a baby. But I feel so much older. I can remember being eight and thinking how tough it would be to be sixteen then thirty-two then forty then fifty then sixty-five and then I'll have grandchildren. I have only one more year of high school and then college.

But I don't have the slightest idea what I'll be. I want to be independent from a man. I've got to be able to take care of myself alone, cause I really don't know if I'll ever marry or what if he's killed!!? I have to be prepared for those kinds of things.

Oh, and I saw Paul Newman and Robert Redford movie, Butch Cassidy and Sundance Kid. I love him and him soooo much. I went with Maggie last night. Gotta go eat supper. Bye, Brandon.

PS. I love BASKETBALL and maybe Mitch.

Mitch avoided me for the next few days but my mind was occupied with the coterie's secret plan to visit New Orleans for the first time. We wanted to see New Orleans because people got drunk there, went to strip clubs, danced, wore strange clothes and partied all the time. When I say "we" it was mostly "me," but Libby and Maggie didn't mind the distraction. Strictly speaking, we were not allowed to go to New Orleans because it was a town of sin and crime. So, of course, we had to go.

Maggie's momma was a nurse, and she often worked at night, so staying

75

with Maggie was the easiest way to sneak out of Soso. One Saturday, we finally had saved enough money to take Maggie's car, Vanilla, on the two-hour drive to New Orleans. It was close but different enough to feel very far away. I wanted to see Cajun and Creole life in action. Cajuns spoke weird English, different from how we talked, and Cajun French, too.

How could France be so close to Soso?

I had watched *This Property Is Condemned,* the movie based on the Tennessee Williams story, a dozen times or more by then. The movie was about a young woman from a small town in Mississippi who yearned to take a train to escape to a more exciting place. You can imagine why I loved the movie. Or did the movie make me want to escape? Natalie Wood—Alva— followed Robert Redford to New Orleans. In the back of my mind, I thought maybe I'd find my Robert Redford in New Orleans, if Mitch didn't work out. We made our way to the city by afternoon and planned to drive home when the sun rose over Lake Pontchartrain Sunday morning.

"New Orleans, here we come," Libby said after we parked Vanilla. We had no idea where else to go, except to Bourbon Street. We walked toward the bright lights and glowing colors of one strip club after another, plastered on the outside with photos of naked women in positions like from the book, *Joy of Sex*, and the porn magazines we collected. Anyone could view the photos from behind glass. We had heard about the strip clubs and the most famous one, Big Daddy's. It had a neon sign with swinging mannequin legs in a window one floor above the club. In 1975, Big Daddy's was the top, topless go-go joint on Bourbon.

We didn't know any girls in our school who had made their way to New Orleans, much less Bourbon Street and Big Daddy's. Listening to jazz, the blues, disco, and rock pouring out of the clubs and looking at stripper photos while walking down the blocks of Bourbon filled with people drinking openly on the street were not things we could do in Soso. Aside from dancers, Big Daddy's also had magicians, contortionists, escape artists, fire-eaters, and live bands. We found out about this place from going to the county fair each year.

We went on a Friday or Saturday night. Black people could only attend on Tuesday nights, even after integration. Buying cotton candy and caramel-covered apples at the Jones County Fair was the first thing we did. We took pictures of ourselves making funny faces in the photo booths, played plenty of games to win teddy bears, and rode on the Ferris Wheel, the Scrambler, and a dozen other rides. But the most exciting part of the fair was the Greatest Show on Earth, where women danced with revealing tops and bottoms on a raised floor outside a large tent. We boldly walked by the tent entrance and gawked at the scantily clad, young and old women, as they tried to lure men and, sometimes women, inside. Some of the dancers exposed their breasts on the outside dancing floor, covered only by tassels. Mostly men packed the space in front of the tent. That's where I had found my daddy one night at the fair. I was six and lost, roaming around alone for what seemed like hours. I remembered him standing there outside the tent, smiling, and I ran and hugged his leg because I was terrified. Years later, we saw plenty of daddies, a few coaches and, even postmen, preachers and principals, standing there with smiles on their faces, too. Some even bought tickets to go inside.

One night at the county fair, the coterie walked up to a stripper who took a break by the side of the tent. We asked where she was from.

"New Orleans is where I live, but I go out to these county fairs, too, to make extra money. Sometimes I stay in New Orleans and strip at a place called Big Daddy's," said the dancer, who looked our age, seventeen, when we got closer to her face.

I said, "Like Big Daddy in *Cat on a Hot Tin Roof*? Do you have a hot tin roof?"

"What is *Cat on a Hot Tin Roof*? Who is Big Daddy on that roof? The only Big Daddy I know is the man who owns it. Big Daddy's club is a gas," she said.

A gas? We wrote that down on our curse list later.

"Can we see this gas place?" I asked.

77

"You are too young. They may not let you in," she said as she climbed up the steps to the stage, ready to dance again.

"Well, Big Daddy let you in. He may let us in, too," I said.

We all looked at each other and I said, "Let's go to New Orleans. I think when she said, 'it's the gas,' that means it's the best strip club ever."

At the doorway of Big Daddy's, even more naked pictures of women adorned the entrance. We concluded real women must be stark naked inside, behind the swinging legs belonging to the mannequin. The mannequin had legs but no arms.

"Why doesn't she have any arms? What does that mean?" Libby asked.

"I have no idea," I said. "I guess legs are sexier than arms, and arms aren't as necessary for having sex as legs are. She's not real, anyway," I said.

A tall, heavy-set man approached us as we stared at the legs outside. We assumed he was Big Daddy. Who else would he be? Big Daddy said we didn't have to show ID, and no one would mind if we were there. Maggie and Libby mouthed to me in a whisper, "No. We can't go in. We're too young."

I said, to them, "Don't be scaredy cats." To Big Daddy, I said, "Sir, how much does it cost to go in?"

"It's free, young lady," he said, voice booming. "But you have to buy drinks."

"How much are the drinks?"

"Five dollars," he laughed.

"Five dollars! We don't have enough money for that. We need our money for gas to get back home."

"Well, I bet there are some men inside who will buy drinks for you. Come on in."

I looked at Maggie and Libby. They were clinging onto each other, shaking their heads frantically. Libby pulled me aside and said, "No! Big Daddy scares the pants off me. I'm not going in."

"The mannequin is scarier than Big Daddy. I'm going in. Maggie, you stay with Libby. I want to check it out," I said.

I was terrified, but I couldn't let the girls know that. The trip to New Orleans had been my idea, after all. Trying to hide my fear, I walked inside the joint. A stripper who looked my age swung around the pole, squatting up and down. Three middle-aged men sat close to her on the stage, staring at her and paying no attention to me. She sat on the stage and spread her legs so they could see her big divide, covered partially with a white panty that she pulled aside to give them a quick peek. They gave her a dollar.

I didn't know what to expect, but it was too much, too fast. I panicked. *I've got to get the fuck out of here.* "Sir, I think we've changed our minds. We're going to find a different place. Thank you, though, Big Daddy."

Outside the club, I looked around at the people milling around on the street, gorgeous women cackling with men on their arms. It was all so loud, so glamorous, so different. So sexy. "I don't understand New Orleans," I said.

"Yeah," said Maggie. "But we don't understand Soso, either."

We got back to Maggie's house in the early morning and skipped Sunday church, sleeping until the early afternoon. Awakened by a knock, Maggie scampered down to open the front door before running quickly back up the stairs to tell me that Mitch wanted to see me.

"What does he want?" I hissed.

"I don't know, but he's downstairs."

I panicked. "Oh, my God, I look like shit."

Maggie laughed and tickled me. "I'll tell Big Daddy you'll be a few minutes." She scampered back down.

I washed my face, threw on a little makeup, changed from my PJs into jeans. I walked down the old, creaky stairs to say hello. Each step felt ominous, like a declaration of some kind.

"Hey," I said, trying to make my voice sound casual. There was a funny taste in my mouth when I breathed out. Had I remembered to brush my teeth? "What's the matter, Mitch?"

"Nothing." He shrugged, easy. "I'm just here to see you. Your momma told me I could find you at Maggie's."

I looked back at Maggie in the kitchen. She shrugged her shoulders. I looked back at Mitch. "Let's go for a ride."

In his car, we listened to music while he asked what I had been doing all weekend. I didn't mention our trip to New Orleans. No one could know, for obvious reasons. If anything got back to our mommas, we'd be in for a whooping.

"Let's go over to the pumpjack and talk," Mitch suggested.

I had a feeling that talking was not his plan. Mitch stopped the car near a horsehead pumpjack, a long, horizontal beam mounted on top of two vertical legs. Drooping down from one side of the beam was the horsehead, which bobbed up and down, pushing the oil out of the ground. I could see and hear the horsehead pumpjack go up and down, up and down. In and out. I was terrified of both directions.

Mitch left the music on. Then he leaned over, took my face in his hands, and said, "You are very pretty." His hands felt different from that night after the football game. Maybe they were firmer, stronger. Maybe they'd changed. Or maybe I'd changed, in New Orleans, somehow. Or maybe my mind was just racing and full of everything or just nothing.

It was nice to hear that he thought I was pretty, of course. I also had imagined, though, for a long time that a boy would say to me, "You are a potent force, Karen," something Robert Redford said about Alva in *This Property Is Condemned.* I told myself to stop thinking about a movie or a book or a song. I was supposed to be on my own two feet, not Alva's.

He kissed me. His mouth was soft and wet—softer and not as wet as what I had expected. He tasted like the cotton candy at the county fair. He started slowly, with a few small pecks, but then he placed his tongue inside my mouth. He didn't force it in, he just moved his tongue gently, against my lips, until I knew that I was supposed to open up and allow him in. I just let it happen, let his tongue circle mine while mine just kind of sat there, unsure, asleep. He had looked really stupid licking the ice cream cone, but his tongue didn't feel stupid. He pressed harder with his mouth, and suddenly I wanted to sink underneath him. I moved against him, not with any intention of sex. I just wanted to be closer.

He put his hand on my breast.

That woke me up, and I laughed. "No, Mitch, we ain't going to titty territory yet. Kissing is good, though, but it's enough for now."

He tried again. Despite the sexual allure of New Orleans — or maybe because of it—I froze from anxiety and worry that I would fail at having sex with him. I needed direction, for sure, but I also wanted to be the one to set the scene and control the action. Janice was on my mind, and I didn't want my first time to be like hers. Not even close.

"Mitch," I said. "Give me some time."

"My balls are blue," he whined.

"They are? I never knew that balls were blue," I marveled. I didn't want to see them—I knew that would be perceived as an invitation I didn't want to give—but this was something I hadn't seen in any of my porn magazines, and I was curious.

"No, dummy. I mean they hurt."

"Oh," I said. "I didn't know balls hurt."

He cranked the car, and we left the horsehead, pumping Mississippi soil for oil. He was pissed. Again. When I got back, I asked for advice from Maggie and Libby about what to do next.

"How do we manage all of our body parts?" I asked. "It's too complicated. I don't know shit about sex."

"We've talked about this before. You just suffer through it the first time," Libby said. "The second and third times get better."

"Remember what I told y'all about Bud and me having sex," said Maggie. "Breathe deeply and exhale, and your vagina will open bigger each time you blow out air. Bud and I were kissing in the TV room when Momma was away. He sat on the TV chair with a pull-out footrest. I was sitting in his lap when he unzipped my shorts. He removed my shorts, and his, too. He asked me to sit on him. I was so nervous. I knew it would hurt extra bad. So, I took a deep

81

breath and when I sat on his dick, I exhaled and relaxed my entire body. And, pop, it went in."

"Oh, my God. That had to hurt," I moaned in pain.

"Yeah," Maggie said. "But I managed."

It was more detail than Maggie might otherwise have provided—more than what she would have given us a year ago—but someone had to fill Janice's role, the frank keeper of all knowledge. Maggie, now the most experienced of the remaining three, had taken it upon herself, initially with some reluctance, but with more confidence as time went on.

Our time at the Midnight Train was different now that Janice had left. We hadn't heard from her. When Janice got the word we wanted to talk to her, she wrote me a letter saying she missed us, but she was happy with Tim. We didn't have her phone number, and her momma either didn't have it or, more likely, pretended not to. Before we went to New Orleans, I wrote Janice a letter, asking her to come with us. She never wrote back.

I knew that if Janice were with us, she would have had the right answers for all my questions about Mitch, including those about sex.

Maggie and Libby were both more experienced than I was, sexually, and if there was one thing I knew from chasing trains all those years, it was that I hated being last. I knew, too, that Mitch was getting frustrated with me, and that the sand in the hourglass was running out with him. If I wanted him to be my first time—and I did, but, really, it was more a practical matter of need, since I didn't exactly have other options lining up. I knew I couldn't lead him on anymore.

The next weekend, Mitch and I rode in Myrtle and returned to the pumpjack. I had the evening all planned out: When Mitch made his move, I would insist we get in the back of the car and take off all of our clothes. Then, we would kiss, and he would touch me so I would be ready for his pecker, his penis, his whatever.

When the time came, I wasn't ready, despite twenty or more kisses and twenty or more touches. His thing hurt me. I was flat on my back in the back of Myrtle. A full, bright moon watched us the first time we tried.

"Mitch," I cried. "Oh, man. I'm sorry, but this *hurts*. I think your dick must be super big."

"No, it's not super big," Mitch said, frustrated. "It's average. Let me try again." He must have really wanted to avoid blue balls; I didn't know any other high school boy who would have told me that his dick *wasn't big*, just to get it inside me.

"Okay," I conceded. "But remember you have to pull it out before you come, or I'll get pregnant, and then you'll have to marry me, and I'll have to marry you, and then we'll have to get jobs even before we graduate high school. Our lives will be completely taken over by our baby."

"Karen, I promise you won't get pregnant."

At this point, the excitement of doing something for the first time had passed. I laid there in the back seat looking at the moon. It was unobscured by clouds except for a few wisps here and there. Oddly enough, Mitch was being very sweet. He had done it before, so he wasn't exploring new territory. He put his arms around me, and we looked at the moon together.

"You think we'll have a lot of moons like this, this month?" Mitch asked.

"I hope so," I said.

We turned to each other and laughed. He didn't try to fuck me after that. We just talked for a while about music, school, our brothers, and Janice, of course. And then he drove me home.

I realized, getting ready for bed that night, I was falling in love with him. The next morning, I woke up with a huge smile on my face, just like Scarlett did when Rhett scooped her up the red-carpeted stairway to bed in *Gone with the Wind*. Some people thought Rhett raped Scarlett, but I didn't think so. Scarlett knew exactly what to say to Rhett to stop him, but she didn't protest.

No surprise, my first attempt at fucking hurt. But I couldn't wait to try again, and I knew Mitch would definitely want to, as well.

Washing Libby's hair in the gym shower after basketball practice that day, I whispered to her through the suds. "His dick went up about an inch and

83

then I completely freaked out because it didn't feel good. I could tell he was excited, but not me. He needs to get that thing in me so we can just be done with it."

"I forgot to tell you this," Libby said. "He should buy this greasy lotion and put it on you. That will make it *much* easier."

"Get me the name of the lotion," I said.

"Make sure you drink something," Maggie added, joining the conversation from the next shower. "A beer or wine or something. It will help." Then, "Let's go chase the train this afternoon after school. Maybe we'll beat it this time."

"Be careful, Karen," Libby said, toweling herself off. "He may be romancing you now, but later, after it's done, he may move on to the next girl. He has that reputation."

"Really?"

"That's what I've heard from Gloria."

Fuck, I thought.

That afternoon, we ran faster and longer than any other chase. The train still beat us. I felt like we had won, though, for the first time since Janice hadn't been part of the chase. I needed to win.

***

Walking from class alone, Mitch snuck up behind me and grabbed my hand. "Let's try again. I want to see you soon. How about this Saturday?"

"Okay, Mitch. I can do that. With one provision. Can you bring a bottle of some kind of booze? I'm gonna need a drink. Also, that gooey lotion stuff. That will help."

Signs of being in charge. Ordering him around. I was making progress. I was winning.

On Saturday night, we were back at the pumpjack in Myrtle. Maggie had been right: Several sips of Mad Dog 20/20, a cheap fortified wine with 20 percent alcohol, calmed my nerves and helped me relax. I had sex on the first try. I was making love with Mitch, as close as two people could be. The world

84

was perfect. The moon was full. The frogs were croaking. The lightning bugs were blinking. The oil smelled like perfume. The car was spinning. And then I leaned out the car to vomit.

"You feel better now that the Mad Dog 20/20 is on the ground and out of your stomach?" Mitch asked a few minutes later.

"Definitely. Why didn't you throw up?"

"I'm used to it. I'm getting used to you, too."

"Oh, my God, I'm still spinnin'. I will never get use to that Mad Dog." I flopped down onto my back and laughed, high and drunk and happy. "Why did you let me drink so much? I'm no longer a virgin, and I'm drunk." I laughed. "And I got the man I wanted to be first."

"Will I be the last?" Mitch asked.

"I don't know. I've got lots of time to decide. I still don't like a lot of things about me. I'm sure you may feel the same way."

"What's not to like? You're pretty, a good athlete, smart, sweet mouth, blue eyes, nice ass, and…"

I smacked him, lightly, on the chest. "Enough bullshit. You're just hopin' for another round. But I need to get home before my momma jumps in her car to track me down."

"I like the sound of the pumpjack. In out. In out," said Mitch.

"Don't use that line again," I said, but I smiled at him as he drove Myrtle away from the pumpjack back to the house on the hill.

Chapter 5

Chasing Trains

The next weekend Libby, Maggie, and I made it to the Midnight train Sunday afternoon before church service. We wanted to talk about changing Midnight's name to Soul Train because we had been watching *Soul Train,* the Black music and dance TV show. We learned how to do the Hustle, and we loved Don Cornelius, the host, and the musician Van McCoy, who sang the song "The Hustle."

Before the chase, we whistled McCoy's song walking to the track, performing some of the Hustle steps, and mimicking the train sound with "tututututututu." We wanted to hustle. We hustled basketball and boys. No more porn magazines. Only the hustle. We were chasing our Soul Train now.

"Damn right we are chasing our soul train," said Maggie to Libby and me at the end of the workout. "Since our virgin holes have been invaded by dicks, we need a soulful song to get us through the day." I said, "How about 'Let's

Get It On' with Marvin Gaye?" Maggie sang Gaye's song a cappella about love and sex. We joined her for the line "Let your love come out…"

"My love is coming out," I said. "I haven't quite figured out the 'coming' part, yet."

The first orgasm I ever had—I just didn't know it was an orgasm—was when Robert Redford grabbed Alva and slammed her against his bedroom door after a fight about calling him a liar, planting a major kiss on her mouth. I felt the throbbing as I watched them look at each other with glaring passion in their eyes. That hadn't happened with Mitch yet.

"Let me explain then," Maggie offered, standing at attention and motioning appropriately. "The top part of your pussy, where that tiny flap is, starts to tingle and then before you know it, you can't believe how terrific it feels. It makes you squirm and groan and scream."

"Scream? Groan? Squirm? Really?"

"Yes. I want to do it again and again and again. And, sometimes when my jeans are too tight between my thighs, it just happens on its own. Bud got it to work."

"What to work?"

"That flap!"

"How?"

Libby laughed, "Did Bud kiss it?"

Maggie responded, "Sometimes. I know Scott has done it to you, too."

"So wait," I stopped them both. "Do I have to tell or ask Mitch to do this? Or will he just do it, without my telling him?" I asked.

"If he doesn't do it soon, then definitely tell him," answered Maggie.

"Oh, the burden," I said, falling back onto my Soul Train seat. I didn't want to think about it. I changed the topic to our upcoming state championship basketball game.

We felt ready. We had gotten stronger and much more aggressive, as aggressive as the girls from Mount Olive. When Coach Michaels wasn't in the gym, most of the team would gather for an hour and do run and guns during study hall, up and down the court, before regular third-period practice. Elbows swung in coordination with each foot move. Eyes shifted back and forth to keep the movement of all bodies on the court in our sight. Look to the right but throw to the left. If the shot was no good on the left, the ball came back to where it started, and someone would shoot and score. That was our plan.

We never stopped for air. We jumped. We turned and twisted. We kept in motion.

Maybe we would pick—part of Coach Michael's strategy—but the pick would happen when we decided. Not Coach Michael.

Without Coach Michaels around, we even practiced bad-ass and sarcastic lines that we delivered to opponents, messing with their minds, especially during foul ball shots.

"Girl, you breathin' really hard. You okay? You need me to tell your coach?"

"I think your teammates don't like you. You want me to tell them to throw you the ball?"

"Next time you get the ball, I'm going to take it from you. I'm giving you a heads-up."

A few days before the championship game, I came down with the flu. I was very sick but was determined to play. I did, but I couldn't run and gun with diarrhea and a temperature. I missed shots I always made. We lost. I lost. I sat in the stands, alone by choice, crying during the boys' championship game. Maggie, Libby, and my momma walked over and sat behind me to comfort me. Momma didn't say a word. She knew better.

The next day at school, I was in my car when Mitch scared me by hitting the front window as he smashed a bug.

"Let your window down," he yelled.

"What do you want?"

"I'm sorry you lost," he said.

"Go away."

I drove to my father's cemetery and cried at his gravestone. I hadn't been there for two years. I cried about losing him and the state championship. Two losses. I was a miserable loser.

The next day I got a letter from Oxford, Mississippi, informing me that I had been accepted at Ole Miss. I felt like a winner, just like that, and I had the acceptance letter to prove it. I still had to try out to be a Lady Rebel, but I knew I could make the team. Because I was damn good or at least good enough.

As graduation approached, I thought about Janice almost every single day. I imagined that if she had only stayed with us—if Janice had told her parents and the school about Coach, if we had told the school about Coach — then Janice would have gotten her high school diploma and gone onto college, maybe even with me as part of the Ole Miss basketball team. That's what I wanted to believe, anyway, even though it was hard to linger on what could have been.

Also hard to believe was when Janice showed up at school unannounced a few days before graduation. Maggie, Libby and I hadn't seen her for over a year, and we squealed with a joy we hadn't known was possible since before she told us she was getting married and leaving. Dodging students between class, we zoomed down the hall to see her outside and gave her huge hugs while other students hung out the school windows to scream, "Welcome back, Janice!" It felt like we were in a movie, sun shining and cinematic. Her hug was as firm and as warm as I'd remembered it was.

After a round of announcements about the latest news about graduation, Janice calmed us down and told us, "I'm back, y'all. I'm divorcing Tim."

I should have felt happy. This was, after all, what I'd wanted, for so long. Instead, I was just shell-shocked. "What?" I said. "Don't get me wrong, girl, we're real glad, but why exactly?"

Janice shrugged, trying to look nonchalant, though I wasn't sure. I couldn't read her as well as I used to, after the time we'd spent apart. "Tim wanted a baby, and I wasn't ready. He was away or worked late, anyways. We fought. It wasn't what I thought it would be. I'm getting a trailer from my parents."

89

"What about finishing school?" I asked.

"No reason to finish." Janice shrugged again. "I'll figure it out. Maybe I'll get a GED."

"Become part of us again," I begged, deciding not to probe into the details of a divorce. "Part of the coterie. Graduation is next week. We don't go to Midnight as much as we used to, without you."

"Let's go now!" Maggie urged.

"I can't," Janice said, smiling. "I have to meet my parents soon. Another day, okay?"

"Yes, yes, yes. We are so glad you are back." I grinned so wide I almost worried it would split my face in two.

That smile would soon fade: Janice was back, but everything was different. Maggie, Libby and me were disappointed that everything was different, but why wouldn't it be different? Obviously it should be different. Janice had been raped, physically and emotionally. We knew that, but why didn't we *get that*?

We didn't get it because we never told anyone. We never told anyone because we didn't think we should. We didn't know any better. We didn't know any better because no one—not our parents or our schoolteachers—ever talked about rape, sexual abuse, sexual harassment. Like most teenage girls, we talked about sex. The kind of sex we wanted was different from the kind of sex we never wanted.

***

Momma made me a dress to wear underneath the graduation gown. I insisted the neck be low so that I could look sexy for parties to mark the big 1976 senior celebration. We entered the gym from the back and walked down the gym aisle, sat in folding chairs, and listened to the Valedictorian for the first thirty seconds, before our minds started to drift. Janice sat in the back, in chairs for family and guests. We waved, laughed and blew her kisses. She smiled and blew us kisses back, but that was all. Invited to every graduation party, Janice declined.

Mitch and I continued to see each other, and I loved him, in my almost-eighteen-year-old way. When Mitch didn't win the Best All-Around Football Player award at the athletic banquet our senior year, I was so furious I drove over to his football coach's home, knocked on the door, and told him, "You didn't do right by Mitch." He thanked me for my thoughts and slammed the door in my face. Even so, I didn't want to leave high school. I didn't want to leave the basketball team, the coterie, Soul Train and the memories of Midnight. I worried about Momma not having me around. She hadn't dated anyone since Daddy died. She crocheted, washed and ironed my clothes, and made Robbie and me breakfast every morning.

Mitch's parents often sat on their porch after dinner in rocking chairs and talked. For a while, I thought I would do the same thing with Mitch one day. That fantasy didn't last long. The summer after senior year, I started wearing a bikini, and Mitch told me I had to stop. It was too revealing, he said, and he demanded I not wear it ever again.

I looked at him as if he had lost his mind. I laughed. Surely this was some grand joke of his. Surely Mitch couldn't have dated me—me!—for a year and still think that I was the sort of girl who would let her boyfriend dictate what she could wear and when.

"What makes you think you can tell me something like that?" I asked. "Of course I can wear a bikini."

"Not if you want to be my girlfriend," Mitch insisted. "You have to respect my request."

"I don't have to respect your request, actually," I countered. "Relax. You should be flattered. I'm showing off my body, but you're the only one who can touch it."

But he didn't let it go. He pouted for days. I felt bad briefly and quickly revived myself after two McDonald's fish sandwiches, a strawberry milkshake, and an apple pie with Libby and Maggie.

"Tell him to fuck off," suggested Libby.

"Tell him to find another girlfriend," Maggie said. "What a shithead."

"What else can we call him?" Libby asked. "Freak. Sexist. Demanding. Punk. Motherfucker."

"Mindless," Maggie added. "Jealous. Controlling. Pain in the ass. Madly in love with you. Will seek forgiveness."

But Mitch didn't seek forgiveness. Instead, he disappeared, and I didn't hear from him for most of the summer. One day, I saw him in his truck on the road to McDonald's. He waved from his truck and pulled over. I did, too.

"I'm headed to Ole Miss soon," I said.

"Yeah, I know that," he said.

"I'll miss you. You know that, right?"

He shrugged his shoulders.

"You look a mess. What have you been doing this summer?" I asked.

"I'm working at a lumber mill. It's hot and dusty. Sorry if my smell bothers you."

"No, of course not," I said, thinking of something to say that would make him like me again.

"Good luck at Jones Junior College," I said, with a big smile on my face. "I'm leaving soon for Ole Miss." But then I realized that I'd already said that and stood there awkwardly in silence as he drove off — my first and only fuck deserting me because I dared to wear a bikini once in 1976.

***

Shortly after graduation, I called Janice's momma at her parent's jewelry store and asked how I could reach her. I finally got a phone number, but there was no answer when I called. Libby, Maggie and I drove over to her trailer and, finally, she answered the door.

We invited her to Midnight with us, one of our last chases before we all parted ways at the end of the summer and went off to college. We went back to calling our railcar, Midnight.

"I will try to meet you there," Janice promised. "I need to take my car, so I can go over to my cousin's house for dinner after." She smiled, but it didn't quite reach her eyes. Her smile had changed. Her eyes, too.

She never made it for the chase. The three of us didn't want to chase without her.

In a few days I'd be leaving Soso. The West Jones High School football season and then the basketball season would begin soon as they always had. Coach would still be there. Coach Michaels, too. A new group of girls would be figuring out how to get in Mrs. Cook's English class and out of Miss Curtis' typing class. Momma would pay her visits to Daddy's grave, again without me. The day we didn't chase the 3:14, I knew I was leaving the Soso tracks for good, except for occasional visits.

It was too hard for me to say goodbye again to Janice. I tried not to worry about the coterie as Libby, Maggie and I said our final goodbyes before heading off to college. I would see them again soon. Maybe we would even chase a train during a school holiday, I kept telling myself.

In truth, I knew that all of us—Janice, Libby, Maggie and me—had new trains to chase, without each other.

Chapter 6

False Colors

Attending Ole Miss was as big a deal to me as attending Harvard or Yale would be for any wealthy prep school kid from Connecticut. Harvard and Yale, though, existed on another planet as far as I was concerned. My ACT score of 21 never bothered me. I made terrific grades, and no one told me to study for the ACT. It was a low score, I finally figured out. It was good enough for Ole Miss, though, and I had been offered a spot on the Lady Rebel team.

Ole Miss had mostly white students and, outside the Deep South, had been branded as a racist institution with a stormy, violent past after its refusal to admit a Black man, James Meredith, in 1962. During the Battle of Oxford, as the riot was called, two civilians and a French journalist were killed, and over three hundred people were injured; seventy-nine of them were U.S. Marshals deployed by President Kennedy to ensure Meredith's attendance. Ole Miss got the headlines, but other Mississippi colleges, public and private, weren't much different in their attitudes about race. Meredith got into class, and many more Black students followed in his path, including Peggy Gillom, who became the first Black woman basketball player fourteen years later, in 1976, the year I joined the team.

My thoughts were elsewhere during the drive from Soso to Oxford with my momma. Leaving home left my heart heavy. Momma drove me in Daddy's gold Chevrolet El Camino, the truck Daddy died in when Robbie drove him to the hospital almost four years earlier. She and I always tried to avoid sitting on the passenger side where Daddy passed; Momma scooted close to me to sit in the middle, and I needed all the room in the back of the pick-up truck to load up my college stuff. At the dorm, we unpacked, and I surrounded myself with my favorite books, music posters, photos, and plants in a room shared with another basketball player.

My roommate wasn't happy about the amount of my belongings, but they were behind the imaginary half-way line that marked off our personal space in the room, and my things made me feel safer. Ole Miss was known as a haven for white kids who had wealthy daddies, went to private academies, and grew up on large plantations in the Delta. Not girls like me who lived in a concrete house with tobacco turds in the backyard. I was nervous—scared, really for the first time—and I felt last in everything. Again.

Before she headed back to Soso, Momma tried to reassure me, as mothers do. "Karen, you always figure things out. You will get over your fears."

And, after being there a week, I did figure out a few things. Most girls were better dressed than me. My Social Security check didn't cover Barbie doll dresses, nice heels, handbags, perfume and make-up. And, everyone but me seemed very comfortable in social settings. They knew how to party, too. I hated beer, but at Ole Miss you needed to love it to make friends. Meeting new people horrified me. When I did meet someone, I didn't know what to say to them. To entertain myself before classes began, I strolled the campus alone, with no coterie to join me. I wasn't alone. I just felt alone, and plenty of other young women felt alone.

95

I saw the campus as historic and majestic. Two of the original school buildings, the Lyceum Building, built in 1848, and Barnard Observatory, built in 1857, reminded me of background scenes from *Gone with the Wind*, before the Civil War. The beautiful buildings overlooked the Grove, where the nastiest, loudest, and drunkest tailgates in the Deep South, maybe in the entire country, took place before football games. After tailgates, the Grove looked less than majestic, covered with beer bottles, broken glass, and the mud dug up and flung by truck tires.

Drunk guys "gatored" on the Grove, as well as on the football field, at half time. Gatoring was imitating an alligator pretending to have sex in the water with another gator. I was never sure how accurate the imitation was because I had never witnessed two gators having sex. Nor had most Southerners, even those living near gators. Nonetheless, human gatoring was extremely popular at Ole Miss.

An Ole Miss frat boy, my first date at college, introduced me to the odd ritual of gatoring. I met him in Western Civilization. After a couple of classes, he asked me to the football game on Saturday. I was more afraid to answer his question than any of those asked by my Western Civ professor. Desperate to make new friends, I agreed.

By the time he arrived at my dorm around noon on game day, he had been drinking since 10 a.m. I made polite conversation with other girls at the tailgate while my date appeared and disappeared on a fairly regular basis. By the time we made it to the game, he was so piss drunk he forgot I was his date. At half -time, I saw him on the field, gatoring. Thousands of other people saw him, too, and everyone sitting around me laughed hilariously and chanted, "Gator! Gator! Gator!"

I left the bleachers faster than any horny gator chasing its mate. That Monday in class, he tried to apologize, but I held my hand up, in front of his face.

"I don't know you. You had a date with a gator, not me."

He always sat behind me in class, but we never spoke again.

Ole Miss represented too many things that scared me, even more than the mysterious voodoo panthers that I imagined stalked our Soso farm. I had no Janice, no Maggie, no Libby. I studied and played ball. That was it.

My Ole Miss roommate and I didn't hit it off, either. Patty complained that my books and plants took up too much space; but other than that, we didn't talk much, primarily because she slept late in the morning when I was already in class and was out late at night when I was already asleep. That problem resolved itself soon enough: Patty got pregnant during the first semester and left school.

I never wanted anyone to become pregnant accidentally, so I did feel badly for her—at least, for the twelve hours between telling me about her baby and being picked up by her parents the next morning.

"Why didn't your boyfriend wear a condom? Why didn't you get on the pill?" I asked after hearing her news.

"I don't know. We just weren't careful one night. I guess I love him. I'm going to have his baby, regardless," she said.

"Why don't you get one of those abortions? My momma said abortions were wrong, but when one of my cousins got a girl pregnant in high school, Momma paid for one."

"Lord, girl! You have got opinions, Karen. I will miss you," she said, and then popped her head up from her pillow. "A word of advice: Enjoy yourself more. You study, workout, play ball, then study, workout, play ball. You're too intense. Sometimes you really get on my nerves."

I didn't like Patty, either, but I took her advice by trying to join a sorority, the great Southern sisterhood. I had little to no idea what a sorority was or what the girls in the sorority did when I applied. During rush, when a Tri Delta sorority sister asked me to submit "recs," I asked, "What is a rec?"

The Tri-Delta member laughed, then smiled and told me, "Sweetie, it's a recommendation from someone you know or knows your mother who has been in our sorority."

"I don't know anyone. My momma doesn't, either."

The Tri-Delta responded, "Have someone in Laurel who knows your parents call us."

My daddy was dead, and my momma didn't know a lot of other mothers from the city, Laurel, and certainly no one who had been in a sorority. Tri-Delt rejected me almost as quickly as I applied.

I got rushed, though, by the "angels" as they called themselves, from Pi Beta Phi. Pi Phi often recruited smart girls from out of state. I wasn't out of state, but I had good grades, and I was on the Ole Miss basketball team. Before Title IX, the sororities didn't care much one way or the other about women athletes as members. But when federal funds started flowing for women's sports teams under Title IX, sororities played a different tune. Having a Lady Rebel as an "active" brought prestige, I guessed, and a pledge invitation came my way.

I paid for the honor, though. They made me do study hall in the sorority house for an hour each day. Other pledges would talk and disturb my attention or ask me questions about the basketball team. I hated it. When mid-term grades came in, I had all A's, and I told my active "big sister" that was it; no more study hall for me.

"Yes, but it will be good for you to be around the other pledges," she said, ignoring my request.

"It may be good for them, but not for me. I have class early in the morning and practice every afternoon. Games start soon. I'm wasting my one free hour in study hall. I need to study alone. Maybe it's best for all if I just quit. Besides sororities don't have any Black pledges or actives. We had Black girls on our basketball team and cheerleading squad."

"No, you can't quit," she said. "It's a huge mistake for you to drop. Oh, my goodness, you just can't. Your mid-terms were all A's, and we need pledges with high grades so the ones who have low grades don't mess up our averages. Karen, please!"

Now I understood my purpose: I was there to make Pi Phi appear smarter. I had A's because I was good at memorizing stupid shit for tests. That didn't make me smart; it just made me disciplined, my true strength. Having discovered the scam, I said to my big sis, "Well, maybe, I'll stay if I don't have to do study hall, and you don't make me collect names on the angel arrow. I just don't have the time." Pledges had to carry a wooden angel arrow, which was about the length of my arm from wrist to elbow, everywhere they went. Pledges then had to strike up conversations with the actives, who then might offer to sign the angel arrow. This signing ceremony required a level of chit-chat to get to know actives, but I had no idea what to say to them.

My Big Sis nodded curtly. "Deal. I'll work it out with the president."

I started making deals very early in life. Once I figured out that the sorority was all about the art of the bargain, I didn't care what they wanted. I knew they needed me for their grade average. Later that semester, they told me I had to wear mascara to class. My big sister said, "You need mascara on both the top *and* bottom. It doesn't look appropriate otherwise."

Appropriate? "Why does it matter?" I snapped. "I make straight A's. Why should lash care be on my to-do list? My classes start at 8 a.m., and I'm tired from basketball. Some mornings I don't have time."

"I know," said my big sister. "But that's just the rules."

"Well, the rules are no good."

The night of the big initiation ceremony, I walked into the Pi Phi house, which was bathed in candlelight, its walls covered in white satin sheets for the occasion. I had gone to heaven with the angels —that, or entered the campus' KKK dressing room.

All of the actives held wands, and the sorority president sat on a large, comfy chair covered with white satin, wearing a jeweled crown on her head. I marched with the other pledges in between two lines of actives, who all smiled and waved their wands over our heads as we marched to the big momma angel up front. I was pinned with a silver arrow, covered with my choice of sapphires and diamonds—I chose sapphires because they were blue like my eyes. Several Social Security checks had paid for that. The president waved her wand over our heads, blessed us, and declared us Pi Beta Phi angels. It was the most ridiculous ceremony I had ever witnessed, including those at revivals at Maggie's church, where people spoke in tongues.

A few weeks later, big sis tracked me down at breakfast, chipper. "New news! We want you to be in the Most Beautiful pageant."

I winced. "I'm not beautiful, and I don't want to go through that. Plus, you don't need any talent to be in the pageant. You only have to be beautiful."

"You are *too* beautiful, especially when you take the time to do your make-up. You'll have a shot at Most Beautiful or runner-up." She was undeterred. "I heard about a rust-colored dress you have. Someone told me you wore it to your senior athletic banquet in high school. Maybe you can wear it in the pageant."

"Yeah, my momma made it on her sewing machine."

"Great! Come by the house tonight to show it off."

I could have cared less about a pageant, but I did want to show off Momma's dress, so I agreed to stop by. The rust-colored satin dress and my momma's sewing abilities generated plenty of compliments, and even I received a few. Despite my misgivings, I was elated that a bunch of sorority girls thought I was at least pretty or cute. Buoyed by the ego puffing, I signed up for the pageant, against my better judgment.

With the pageant approaching, my big sis mentioned to me she had a pink chiffon dress with a fluffy skirt that she thought might be even nicer on me than my Momma-sewn, rust-colored dress.

Struggling to pull the pink chiffon with the fluffy skirt over my head wasn't easy, but I finally managed in front of five sorority sisters at the Pi Phi house in my big sis' bedroom. I thought I looked silly. Everyone else agreed that pink was clearly my color.

"I hate pink," I grumbled. "Rust is better."

"No," the queen of the sorority insisted, "pink is best for you."

A few days after that, my big sis casually asked me if Bridget, a senior, could wear my rust-colored dress, since I wasn't wearing it for the pageant.

"Fine by me," I said.

100

I called my momma a few days later to tell her I would be in the Most Beautiful pageant. She was tickled, I think. But when I mentioned the dress exchange, her amusement quickly turned to outrage. I could hear her fury crackling down the phone line. "Judy Karen, they are trickin' you and lyin' to you. Get my dress back."

"Naw, Momma," I said. "Why do you think that?"

"It's a beautiful dress, and I made it for you, not Bridget. She may win, and you won't. They flyin' false colors, like you always say," she said.

I thought that she was making a lot out of nothing, and I didn't say anything to my sorority sisters. But, like she usually was, Momma was right. Wearing Momma's dress, Bridget made the top ten in the competition for Most Beautiful. I didn't make nothing.

Competing in basketball demanded most of my time and my energy; competing to land time in a ballgame was legitimate. Competing over a dress was a false color; a trick and a lie. For a while, I tried to juggle the two worlds, but by the end of my first semester my roles as a Lady Rebel and a Pi Phi Angel collided. Literally.

One of my Lady Rebel teammates was Peggy Gillom, who was the first Black woman to play at Ole Miss and later coached at Texas A&M and Ole Miss and inducted into the Women's Basketball Hall of Fame. I was West Jones tall, but she was Ole Miss tall, sporting a significant height advantage over me. One afternoon at practice, Peggy and I competed to pull down a rebound off the backboard. She jumped so much higher than I did that she not only snatched the ball, but also rammed her elbow down on my lip as her feet hit the floor. In the locker room after practice, my lip had swollen so large I couldn't close my mouth.

Unfortunately, before basketball practice, my big sister had begged me to go to a swap that night, when a sorority and a fraternity throw a party together. It was meant for the attractive individuals of similar ages to mix and mingle.

"I'll fix you up with a really good-looking guy, a friend of my boyfriend who's in the fraternity," she promised.

101

"I can't," I protested. "I won't know anyone."

She interrupted me. "We'll pick you up around seven tonight. Just talk about basketball. They'll love that you are a player."

But when I got back to my room from the gym, my lip was bloated like a pufferfish. I called her back. "My lip is swelling from practice. I got hit. I can't do this swap tonight. I'll look ridiculous."

"I'm sure you'll be fine. We'll see you soon." Click.

Big Sis and the two dates met me in the lobby of the dorm to escort me to my date's car. All three of them looked at me like I was some strange creature from another galaxy. I wanted to run back to my dorm room. My date looked at his friend, smiled at my big sister, and opened the door to the car for me. He didn't utter a word, and neither did I—except to explain why my lip was huge. He didn't seem amused.

When we walked into the frat house, he told me that he had to say hello to a few people, and that he'd be right back. I didn't see him for the rest of the night, just like the gator date. I'd failed again.

After searching for the restroom to hide, I exited the fraternity house from the back door and ran into a couple fornicating on the steps, both highly intoxicated. So drunk, they didn't notice me. I found my way back to campus and walked all the way back to the dorm, alone.

Plopping down on my bed, I cried for five minutes straight. It was maybe the longest I had ever cried, aside from when we'd lost the state championship in high school basketball.

The next day, I went to see the queen. She had no wand this time and didn't look at all queen-like. I told her I was getting out and wouldn't return.

"Karen," she said, almost amused, "to drop out, you have to give us your active pin. You know you can't keep it."

"You can have the arrow back, but not the sapphires and the diamonds. Those are mine. I don't give a shit about the arrow."

It was worth it to leave just to see the shock on her face.

"Karen!" she scolded. "Don't speak like that."

"You're right," I said. "I shouldn't say 'shit.' What I should say is that you lied to me about that frilly pink dress you made me wear in the beauty pageant, and you stole my rust-colored dress that my momma made for me."

I did return the arrow, but I kept the gems. Eventually, I had a lovely ring decorated with the sapphires and diamonds. A couple of years later, a painter hired by the owner of my college apartment to repaint the exterior of the building knocked on my door, asking to use my bathroom. After he left, I discovered he'd stolen the ring from my jewelry box. I swear to God he changed the color of the outside of the apartment complex from rusty brown to a muted pink.

I was right about pink: stuck with that fucking false color once again.

***

As a Lady Rebel, my colors weren't false—they just weren't as true as some of the other players on the team. I still loved basketball, but it began to feel less central to my life than at West Jones, mostly because I wasn't as good as my teammates. I wanted to love Ole Miss and feel special, but mostly I felt that the Ole Miss crowd looked at me like I was just white trash from a town full of trailers. My first semester of college, I'd lost my basketball skills, my rust-colored dress, and my angel pin. Gossip about my swollen lip blocked my dating rotation. I had yet to be kissed by an Ole Miss boy.

All was not lost. That year, I saw the movie *All The President's Men*, mostly because Robert Redford was the star. But the fast-paced world of the *Washington Post* and the work of investigative reporters Bob Woodward and Carl Bernstein soon captivated me. Rather than imagining myself as Robert Redford's girlfriend—as I had done when watching every Robert Redford movie previously—I watched each scene picturing myself as Robert Redford himself, the reporter. I was taken in not just by Redford's looks, but his confidence, his doggedness, his way of reading people and getting to the truth of what they were saying and doing. Sitting in a dark theater that afternoon, I fell in love with the idea of becoming a reporter. That was the movie that clinched my plan to major in journalism and political science.

I started writing for the *Daily Mississippian,* the Ole Miss student paper. The editor was a senior, and the assistant editor was his girlfriend, Katie, who really ran the paper. The boyfriend just thought great thoughts in his office, which I'd soon learn was typical of many men in charge of just about everything. Katie became my journalism teacher outside the classroom, editing my stories and helping me learn how to talk to sources and write a lede.

The journalism building soon became my dorm away from the dorm. It was one of several buildings used as hospitals for Confederate soldiers during the Civil War, with beautiful walnut doors, which I ran my hands over every day, thinking of the wounded soldiers who'd passed through them. Unlike many Ole Miss students, I was no Confederate apologist. I was embarrassed by the emblem of the Confederate flag that was incorporated into our state flag. Still, I reckoned that some wounded and dead Southerners who entered those doors had been victims of profit-hungry white slave owners who marched poor soldiers toward death for their own lost cause.

When the college made plans to raze the building for a more modern space, I wrote a piece for the *Daily Mississippian* about the history of the building and the dumping of the walnut doors. It was largely ignored, but the doors survived. It was my first journalism victory.

Protests, poverty, riots, Vietnam, and Richard Nixon headlined the front pages of newspapers in most states. But not Mississippi, where local news was all that mattered.

Still, I had big dreams. I read one news story about Israel in *Time* magazine and, after that, felt informed enough to write an editorial about a country I knew nothing about and could not find on a map. One of the few liberals who existed at Ole Miss came by the *Daily Mississippian* to meet with me to talk about the published editorial. He was a short white man with a long beard from Maine or Massachusetts or another foreign country I knew nothing about. He said he was in Mississippi to write a book about civil rights as he worked on his doctorate.

I asked him, "Why don't you write about where you're from? Doesn't that matter most?"

"You wrote about Israel," he countered. "The history of civil rights is happening right here, and this is the place to concentrate on."

"No one concentrates in Mississippi or about Mississippi," I said. "Most of the national news right now in Mississippi is about Boston and busing."

"I think that's incorrect," said Harold, my about-to-be new, older liberal friend from the Far East Coast. "There are important racial movements happening here, too."

"I suppose that's true." I shrugged. "My daddy's Black workers used to have union protests outside of his construction sites when I was growing up."

"Did the protests upset you?" Harold asked.

"Yeah," I admitted, "because they said bad things about my daddy that I knew weren't true. They said he was a racist. But one night when I was about ten years old, we were at the dinner table, and the news was on, and there had been something about Blacks protesting in Memphis. I never said the word before but, for some reason, that night I said to my daddy, 'Those n-----rs need to stop protesting.'

"My daddy always read *US News & World Report* during dinner, but that night he looked up from the magazine at me with fire in his eyes. He stood up at the table and pointed to the TV room, where our Black cleaning lady was ironing. He didn't say a word to me. He just stared me down, and I ran from the table to my bedroom. Not a word was spoken, and I never said that word again."

Harold hummed in thought as he twirled and stroked his beard. "Complex. White people have to acknowledge their racism."

"I think you can't be a little bit racist or a lot racist," I argued. "You either are or aren't. We have to get over it. Everywhere, including Boston." I was trying a new vocabulary on for size.

"Was he not a racist because he didn't say the n word? Or was he a racist because he wouldn't hire Black union workers?"

"Some of the union workers were whites. But it's complex."

Jones County, where I grew up, was the most conservative county in the most conservative state in the country. It was hard to explain how I became a liberal rebel at one of the most conservative colleges in the country. I always said Fannie Lou Hamer and Medgar Evers, both well-known Mississippi civil rights activists, influenced me. It was a believable reason, but only part of the story.

The complexities of mixed-race families in the South after Native Americans lost their tribal lands were the makings of Southern literature, especially in Mississippi—or so Mrs. Cook, my high school English teacher, told me. And that mix resulted in one of the most fascinating stories about Jones County, one that I devoured way before I left for Ole Miss. Jones County was a segregationist hotbed, a place of racial violence where the Klan was as strong as anywhere in the South. I learned much later that my own uncle had been head of the Jones County Klan and involved in terrible violent acts against Blacks during the 1960s. Amazingly, though, a century earlier Jones County had seceded from the Confederacy during the Civil War. A group of poor Jones County whites joined Black slaves to fight against Robert E. Lee's troops on the side of the Union, declaring itself the "Free State of Jones."

On the rolls of the Free State's rag tag army were Hintons. I liked to think those were my Hintons.

Stories about race, gender and religion drew me to Southern literature in high school and college. I read a lot of Tennessee Williams, spurred by my obsession with *This Property Is Condemned,* as well as William Faulkner, Carson McCullers, Eudora Welty, Flannery O'Connor and Richard Wright. Not easy summer reads, but either Janice or Mrs. Cook explained them, or I read without them in college. O'Connor in particular surprised, shocked, and scared me with her troubling, contradictory endings.

In *Good Country People*, a Bible salesman stays for dinner at the home of the Hopewells, even though they did not want to buy the Good Book. Mrs. Hopewell thought he was "good country people." After dinner, the salesman invites the young daughter, Joy, for a picnic the next day. Joy, who says she is

106

an atheist, wears a prosthetic leg and glasses. During the picnic, the salesman convinces Joy to go to a barn loft where he removes her leg and glasses and offers her whiskey, pornographic cards and condoms, hoping for sex. Joy spurns him, so he leaves her alone in the barn loft without a leg after telling her he's nothing but a lawless heretic. Conflicts, misunderstandings, lies, and unanswered questions surfaced in all of her short stories, but I couldn't stop reading them regardless of her head-banging narratives. I definitely could stop reading Faulkner's books in high school and did. I finally conquered a few: *As I Lay Dying, Barn Burning*, and *The Sound and the Fury*. The leftish news magazines that Harold gave me at Ole Miss, *Mother Jones, Seven Days,* and the *Village Voice*, added another, very different layer of liberalism.

But what pulled me further and further away from the overt racism of Jones County was the world I read about through the writing of and books about Fannie Lou Hamer, Medgar Evers, Martin Luther King, Jr., and Malcolm X, especially Hamer's 1967 autobiography, *To Praise Our Bridges*, which the owner of Square Books in Oxford, Richard Howorth, helped me find.

Hamer was one of the first civil rights workers to write about her personal life, working in the cotton fields of Ruleville, Mississippi, fighting not only for the right to vote but to have the money to eat and buy a pair a shoes for the winter. When white men threatened to kill her and her family, she put a shotgun on every wall in her bedroom, ready to protect herself and her loved ones. Although the history of this world existed all around me in Jones County, it took Hamer and the others for me to see their world—and mine—one which I barely understood existed in Soso, though it was right there in front of me.

Others guided me in person. One was Willie Morris, one of my professors. Willie was a writer-in-residence at Ole Miss and a native of Yazoo City, Mississippi, who had returned to his motherland after serving as editor-in-chief at *Harper's Magazine* in New York during its heyday in the '60s and '70s. Willie wrote *North Toward Home,* a best-selling autobiography that won him the Houghton Mifflin Literary Fellowship Award. At *Harper's*, Willie published leading writers, many Southern, such as William Styron, Norman Mailer, Truman Capote, Gay Talese, David Halberstam, Ralph Ellison, and Arthur Miller. He was pals with most of them and convinced a number of them to come to Ole Miss to hold forth to his students. Luckily, I was one of those students in 1980, my senior year.

Aside from Willie himself, the visiting writer I was most intrigued by was the least-known and youngest writer in Willie's collection, Winston Groom, the first author to arrive in 1980. Six years later, he wrote *Forrest Gump,* which became the hit movie starring Tom Hanks and Robin Wright. Groom was born in D.C. but raised in Mobile County, Alabama, about a two-hour drive from Jones County. He thought of becoming a lawyer like his father, but writing became his passion. He served in the Army from 1965 to 1969 in Vietnam. After the war, he became a reporter for the *Washington Star* but resigned to write novels. His first was *Better Times Than These*, about a rifle company in the Vietnam War. As I read his book, twice, before his arrival, I thought of my neighbor Tony, who'd killed himself in Cambodia after being drafted to Vietnam. In Soso, he pushed me so high in a swing set I could see him upside down when I swung back to him.

Winston Groom was a good writer—funny, but not stupid funny—and very good-looking. I wanted to write like him. I was nervous about asking any questions, but I had to hear his views about Tony and what happened to him. "I knew this boy who went to Vietnam and killed himself. Why do you think he did that?" I asked.

Stunned, Groom hesitated, took a sip of whiskey, and explained: "I knew a Tony. Not your Tony, but another. I don't know why soldiers kill themselves. Suicide happens everywhere to someone. Loss of hope and a belief in yourself are signals or signs. That was Vietnam. Honestly, though, I have no idea. It's impossible to know the real reason."

This answer was most unsatisfactory to me, but I was too shy to press further. Tony killed himself because he didn't want to be there. At least, that was what I thought.

After Groom left, George Plimpton arrived. He was charming, but we didn't know what to do with him, because he was not really a Southern boy — even though he tried to be. He wore a bow tie, had a professorial laugh, and wore a seersucker suit. That could work in certain Southern venues, mostly in the Mississippi Delta, but definitely not in Soso, Mississippi. "Is someone cookin' me some collard greens and fryin' catfish for supper?" he asked us in Willie's class, with a bad attempt at a Southern accent.

Willie also was a close friend of Bill Styron. Willie had published several of Styron's pieces in *Harper's*, including a 45,000-word excerpt of Styron's *Confessions of Nat Turner,* which accounted for the entire edition of *Harper's* that month. Just before he came to Ole Miss, I read Styron's 1979 novel *Sophie's Choice.*

Styron was the most famous of the writers who visited us that year. I imagined questions to ask: Did you know a Sophie? Was she as beautiful, as sad, as happy as Meryl Streep was or wasn't in the movie? Why did you want to be a writer? Does writing make you feel good? Or does it drain you of energy? I memorized his quote about the essence of writing: "Writers ever since writing began have had problems, and the main problem narrows down to one word—life." He was a godlike author to us wannabes seeking entry to the gates of literary heaven.

By that point in the year, Willie and I had become close, and he invited me to dinner with Styron and William Faulkner's niece, Dean Faulkner Wells. She and her husband, Larry Wells, a publisher, opened their cozy and welcoming home to Willie, Styron, and a few students. Faulkner's home in Oxford was walking distance from his niece's home and had become a tourist stop for Europeans and Asians discovering American Southern writers. They were among the many visitors to campus who cared more about Faulkner than the Ole Miss Rebels cared about Faulkner.

I kept my mouth closed for much of the evening during dinner, as I often did, listening to Styron, Willie and our hosts. Absorbing quotes of wisdom about literature for my diary was my priority, my notebook and pen always close by. Styron spoke about his work a bit, but mostly he joked with Willie about the South. After the laughs about Mississippi politics and its segregationist governors of the past had died down, though, he got serious, moralizing on the tensions between whites and Blacks and what he called that night, "the sadness of time passing by the South." Definitely a diary quote. I wrote quickly.

By the time we were leaving Dean Faulkner Wells' home, Willie asked me if I would drive them home and drop Styron off at his room at the Inn at Ole Miss, a lodge on campus for special guests. I told Willie I'd be pleased to chauffeur, but I was driving my new convertible Volkswagen beetle, paid for by my soon-to-end Social Security checks. There wasn't much room in the bug. If we let the top down, it would be roomier, but it was winter, providing the worst kind of cold: humid cold, the wet cold you get in the South that gets beneath your skin and won't let go.

When he got into my car, Styron was full-on drunk. I knew he'd had many glasses of wine, but I didn't realize the impact the wine would have on Styron's ability to walk. I managed, with a little help from Willie, to walk Styron unsteadily to the car and get him in the backseat. Willie hopped up front and joked with Styron about my VW bug.

I drove Willie home first. As he navigated his way out of the car, Willie directed me to "take good care of my good friend Bill. Make sure you take him inside to his room. I don't want anyone to see him in the shape he's in."

Styron stayed in the back with his eyes closed and his mouth open. But driving through campus, I heard him stir. "The beauty of the white oak trees, the smell of dirt, the fireflies, the moon, my God it's a creation," he said. I decided I would write that one down in the diary. Maybe a writer is most eloquent when drunk.

I said, "Yeah, I know. It's a creation of both good and bad things."

"Of course, I understand. Many terrible things have happened here. You do know," he said, barely getting his words out of his mouth and slurring most of them.

"Yes," I said. "I know."

"But the women! They are gorgeous. Spectacular. Beyond belief!"

"Some say." More for the diary.

"*You* are gorgeous," Styron insisted.

"No, I'm not. I'm very average," I sputtered. I hadn't learned—and still don't know how—to accept a compliment, even from a drunk man. I also felt, instinctively, that accepting Styron's would have put me in dangerous territory.

"Average? What does that mean?" he slurred.

"I'm not sure," I admitted. "Just that I'm not spectacular. I don't think I'm downright ugly. I was in the Ole Miss beauty pageant, though."

"You probably won!"

"I didn't."

"Well, I am insulted that the judges did not value your very attractive appearance."

I didn't know what to say to him, so I brought up the old sorority story. Perhaps he would be entertained by it, as told by someone who hadn't spoken all evening, afraid she would say something beyond stupid. By the time I'd gotten to the part about the dress swap, Styron had fallen asleep again.

When we arrived at the Ole Miss Inn, I had another problem: a dead drunk William Styron crammed into the back of my little VW bug. First, I tried politely to get him out of the car, nudging him a bit. No movement. I grabbed him by the shoulders and tugged. He gave a snort but didn't budge.

I decided to go all in, bracing myself with my hips against the side of the car and yanking as hard as I could. That woke him up, more or less, and I got his feet on the ground, as quietly as I could, hoping security wouldn't hear or see us.

He threw his arm around my neck to steady himself as we walked inside. It was early morning, around 4 a.m. I finagled his keys into my hand and, finally, we staggered up to his room. I unlocked the door and sat him on his bed, praying that he would lie down so that I could tuck him in and leave. Instead, he looked up at me very sweetly, with an intent and mischievous

111

glimmer in his unfocused eyes: He wanted a kiss. He tried, too, but he couldn't pull his lips high enough to reach mine.

He smiled. I smiled back.

"Stay with me," he begged. "I'm all alone."

I couldn't tell if he really needed companionship or was just so drunk he didn't know what he was saying. "I can't stay. I have to leave," I said as I draped a quilt around his legs and up to his chin.

Suddenly, he lifted his head and tried to bring mine to his. I pushed him away, more easily than I thought. He didn't have the strength to stop me.

"You are a great writer," I said, firmly. "And you have been drinking too much. Now go to sleep."

Driving home, I thought of Janice, wondering why I wasn't upset or hurt by Styron's wine-soaked moves. Did I give his flirtations a pass because of the alcohol? Was it because he was a famous and a highly-praised writer whom I'd wanted to meet? Or did I need to protect him since he was somebody, and I was nobody? I only knew that I didn't feel abused, like I knew Janice had been. What was the difference between Coach and Styron, between Janice and me? Janice was only sixteen then; I was now twenty-two. Styron was famous. But so was Coach, at least in Soso.

The bookroom kiss—the rape that I at that point understood it to be— was black-and-white in my mind. The night with Styron was somewhere on the gray side. Back in my apartment, I stayed awake past dawn, thinking about the different shades of sexual overtures that had colored my girlfriends and me: a rape, a blowjob, a drunken pass. No easy explanations came, even in my dreams. I never told Willie what happened.

During my senior year Willie became a mentor and a professor to drink with while the Chair of the Journalism Department, Ronald Farrar, was a professor to avoid. I never paid much attention to him until he took a trip to South Africa to visit with members of its all-white, apartheid government. Farrar returned and wrote an article supporting the white government and criticizing Nelson Mandela, who was in prison for leading the anti-apartheid movement. Harold brought his liberal crew together to discuss the Chair's visit, including me. I didn't know much about South Africa, but we discovered the South African government had paid Farrar for the trip, as well as his article. Post-Watergate, exchanging money for positive news coverage was considered unethical in journalism.

As a result we showed up for one of his classes and protested, loudly, with signs—my first protest ever. I had only seen the labor union protests against Daddy's construction business. Later, my journalism professor, Will Norton, told me the Chair was not happy with me. "But good for you. You did the right thing," said Norton, who made me feel like I could one day be a Woodward or a Bernstein.

The next day, I had my regular class with Farrar, and he didn't look at me or call on me when I raised my hand. Everyone in the class, though, looked at me for the first time. Farrar resigned later that year.

In addition to my lefty friend Harold from up North, my classmate Linda Monk became a strong influence. Like me, she grew up in a family with little money. From Vicksburg, Mississippi, she made her way to Ole Miss on her own, interested less in the Grove and sororities and more in literature, history and the law. Use of the phrase "white trash" or "trailer park trash" stung us both; the term was more judgmental and symbolic about poor white people than about actually living in a trailer park. Neither of us had ever lived in one, but Ole Miss sometimes made it feel that we had.

Linda was majoring in political science and English. I met her in a constitutional law class and listened to every answer she offered to our Ole Miss political science professor, John Winkle. I took notes from her answers more often than I took notes from Winkle—and he was a top-notch professor. Linda and I explored the history and complexities of women's rights and human rights in a way that reminded me of how Janice and I dissected growing up and having sex in high school. During our junior and senior years in college, we both won Ole Miss' highest academic award, the Taylor Medal. Linda was brilliant and wanted a law degree from Harvard Law School, and she got one.

She later worked for the American Civil Liberties Union and wrote books on constitutional law and the Bill of Rights.

Janice, I often thought, could have become a Linda Monk or a Peggy Gillom, the Ole Miss basketball star, or Katie, the *Daily Mississippian* assistant editor, if not for that bookroom kiss and her marriage to Tim. I thought of her often. I wondered what she was doing, and how she was feeling, four years after her divorce. We hadn't stayed in touch.

During my last year at Ole Miss, my new coterie of friends encouraged me to start an alternative and unofficial magazine that would focus on telling stories they wouldn't see in the official school paper. My then-boyfriend, Aaron, and I, both seniors, decided to publish as a team. I'd met Aaron at the *Daily Mississippian*. He wanted to write. I wanted to write. Reason enough to date. We pushed each other and supported each other in equal parts, always knowing when a lighter or firmer touch was needed. And, importantly, I knew that he would never tell me that I couldn't wear a bikini if I wanted. We named the publication *Hotty Toddy,* after Ole Miss' fight song, "Hotty Toddy, Gosh Almighty, Who The Hell Are We?" And who the hell were we? Me, Aaron and my other friends?

Our strategy was to attract readers by putting some celebrity or controversial topic on the front page. On the front of the first edition, we plastered a flattering picture of the popular Ole Miss quarterback, John Fourcade. Inside, we featured a photo of his butt in jeans while climbing up a tree. Aside from having a great ass, he would soon break the career record of Archie Manning, father of Peyton and Eli, by gaining 6,713 yards at Ole Miss from 1978–1981. After playing for the Rebels, Fourcade joined the New York Giants and then the New Orleans Saints. Even though he hadn't achieved those career milestones yet, we could see clearly that he was on his way, and that he was worth front-page placement.

The article wasn't all about his ass, impressive as it was. We also wrote about Fourcade's support for abolishing the Greek fraternity system on campus. I was all for that, after my Pi Phi experience, but it was tantamount to

114

treason at Ole Miss—almost as bad as a Southerner criticizing the Confederacy. Fourcade gave us his views as I took photos and Aaron took notes. We published them in *Hotty Toddy*: "I don't believe in the things that they [fraternities] do. It's just not my bag. I just can't see how somebody gets off on making somebody else do crazy things. I mean, sometimes they treat you like a dog. I'm friends with some of the frats, and they treat me great. But there are some things that go on there that I don't like.''

He declined to cite specifics, but we knew: drinking, hazing, humiliation. Frat boys learned early.

In the second edition of *Hotty Toddy*, we printed the salaries of the ten highest-paid professors at Ole Miss on the front page, which stirred up big trouble with the professors. They complained to the journalism department about their salaries being placed in a campus publication. Of course, their salaries were public, and all I had to do was walk into the college library and ask for them. Clearly, they didn't think that anyone would—or should.

I wrote that salary story, as well as a back cover piece about oil prices. An owner of a Chevron oil station in Oxford complained about how "oil companies own the country" in 1979, when oil prices spiked. I accompanied the piece with another story about the cheapest place to buy gas in Oxford, Bob's Texaco, to the west of Oxford on Highway 6, across from Mobile City, a local trailer park.

Thirty years later, I would lead a media campaign to expose toxic oil contamination of the Ecuadorian rainforest by companies like Texaco and Chevron, only this time in outlets like the *New York Times* and *60 Minutes*. The poisoning of the rainforest occurred in the '70s—almost the exact same time I was writing about Bob's Texaco and Chevron's price gouging in *Hotty Toddy*.

We all knew that *Hotty Toddy* wasn't the *New York Times* — but it didn't do too badly. James Dickerson, a *Jackson Daily News* reporter who helped me with a summer internship at the paper, made *Hotty Toddy* the subject of his own news coverage. "*Hotty Toddy*—it'll never be the same," he wrote. He quoted me in the piece: "We take a liberal stand, and that will turn some people off... [but] I think we realize who our readers are."

I may have misjudged the reading public at Ole Miss. While we sold all of our whopping 4,000 copies, forty was a more accurate count of the Ole Miss liberal population in the late '70s. The 4,000-plus readers were largely conservative white Democrats inexorably converting to Republicans. They just wanted to know what we two liberals were up to.

In the end, we only published those two editions of *Hotty Toddy*, but writing for that magazine and the *Daily Mississippian* made me a writer—not a great one, but at least I had begun. I'd started Ole Miss as a Lady Rebel but left more rebellious than ladylike.

Part Two
The Capitol Hill Stable

Chapter 7
The Past Is Never Dead

Whatever demons haunted Willie Morris, no one could fault his loyalty to his friends. He recommended me for a reporting job at Jackson's flagship paper, the *Clarion Ledger*. In 1980, Jackson, Mississippi had two daily newspapers; the *Clarion Ledger* was the morning paper, and the *Daily News* was the afternoon paper, both owned by the Hederman family. The Hederman family—and their newspapers—had been staunch supporters of white supremacy and segregation throughout the 1960s, unashamedly promoting outright racism. In the wake of Martin Luther King's 1963 March on Washington, the *Clarion Ledger*'s coverage proclaimed that "Washington Is Clean Again With Negro Trash Removed." The newspapers and their owners opposed the integration of Ole Miss and tacitly encouraged violence to prevent it. However, the direction of the coverage changed dramatically in the early 1970s, when Rea Hederman, the scion of the publishing family, took over as editor of the *Clarion Ledger*. Under Rea, the paper hired a new team of young reporters and started producing award-winning journalism on racism and discrimination. Naturally, I wanted to be one of those reporters.

Willie was a friend of Rea's and talked to him over dinner, trying to convince him to hire me. Willie followed up with a letter to Rea on my behalf: "What you're doing is probably the most important thing that can be done in Mississippi, or America, right now. I appreciate your courage, imagination and dedication.... [P]robably my best student out of the sixty or so students in my writing and novel classes [is] Karen Hinton. Karen's talent is first-rate. She uses the language beautifully .... Of all my students... I'd recommend her to you the most for a full-time job .... [She] is the best young person you can hire for the *Clarion Ledger* out of the Ole Miss class of 1980."

His compliments were a very big stretch, but Willie always went all-out to help the students he favored.

The stretch wasn't enough. Rea was hiring mostly non-Mississippians, mostly white and mostly from Ivy League Schools in the Northeast. And he already had one home-grown Mississippi girl, hired a few years before. A graduate of Ole Miss, Stephanie Saul grew up in New Albany, Mississippi and later won awards for every newspaper she worked for: the *Clarion Ledger* on jail conditions and corruption; the *Plain Dealer* in Cleveland about a judge's corrupt practices; *Newsday's* 1995 Pulitzer Prize for Investigative Reporting on disability pension abuses by local police. She joined the *New York Times* in 2005. Her writing on the Deepwater Horizon oil disaster was the basis for the 2016 blockbuster film. All in all, not a bad person to lose a job to.

I did, though, get a consolation prize: a job with the afternoon paper, the *Jackson Daily News*, where I had interned the summer before graduating from Ole Miss. With the same run and gun competitive streak that helped me control the basketball court in high school, I made it my mission to beat every *Clarion Ledger* reporter who covered the same beats as I did—*especially* male journalists from the North.

At the *Jackson Daily News*, I dove headfirst into my beat on City Hall and the intricacies of local politics and policies. I chatted up sources and made friends with the City Attorney, agency heads, lawyers, engineers, contractors, and other employees in city departments. I made a mix of friends and foes in the Mayor's office and with the City Council, too. Any place where a good story might lurk, I tracked it down.

I even kept my ears open for conversations taking place in the hallway between the *Clarion Ledger* and the *Daily News* offices and often took the newspaper's "shared" photographers out for beers to shake out tips about what the *Clarion Ledger* was working on.

Even so, the *Clarion Ledger* reporters intimidated me. They were smarter, more aggressive, funnier, more talkative, and not at all interested in getting to know me. I did, however, become friends with a few of them. Marty Zimmerman, who later left the *Clarion Ledg*er to work at the *New Orleans Times Picayune* and then the *Los Angeles Times*, was my best friend. He was from Indiana and wasn't Ivy League. Road trips bonded us, in addition to rounds of drinks, an occasional toke, and working on our stories together in secret so our editors wouldn't know we were helping each other.

And then there were the music festivals.

In September 1981, I crammed five reporters into my VW convertible bug and headed to the Mississippi Delta Blues Festival in Freedom Village, near Greenville and Leland, Mississippi. I told my fellow blues travelers that we were "driving down Highway 61 to give our poor hearts ease."

B.B. King often sang "Give My Poor Heart Ease," following a number of lesser-known blues musicians also living in the Mississippi Delta, the home of the blues.

My little VW bug dipped us down from the hills of Yazoo City, Mississippi onto the flat, fertile ground of the Delta until we reached Freedom Village, the location of the festival, with thousands of acres covered with cotton, soybeans and rice in between. Freedom Village was a community founded in 1966 as a refuge for Black sharecroppers when industrialized agriculture pushed them out of traditional plantation jobs.

The reporters didn't fit in my bug any better than Styron had, but they were infinitely more sober as we let the top down to breathe the hot air and smell the dirt. At least we were sober until we arrived at the Blues Festival, where we washed down an enormous number of hot tamales with a non-stop river of beer. In those days, most festival fans were Black, and our group of whites stood out. We didn't care. We danced with anyone who would dance with us. I even danced with Son Thomas who was born in Eden, Mississippi, in 1926 but lived in Leland most of his life, working as a gravedigger to make money. By the time of his death at sixty-six from a stroke and heart attack, he had become a beloved international blues musician. He also was a sculptor. I bought one of his sculpted skulls before he died but lost it, stupidly, during one of my many moves.

When we weren't dancing we were drinking and eating. The reporters who had cuddled up in my bug for the four-hour drive from Jackson to Freedom Village sat on blankets soon covered with hot sauce, spilt beer, bits of corn on the cob, grease from fried catfish and sticky juice from watermelons. We peed in the woods and pooped in the nasty porta potties. But it was the music, not the food or even the dancing (and definitely not the porta potties) that captivated me.

I had never heard blues and soul played live, instead of on a record or a cassette. The musicians seemed to sing and play directly from their souls, not just their lungs, and that gripped me. When the sun was setting and the stars appeared, slow soul music lulled me to sleep until snapped back by headliners hitting the stage, performing late into the night. Over the years, a dozen or more times, I returned as the festival became more elaborate, more popular and the audience more white. The musicians, though! As Styron said about the Ole Miss campus, "my God it's a creation," so were Willie Dixon, Koko Taylor, Carla Thomas, John Lee Hooker, Muddy Waters, Son Thomas, Sam Chatmon, Bobby "Blue" Bland, Little Milton, Bobby Rush, Lynn White and dozens of others who played deep into the Delta darkness, when everything disappeared but the wailing of singers and guitars.

121

The Mississippi Delta put its spell on me during the first trip. The music and the cotton were as interwoven as the burning sun and blue skies which could suddenly turn to pounding thunder and the curious lightning that struck left to right in the sky instead of up and down. The rolling hills, pine trees and swamps of Jones County were my home, but the Delta sprouted something bigger and more profitable than our peas and butterbeans. Rice, soybeans and cotton turned the deep brown dirt into long green rows of crops that whispered of history, slavery, blues, tenant farming and civil rights. The Delta seemed unending from top to bottom, almost a six-hour drive from Tunica, near Memphis, to the Gulf of Mexico, near New Orleans.

Our music road trips also sparked ideas for news stories in unexpected ways. I always felt desperate for another breaking or insightful story to make a name for myself. A trip to New Orleans to see The Clash in 1982 indirectly produced my first clash with an editor. The Clash were playing in a now defunct club called The Warehouse down by the port (Jim Morrison's last show with The Doors was there in 1970, one of many legendary concerts to take place there). As The Clash belted "Train In Vain," a gang of white guys with spiked hair and no shirts started pushing and shoving each other for no apparent reason near the stage where I was watching the show.

I took an exit to take a few tokes outside in the humid June air. Suddenly, a foul smell almost made me retch. New Orleans was largely below sea level and had to pump everything that went down, back up, including the sewage. I recalled that a similar sewer smell permeated the backyard of my rental house in Jackson.

Back in Jackson after The Clash trip, I spent a week interviewing people who worked on Jackson's sewer system, professors knowledgeable in water and sewer systems, city council members and engineers who oversaw public works for the city, and residents having problems with their toilets. I was a sewer sleuth. I proudly wrote forty inches of information about sewers. I thought I had a major story.

My editor cut it in half.

Reporters write, editors cut. That's the way of the newsroom. So it didn't go over well when I threw a public fit in the newsroom. My editor ordered me to the roof. There, standing toe-to-toe, he lectured me about why no one would read forty inches about the "shit in their toilets." We stood tensely in silence for a moment. Then I burst out laughing.

"That's the funniest, meanest thing any editor has ever said to me in my nine months of journalism."

"It won't be the last," he promised.

I promised, in turn, no more stories about shit in people's toilets. I also thought his line would make a good title for a Clash song, and I might not be cut out for journalism. When you are a reporter, you open yourself to a non-stop torrent of criticism not only from editors but readers and the people you cover.

A Rolling Stones concert, also in New Orleans, led to an actual scoop for me. On the floor of the Superdome, I danced to a few songs with an engineer from Jackson. A few days later, he called—and gave me a great leak about the City Attorney, Howard Ross, who himself had occasionally been a source for me. He told me that Ross had handed a couple of longtime friends hundreds of thousands of dollars in city contracts for right-of-way work. He didn't compete the contracts, though the law required it.

I wrote in the *Daily News:* "*... their personal relationships, Ross said, had nothing to do with him giving them a majority of the legal work to acquire right of way for the city since March 1979. Robinson and Barkley, neither of whom worked for the city until Ross became city attorney in 1978, say they have no idea why they got so much of the legal work on right of way. 'Howard Ross just called me,' Barkley said. 'We're friends,' said Robinson, 'but no more than numerous other lawyers. They [the city] seemed pleased with my work.'.... Ross recalls, 'It was just a name I threw out.'*"

After the story ran, Ross started giving exclusive City Hall stories to my competitor the *Clarion Ledger*. "The Big Payback" is what I called Ross' move, after the James Brown song I danced to about two yards from the

Godfather of Soul at a Brown show in a small Jackson club that winter.

I lost Ross as a source, but I was on the front page for the first time. Also on my mind around this time was my salary, maybe $14,000 or so. I hadn't given it much thought until Jay arrived, and I sent my front-page story to my momma for her to see. With a master's degree in journalism from Fordham University in New York and the title of "investigative reporter" at the *Jackson Daily News*, he made more money than me and "investigated" fewer stories. I made less, worked harder and had more experience. Given the pay gap and blatant discrimination, he and I didn't become good friends for several months. Eventually, though, we bumped into each other after a few drinks and became more intimate. Our romantic hangovers turned into a semi-relationship of sorts.

On a roll to improve my status at the newspaper, I reconnected with Harold, the Northeastern liberal who befriended me at Ole Miss. I'm not sure when he stopped getting degrees at Ole Miss, but one day in 1981 he called from Oxford and said I needed to look into the Jackson Chief of Police, Jim Black. Harold said Black, a white man, had shot a Black man in the back at a protest at Jackson State College in 1967 when Black was a street cop. The Black man, Benjamin Brown, was a twenty-two-year-old truck driver and had been active in the civil rights movement. He died from the shot, and no one was ever charged. Black eventually made his way to Police Chief fifteen years later under the Mayor who I had been covering, Dale Danks.

Harold hooked me up with people who knew Brown and also gave me evidence that had been redacted by a Mississippi court. From interviews with people who were with Brown that day, combined with court evidence that wasn't redacted, it was clear to me that not only was Black the primary suspect in the shooting, but that the court system and police department had protected him from being named a suspect.

I took a few weeks to investigate the shooting, still keeping up with City Hall daily coverage the best I could. Bill, my top editor, came by my desk one day to pull me aside. "You need to focus," he told me, "on the day-to-day City

Hall stories. That's your job." He paused. "You don't want to be getting jammed up in this Black, Brown' story."

I stared at him for a moment. "The mayor called you, right?"

"Yes."

I kept staring. I was learning about journalism, and I was learning about politics. I discovered there was plenty of politics in journalism, dumping a story, a great story, to keep the Mayor happy. I heard Coach Michaels' voice in my head: "You can't run and gun, girl." Mitch's voice: "You can't wear that bikini, girl." Even Janice's voice: "You can't tell anyone, ever."

Can't. Can't. Can't. That's why I wasn't going to — I couldn't — back down.

Bill said, "The Mayor calling me is not why I need you to spend more time on City Hall. You're missing good stories."

"Naw, I've got a good story. You want to read it? I'm almost done." I gave it to him, but it never made the pages of the *Jackson Daily News*. Bill and other editors turned it down, and I was angry. A decade later, Stephanie Saul, after she started working at the *New York Times*, heard about my draft story and called, wanting to see it. I told her what I remembered, but I had misplaced or thrown away my draft and notes of the evidence—another important loss in my life of trying to win.

The shooting and murder of Benjamin Brown was never thoroughly investigated, and no one prosecuted.

Getting chewed out over the sewer story was moderately humiliating, but this time an editor killed a story that I knew was right. The story mattered to me, not only for professional reasons. Exposing the hidden story of a racially motivated police killing was something I wanted to do to address the injustices that permeated Mississippi and had followed me all my life.

***

My introduction to racism began early in Mississippi. A few months before my sixth-grade elementary school year ended in April 1970, big news broke. Black students would go to school with us in September for the first time. My elementary teacher, who at eighty had to be the oldest teacher in the world, proudly announced to me and my classmates, "The day the first Black child walks into this school, I will pack up my things, walk up that hill and never return." She kept her promise.

A single Black boy came to our elementary school a few weeks later. He wore basketball shoes that were too big for him, and they flopped off his feet. I waved at him one day, and he waved back. I had no Black friends, and neither did Janice, Maggie and Libby. Rachel, a Black woman who worked as a cleaning lady for my momma from the time I was a baby until after elementary school, was the only Black person regularly at our house. Rachel was in her twenties, very smart and beautiful. She taught me how to read and write as much as my schoolteachers did. My daddy helped Rachel pay for college so she could be a teacher. When she got a teaching job and left, I missed her badly for a long time.

Another memory kept nagging at me when I was working on the story of the police chief involved in the shooting of the Black protester. One night, in 1965 when I was seven, a loud knock on the door woke us up after everyone had gone to bed. I was so frightened I ran into my bedroom closet to hide from people who might be breaking into the house. Daddy, Momma and Robbie hurried to the door. It was my uncle Benjamin Franklin Hinton. Everyone called him B.F. He had been drinking. Daddy told Momma and Robbie to go back to bed, but I snuck out of the closet and crept into the living room to hear the conversation coming from the kitchen.

"Red, you don't want me in the Klan, but I'm in it to stay. Don't tell me what to do," said Uncle B.F.

"All I'm saying is it's a dangerous business for you and your family. Stay out of it. The men you're with cause trouble," I heard my daddy say. I had no idea what the Klan was, but I knew my Uncle B.F. I knew he was mean to his wife, Aunt Jean. My momma and I would visit Aunt Jean at their house in Laurel, and it was always a mess. Dishes everywhere, Uncle B.F.'s cigarette butts, dripping, moldy showers, unmade beds and clothes scattered

126

everywhere. It was difficult for Aunt Jean to keep up with three boys and her husband. When he and their oldest son hollered from the TV room for food and something to drink, she went running for them. They hollered for clothes from the dryer. She went running. They hollered for something from the grocery store. She went running. Either Uncle B.F. couldn't afford a Black cleaning lady or didn't want a Black near him. A white woman who would clean his house, feed him and give birth to his three sons was all he did need, and she was Aunt Jean. Aunt Jean was a nervous wreck most of the time. Her only break was when Momma and I visited. They drank coffee, and Aunt Jean had one cigarette after another. She smoked to calm her nerves.

Uncle B.F. was a racist and a sexist. Much later in my life, I saw firsthand how the two prejudices connect. Basically, you are both if you believe some people, mostly white men, are much smarter, better at what they do and if you are willing to do as instructed by the racist and the sexist person deciding who is superior and who isn't. I concluded that a sexist is a racist by nature.

By the time I read about my uncle in *When Evil Lived in Laurel*, a book published in 2021 by a Mississippi boy turned award-winning journalist, Curtis Wilkie, I had seen the connection over and over again. Wilkie, who had written several books before this one, detailed Uncle B.F.'s plans to have the Jones County Klan murder, beat up or run out of town anybody, Black or white, man or woman, who didn't do as told.

Wilkie wrote that Uncle B.F. said, "'We got the names of eighty-two nigger parents who signed up their children to go to white schools, and we have methods of getting them. They have creditors and charge accounts at grocery stores, and we're going to tell these folks that those niggers are bad credit risks, and that the Klan will be after them.' Hinton hitched up his trousers in a gesture meant to add to his stature. 'I want to tell you that any man that double-crosses the Klan better be careful. If we feel a man might talk, we will take action, though it would be a shame to have to kill a white man.'"

Before Wilkie's book came out, I learned that Uncle B.F. was not just a member of the Klan, he was the head of the Jones County chapter. Or, in Klan-speak, the "Exalted Cyclops of the Klavern." The Jones County Klan operated under cover of a Hunting and Rifle Club, as did many of the Klan chapters in Mississippi. Uncle B.F. was called "one of the White Knights province giants" by the House Un-American Activities Committee in Washington D.C. in 1966, when it investigated Klan activities in the South. In an eighteen-month period in 1964 and 1965, the investigation found that the Klan in Jones County was responsible for over fifty acts of violence, everything from phone threats to house burnings, shootings, assaults and bombings. This was when Daddy told him to get out of the Klan. Clearly he didn't.

Racial hatred lurked within many of those modest homes where I grew up in Laurel and Soso. I had a next door neighbor named Charles Clifford Wilson. He made artificial limbs for a living. In 1966, he helped murder one of the most prominent civil rights leaders in our area. Vernon Dahmer, the grandson of a white slave owner and a slave, was the head of the NAACP in the neighboring county. Dahmer led voter registration efforts with the mantra, "If you don't vote, you don't count." Wilson and several other men went to Dahmer's home one night and threw gasoline and torches into the house. Dahmer was badly burned and died of smoke inhalation after rescuing his mother, his wife and children from the fire. A Mississippi state court found Wilson guilty of murder and sent him to prison, three years after the murder.

Two days before Wilson was indicted, he received the distinguished service award from the Junior Chamber of Commerce in Laurel. After being convicted, he spent a good part of his prison time on work release, sleeping most nights at his home, two houses down from ours. Wilson served three years of his prison term, and then Mississippi Governor Bill Waller released him. Waller had been one of Wilson's lawyers before being elected Governor. Waller said that Wilson's "skills as an artificial limb maker were sorely needed in Laurel."

My preacher, Preacher Brent, who warned me and the coterie about the evils of demons and spirits, spoke up for Wilson when he was released. "I think any Black person in Jones County could lie down beside Clifford Wilson and go to sleep and not have anything to be afraid of, because Clifford's not that type of fellow," Preacher Brent told the *New York Times*. "He's had an experience with the Lord."

After Wilson's release from Parchman, the Mississippi prison, he went back to selling artificial limbs. My momma went to work for him after Daddy died in 1973. The day she told me she was working for Wilson, I was doing wind sprints in the backyard, getting ready for school and basketball season. She walked out to see me. She looked happier than most days and prettier, chewing gum and smiling, looking forward to her first job since Robbie and I were born, something Daddy had forbidden.

I sometimes saw Wilson at his arm and limb center when I occasionally picked up Momma from work. A few times I wanted to ask him why he killed a Black man, but I didn't have the courage, and Momma wouldn't let me anyway. Momma liked Mr. Wilson, as we always called him, and said God, not Governor Waller, had granted him the prison release. Momma remained an employee of Mr. Wilson's for several years until he closed his store.

I asked Momma why Wilson killed a Black man. She didn't know, but she told me about a 1919 lynching in Ellisville, next to Soso.

Ten thousand white people watched a lynching that captured the depth of their hatred of Black people. The newspapers let their readers know the sheriff would hand over John Hartfield, a Black man, for them to hang. A paid posse hunting Hartfield down shot and wounded him. A doctor patched him up to make sure he would be alive for the hanging.

"They hanged him good but they also shot him with dozens of bullets. He had a white girlfriend, and people didn't like that," said Momma.

"What happened to his girlfriend?" I asked.

"Don't know," Momma answered.

I read that they also slaughtered him and took his body parts as souvenirs.

I had never heard about it in school or from anyone else. Ever. Momma told me the story. Even so, she and Daddy played no role in the civil rights movement in Mississippi. They wanted to ignore it, as much and as often as possible, like most white Mississippians did and still do.

***

After my fight with my editor over the story about the shooting and murder of the Black protestor allegedly by the police chief, my editors moved me to the politics beat. Booting me from the City Hall beat was meant, perhaps, to improve the newspaper's working relationship with the Mayor. I was disappointed at first, but the move thrust me into a front row seat to experience Mississippi politics, where battles over race, power and control of the South were being fought at a critical moment. By the early 1980s, Democrats' longtime hold on power was fading fast in Mississippi. Republicans—the party of Lincoln, as they wanted it known, far and wide—were finding new ways to take advantage of the white Southern rebellion against Black civil rights that had started with JFK and LBJ. The white flight from Democrats took off full throttle during the Reagan era. Who was the ghost of Lincoln hanging out with, I wondered: Republicans or Democrats?

I started covering two parallel federal election stories. One was the attempt by Robert Clark, a state legislator, to become the first Black man from Mississippi to win a Congressional seat since Reconstruction. The other was the final re-election campaign of Democrat John Stennis, the most senior member of the U.S. Senate and an unrepentant segregationist.

Mississippi had—and still has — the largest percentage of Black residents in the country. But the state's original five congressional districts were drawn horizontally across the state to ensure that no Black was elected to Congress. The majority of Blacks lived on or near the banks of the Mississippi River, where their ancestors had been brought as slaves, many from slave markets in New Orleans, to serve white plantation owners. After the Civil War, many became poor sharecroppers and tenant farmers on the same land and picked the same cotton. By gerrymandering the land across the state into separate districts, the Black vote split; thus, whites had won every Congressional seat in the state in the twentieth century, as well as every statewide election since Reconstruction. After the 1980 census, though, a federal court oversaw the

130

redrawing of the lines and ran the boundaries of the district north to south, from the state border near Memphis all the way down the river to Vicksburg. The move meant that the newly drawn Second Congressional District had a much larger Black population, finally providing a seat designed to give Mississippi Blacks a voice in Washington and in their own state.

Robert Clark had been the first and for years the only Black state legislator in Mississippi. That alone was a shocking fact, given that over one-third of the state's population was Black. Clark was the natural choice to run for the congressional seat in 1982 against Republican Webb Franklin, a white lawyer and judge from the Delta. I followed Clark and Franklin as they campaigned around the Delta.

The first trip was in the small town of Moorhead at the Yellow Dog Festival. Near the intersection of the Yellow Dog and Southern railways, it was one of many festivals, flea markets, and catfish suppers in the mostly rural, poor district where a candidate could glad hand both Black and white voters. Townspeople told me the railroad was dubbed the Yellow Dog because yellow mud stuck on the train's wheels as it rumbled down the hills onto the flat land of the Delta. Others said it was simply because a yellow dog used to chase the train.

Franklin was late, and Clark, donned in a brown suit and tie in the afternoon heat, wiped the sweat from his brow and addressed the small crowd first, never mentioning Franklin by name and keeping a polite, even tone. A few minutes later, Franklin jumped to the podium, rolled up his sleeves and roared, "I didn't fall out of a watermelon truck! I know most of you are Democrats—but I'm conservative, like you are! I'm not going to Washington to associate myself with the likes of liberal Ted Kennedy and Tip O'Neill, like Mr. Clark will."

Franklin knew exactly what he was doing with the watermelon truck reference. He spoke for forty minutes while Clark mingled with folks near the homemade quilt booths. Clark complained to me, "Franklin is deliberately late. He hangs around in white crowds and shows up late so he can be last, and I can't defend myself."

I wrote the story, watermelon truck and all, and this time they printed it.

The Senate race, meanwhile, had a different kind of drama. John Stennis had been elected as a Democrat in 1947 and was running for re-election at the age of 81, still a zealous supporter of racial segregation. His lock on the Senate seat for another term was virtually assured given his power, influence and strong support, both in Mississippi and Washington, D.C. But the Republicans figured they had a real shot at his seat in the next race, in 1988, when Stennis was expected to retire, and they wanted to use the 1982 election to position themselves. They chose Haley Barbour as their nominee, born the same year that Stennis entered the Senate.

During the Stennis and Clark campaigns, I got an invitation from Willie Morris to join him at a Republican fundraiser he was attending with his author buddy, Texas writer Larry King. As one of a small number of female political reporters in Mississippi, I jumped at the chance to meet the white men who controlled the state's political machine.

Willie and King, who wrote *The Best Little Whorehouse in Texas,* had been friends since Willie was editor-in-chief at *Harper's.* King also had written *Confessions of a White Racist,* which had been nominated for a National Book Award in 1972 and praised by the poet Maya Angelou and other well-respected writers. I wanted to know more about King's view of the Mississippi elections and to talk to the growing number of Mississippi Democrats turning Republican since Reagan's election in 1980. Willie helped me work the room and introduced me to the white political movers and shakers in the state. They took little interest in talking to a twenty-three-year-old girl from Soso working for the afternoon paper, generally smiling politely and turning to the more established male reporters, including my competitor from the *Clarion Ledger.*

The only person who did focus on me—aside from Willie and Larry—was a man named Quinn, a lobbyist for large farmers, otherwise known as plantation owners. Quinn dressed like an Ole Miss frat boy, was handsome with light blue eyes, and a smile that rarely faded from his face. He walked over and introduced himself to me as I stood alone in the corner of the room. It was a pleasant conversation, but produced no intelligence on Franklin and Clark or Barbour and Stennis. He wanted mostly to flirt, but maybe he also thought he could get some information from me about the Franklin/Clark race. I was the one who needed sources with information, not a boyfriend, so I broke away quickly. That was Quinn's strategy, I later learned: Your race, party affiliation, level of intelligence, and even gender were of no concern to him, as long as you could help him help Mississippi farmers and the Delta economy.

Finding no one with a scoop for me, I circled my way back to Willie and Larry. They both drank, told stories, and laughed. But they also produced an offer for me to fly with Haley Barbour on what campaigns once called a "round robin" plane trip to several campaign stops around the state. My first fundraiser wasn't a total loss.

The campaign trip included another reporter, Jim Young of *The Commercial Appeal* in Memphis, on Barbour's small plane. I was anxious to spend time with Barbour, but also Young. He was the most senior political reporter covering Mississippi politics. I arrived at the Yazoo City airport and met Barbour on the walk to the plane. I told him it was the first time I had been on a plane. Young hopped in, but Barbour stopped me and showed me how to position my legs and skirt as I stepped into the plane so that I wouldn't accidentally reveal anything underneath.

"Step with your right foot here, and then place your left hand here, and bend. That's the lady-like way to get into the plane. I thought you would want to know," said Barbour, a polite smile on his face.

"You're right, it didn't occur to me. Thank you so much for teaching me. I hope you did the same for Jim. A man needs to get into a plane like a gentleman, after all," I said.

Once in the air on the way to our first stop, Barbour quickly focused on Young. I interrupted a few times and threw my own questions out for consideration, asking him about why he thought he could beat Stennis or was he just preparing himself for another political race? Barbour's answers were terse, as he turned his attention back to Young. Finally, clearly irritated with my interruptions, Barbour said, "You want to learn how to fly a plane? You can sit up there with the pilot."

"No," I said, as sweetly as possible, "I'm here to interview you. Let me ask you a few more questions and then I'll join your pilot so you can talk to Jim alone. Maybe the pilot will have an interesting story or two about you."

Barbour gave me a few responses on campaign funds and polling numbers but he never asked where I was from or what kind of story I was writing. So when we arrived at our first stop, in Jones County, he had no idea it was my home. I said nothing to illuminate him.

In the car, Barbour said, "We're going to see Gardiner Green in Laurel. He's a Republican who will help me. You can meet him."

I said, "That will be interesting."

Barbour didn't ask me why I thought so.

I had met Green long ago when I was kid because my daddy worked for Green as a contractor. Green made his money from lumber and oil and was a Princeton man, the richest man in Jones County. I knew he would never support Barbour. Stennis, as chair of Armed Services and Appropriations committees and *president pro tem* of the Senate, still had power and had done a lot of favors for a lot of people over his forty-one years representing white Mississippians. Green would stick with him.

We walked to Green's front door with Barbour. Barbour knocked. No answer. Barbour looked around. He knocked again. Still no answer. Barbour turned to his driver, "Check on this for me. Maybe we got the date confused."

I would check, too, but I knew what my lede would be: "Haley Barbour traveled to the most Republican county in the state of Mississippi to campaign, but nobody was home, including the richest Republican there, Gardiner Green."

Once I returned to the newsroom, though, someone from Barbour's campaign must have called my editor to complain about me. When I turned in my story with the "nobody was home" lede, it was changed to a much more complimentary version: "Despite a day of rain and several missed meetings with financial supporters in the oil-rich producing area of Jones County, Haley Barbour stepped into his small plane last night with a big smile on his face. 'I want to stay in Jones County. It helps my ego,' he shouted at one supporter at the county fair."

Screwed again. The county fair line had been near the end of my story, as a way to say that the county fair was the only place he could get a vote. Haley Barbour was going to lose to Stennis, but Barbour was going to be around for a long while, so the editor wanted to button up the relationship long term by softening the story. Suddenly there was a lot more shit in the toilets.

While Barbour won only two of the eighty-two counties in the state — his home county of Yazoo and Rankin—his defeat wasn't a loss. In fact, it was the beginning of the end for Democrats in Mississippi. In 1984, Ronald Reagan campaign manager Ed Rollins and his deputy, Lee Atwater, hired Barbour to turn out Southern votes for Reagan. After Reagan's re-election, he appointed Barbour the White House political director. Rollins told NPR in 2011 that Barbour "is by far the best political strategist in the country."

Barbour never made it to the U.S. Senate, but he later ran the state and national Republican parties, won a Mississippi Governor's race and began a long career as a mega-lobbyist. Barbour also played a critical role in helping Atwater, a political fixer from South Carolina, implement Atwater's "Southern strategy" to permanently take the South from Democrats. As Atwater himself described it:

> **You [Republican politicians] started out in 1954 by saying, "Nigger, nigger, nigger." By 1968, you can't say "nigger" — that hurts you, backfires. So you say stuff like, uh, forced busing, states' rights, and all that stuff, and you're getting so abstract. Now, you're talking about cutting taxes, and all these things you're talking about are totally economic things and a**

135

byproduct of them is, [B]lacks get hurt worse than whites ...'We want to cut this,' is much more abstract than even the busing thing, uh, and a hell of a lot more abstract than "Nigger, nigger." So, anyway you look at it, race is coming on the back burner.

It was a strategy that Barbour helped to perfect. Barbour and Atwater not only re-elected Reagan and elected George Bush Sr. but also built the road for Donald Trump to take and win and then lose the White House.

William Faulkner famously wrote "The past is never dead. It's not even past." Not surprisingly, he was talking about Mississippi.

That was crystal clear to me as I covered the Robert Clark campaign, where race boiled on the front burner in his effort to be Mississippi's first Black Congressman in modern times. By the time Clark entered the congressional race, Mississippi's infamous U.S. Senator Jim Eastland had retired. Described as the "Voice of the White South" and the "Godfather of Mississippi Politics," Eastland was a Democrat because most Mississippi politicians always had been Democrats—until Atwater's Southern strategy changed the face of politics.

As Chair of the Senate Judiciary Committee, Eastland cast no doubt on his racist views by putting the Civil Rights bill in his back pocket and literally sitting on it for a very long time. He killed more than one hundred proposed civil rights bill in the late 1950s and early 1960s.

"'That's their fight [Clark and Franklin's],' Eastland says, sucking on his cigar. He will only observe Delta politics from newspaper headlines and his color TV 'unless I change my mind,' he says as a devious grin spreads around the cigar. 'A man can talk himself into trouble rather quickly,' says Eastland.

"'Will less conservative stands [by Mississippi Democrats] in the future cause more traditionally conservative Democrats to turn Republican?' I asked him.

"'It could hurt the party,' he said, pausing for a long moment, 'but it could help, too.' A devious grin spreads around his cigar again."

Which party, I asked. Democrat or Republican? What hurts? What helps? I got no answer.

I didn't include a conversation about federal subsidies in my story about him because it took too much space—something that I was now mindful of after the fateful forty-inch cut. But, when I asked him why white voters in Mississippi were so critical of subsidies for low-income people, like food stamps, he said, "Farmers get subsidies, too, for cotton, soybeans and the rice they grow. Everybody's got a subsidy. No matter their color." And then he laughed.

Willie Morris told me that he thought I was doing a good job covering the politics of race. Willie was the first man I ever wanted to impress and mimic, aside from my daddy. He wrote me on October 21, 1982, close to the election:

> **Your work is very good. Your column on the subtle racism of the Second District race is the best and most perspective piece you've done to date. This was a highly difficult matter to write on, and you did it with dignity and responsibility. The piece on Eastland is superb. You're learning as a writer and reporter in pieces like this. I suspected the piece on Larry King had the guts cut out around the middle by an editor. Continuing such work, you will make the *New York Times* or the *Washington Post* if you so choose. Of course, I don't know where your heart lies. I remember the girl who wrote the interesting short stories ... I'm rather forced to say that I am in love with you. I don't pretend to comprehend the strange origins of love, in whatever origin or age. All I know from my heart is that I am in love with you. This may sound strange, and you may not want to see me again. But you have always been the most beautiful and wonderful girl to me, the most brave and golden girl.**

I highly valued Willie's praise about my writing. Few other male writers or editors at the *Jackson Daily News* had much to say about my work. As for his romantic musings, I ascribed those as much to a few glasses of bourbon as to his need for someone to love and to love him. If Janice and the women I had read about or watched in the movies were the women I wanted to become, Willie was the writer I wanted to be. If he hadn't been drunk so much and, maybe if I were older or younger, I could have loved him as a woman loves a man. And he never listened to my pleas or those of his wide circle of friends to stop and take care of himself.

A few weeks after my round robin with Barbour, my desk phone rang at the *Jackson Daily News*. It was Quinn. I had forgotten him by then, and he had to jog my memory about the fundraiser. He asked if I would go out with him.

I said, "I don't think I can."

"Why can't you?" he asked. "I can help you with your news coverage."

"I'm sure you can," I said. "The election is a few days away, and I have a lot going on. And, in November, I'm heading to Colorado. I'm taking a break from Mississippi. Maybe forever."

"Not forever," he said. "You'll never leave forever."

Maybe not," I admitted, "but I want to see places far away. Plus, an ethical journalist never dates a source. If you want to have lunch and give me some details on the election, then okay."

This time, Quinn just laughed. "Girl, you're headed far away. But you let me know when you get back."

Chapter 8

He's One of Us

At twenty-four, I'd only seen snow on TV and one winter when I was about nine. The Southern clouds dumped just enough white flakes for Robbie and me to build an emaciated snow man. We wore just rain jackets, underwear and boots, and the snowman was mostly melted before we had even finished giving him a carrot nose. While I was covering the 1982 election season, I read an article about Aspen, Colorado. It looked magnificent and perfect from the pictures, and the writer made the town sound mysterious, its inhabitants gorgeous, sophisticated and rich beyond belief. A different world than the one I knew. And as much as I loved my budding career as a journalist, I wanted to take a break and learn something new after the election. Mostly, though, I just wanted to be somewhere else. See someplace else.

I made plans to go to Aspen with Jay, my colleague at the *Jackson Daily News,* the one who made more money than me, undeservingly so. We loaded up my VW bug and attached a U-Haul to the tiny car to head west. I was chasing snow, and Jay was chasing me, angering his editors by following a Mississippi country girl to Colorado.

Aspen was indeed full of beautiful women in expensive clothes. Their husbands were mostly older men. A few were handsome, but most very rich. The really gorgeous men were on the slopes working as instructors or in the restaurants as waiters. I decided I needed an Aspen strategy. I had no job there and no contacts. The *Aspen Times* didn't need any more reporters.

I figured the quickest way to meet people, especially ski instructors, would be working as a waitress in a bar or restaurant, which was actually the only relatively good-paying job there. I quickly rejected the prospect of waiting tables in a bar. Bars smelled, were crowded and demanded hard work and a certain amount of respect for a customer's sexual interests. I settled on what I called "the Hardee's strategy," named for my first job experience after high school when I quit the busy, smelly, crowded McDonald's for the far less popular Hardee's. At Hardee's, I could make the same amount of money while serving fewer customers and doing less work.

My resolve ran out about as quickly as my money, so I took a job as a cocktail waitress at a very nice restaurant, called the *Arya*, which in the 1980s produced nice tips—at least I thought so—from Texas oil men and the sons of dictators from the Middle East and South America, buying over-the-top dinners often followed by a dessert of cocaine in the elaborate private dining rooms with American blondes.

A shout of "let it snow!" took on a whole new meaning. I spent my days skiing and my nights partying and soon broke things off with Jay, who never quite forgave me.

Meanwhile, after three months of Aspen, I was beginning to wonder where all this was leading when, out of the blue, I got a letter from the *Rocky Mountain News* in Denver, requesting a job interview. I was shocked but I soon discovered that the reporter who accompanied me in Haley Barbour's small private plane, Jim Young, *The Commercial Appeal* reporter, told a *Rocky*

Mountain News editor that I would be a good hire. Staying in touch with Jim paid off for many reasons, including a real job.

Scripps Howard News Service owned the two newspapers then, and they knew each other. After a two-hour interview, the *Rocky Mountain News* editor hired me on the spot. I couldn't believe it. I even said so. "Are you sure I'm hired?" I asked. "Does anyone else need to talk to me?"

"Nope," he said. "I make the decisions."

Of course, a week later, I got a call to inform me I needed to return for additional interviews. I waited three hours for a fifteen-minute interview with one male editor and then had a phone interview with another male editor. The one I talked to over the telephone became my boss.

He told me, "Well, we're going to give you a shot, but if you don't work out, we can and will fire you."

Great. The editors in Denver were no different than the ones down South in Jackson, Mississippi. The *Rocky Mountain News* editors had my clips from the *Jackson Daily News,* and I knew they were solid. Part of the issue was the younger editors were annoyed that the senior—and much older—editor who I first spoke with made a stand-alone decision that involved the day-to-day management of the newspaper. The other part was easy for me to recognize and understand: I was a woman, and a Southern woman at that. Was I smart enough? Aggressive enough? What did I know about Colorado?

They were right about the Colorado part. I didn't know shit about Colorado, except for Aspen. But I learned fast and brought my country girl perspective into play covering the wide-open rural areas of the state.

My beat was northern Colorado, so I was traveling most of the time, from Boulder to Loveland to Fort Collins to Greeley and even to Cheyenne, Wyoming. In Cheyenne, I covered the Cheyenne Rodeo, known officially as Cheyenne Frontier Days, which bills itself as the largest in the world and has been held annually since 1897. I interviewed a bull rider, in his mid-twenties, the side of his face badly scarred and dented in the cheek after falling off of a bull in his teens. To get himself psyched, he slapped his face over and over again before every ride. His strategy for riding the bull involved dominating the animal, gripping its torso firmly between the inner thighs and balancing through the bucks. Some cowboys had a certain allure.

During my reporting trips to northern Colorado, I stayed in motels and filed stories from what I called a phone typewriter. The machine had the body of a typewriter, but at the top was an old-fashioned phone receiver, with a big round rubber mouthpiece and earpiece. A regular phone connected with the rubber gaskets on the phone portion of the typewriter and sent a signal over the phone lines to a receiver at the newsroom, replicating my story on the other end. The gizmo probably resides only in a museum today.

When a veterinary professor at Colorado State University in Fort Collins issued a new academic report about bulls mating cows, my editor asked me to write about the vet and his work. I prepared a list of questions and met him at the university barn. He took me to the corral, where he promptly stuck his hand in the vagina of a cow and helped pull a calf out.

As he walked back to me without an explanation, I asked him, "What was the point of my seeing that?"

"This is what I do, and if you're writing about bulls and cows having heifers and calves you have to see it. I wouldn't expect you would know much about mating and birthing on a ranch."

I smiled, but the dozen other male veterinary students standing nearby laughed, loudly. The professor abandoned me to have a conversation with a colleague. I waited with the momma cow and thought about the time my daddy wouldn't let me come into the barn to see a momma cow have her calf. I disobeyed and walked into the barn, anyway, and watched as she gave birth.

A few minutes later, I watched the Colorado momma cow eat her placenta, which momma cows usually do. I saw that many times on the Soso farm. I hollered at the professor, "Your momma cow is cleanin' up her placenta. You wanna watch with me? I can tell you all about it."

I finally got him to laugh. Turns out I was much more at home in Cheyenne and Fort Collins, Colorado than Aspen.

142

***

I loved Colorado, but in my heart, I wasn't a Western girl — even though I'd met a few nice cowboys. More than that, though, I was finding that reporting the news wasn't enough. I wanted to be more than just a paid observer. I wanted to be in the fight.

I got my chance from Robert Clark, the Black state legislator from Mississippi whose congressional race I covered for the *Jackson Daily News* in 1982. When I heard Clark was planning a second run at the seat in 1984, I reached out to him with the idea of taking me on as his press secretary. I liked Clark when I wrote about him as a reporter and thought this would be a good chance to jump off the bench and into the game. He immediately agreed. I'd always known that it would take a good reason to bring me back to Mississippi. Going to work to help elect the first Black House member from Mississippi since Reconstruction was as good as it gets, I thought.

The racial smears that the Republicans had used against Clark in his first run for the seat were nothing new to him. In the late '60s, white legislators once secretly poured vodka into his glass of orange juice and placed it on his legislative desk at the statehouse. Clark wasn't a drinker and wasn't used to alcohol. He did not taste the tang of the vodka under the orange juice's pucker, putting him quickly to sleep with his head on the desk. One day he found a watermelon on his desk, too. He had never fallen off a watermelon truck, either. He didn't eat it.

Clark had been a Mississippi politician since 1967 and had made deals for years among mostly white elected officials to negotiate a tiny bit of assistance for poor Blacks. He not only worked hard but he also was very clever at politics. He had been a small farmer, and he still had a lot of country in him. His clothes were always a little baggie, but he knew how to work the "power brokers" of Mississippi, a term I learned from Robert Caro's book on Robert Moses in New York. It was the first detailed book I read about politics.

Sitting in the Clark campaign headquarters one Saturday afternoon, a white man dressed in green pants and a pink-and-green jacket ran up the stairs

143

to Clark's campaign manager's office. He had a suitcase with him. Our headquarters was in a closed, empty bank, and the campaign manager's office was in the vault. I was writing a press release when I looked up to see mister green pants open up his suitcase, filled with cash. Lots of it.

Well, the vault was indeed a place for cash.

"Cal," I said to the campaign manager, "where did this money come from? Why do you have it? What is it for?"

The man didn't even look at me. He just kept removing the cash from his suitcase.

"We'll talk about it later," said Cal. He closed the vault door to a bank that once kept millions of dollars for plantation owners whose ancestors owned slaves. The money arriving that day was for a different purpose. Pink and green jacket left, and a few minutes later, Black men in their Sunday best suits walked in and took seats in the chairs Cal had lined up in the main seating area of the bank.

"Hello, sir. I'm the press secretary for Mr. Clark. How can I help you?" I asked one of the first of two dozen or more Black men to enter the campaign office.

"I'm here for the walkin' around money," he said.

"What's that?" I asked.

"It's money we ministers need to turn out the vote. Mr. Barbour has arranged it."

The money was for more than walking around, and Haley Barbour wasn't the first white man to come up with a plan to provide cash to Black ministers to convince them to support certain white candidates running against other white candidates. The white candidate who got the majority of Black votes would beat the other white candidate, with the help of Black ministers and their "walkin' around" money.

In my experience, the ministers often used the money to improve the condition of their churches—new roofs or new pews or a new piano or organ. If a white Republican power broker wanted to make it possible, so be it. They

144

also paid for the gasoline and lunches needed for drivers to take Black congregation members and their neighbors to vote for the white man.

Clark had helped Barbour with his white candidates in the past. Betty Jo Hines, a Clark supporter and one of the few white women in Greenville who knew about Democratic politics and talked about it openly, explained how white candidates paid Black ministers for votes and only when no Blacks were in the race. "The money helps the churches. That matters the most to me," she said. "It's what white candidates have always done and will always do."

Now Barbour was helping Clark, secretly, since Clark's opponent Webb Franklin was a Republican and a sitting member of Congress. Barbour saw the money as an investment in protecting his long-term plan to keep the rest of the state Republican. The state had the largest percentage of Blacks in the country, and a U.S. federal court had made it clear that the Second Congressional District would be configured to elected a Black congressman. Barbour, a power broker to rival any in New York or the nation's capital, understood that the state was going to have at least one Black representative, and he wanted to hedge his bets by helping that nominee. He would happily pay that price to keep the rest of the state in white Republican hands.

A few days after the walkin' around money arrived, I visited with a plantation owner in Clarksdale whose support we wanted to solicit for the Clark campaign. Sitting in his beautiful historic home, surrounded by thousands of acres of cotton, rice and soybeans, the owner said to me, "I'm glad to hear the darkies are turning out for Clark. I don't think the whites will, though."

I didn't know how to respond, or maybe I didn't have the courage. Even in Mississippi, one rarely heard that term and I remember having to look it up after the meeting. The word was tied to a 1931 song, "That's Why Darkies Were Born" popularized by the white singer, Kate Smith. The word wasn't a product of slavery but of a 1930s effort to describe Black people as "fated to work the land, fated to be where they are, to never change." Would Mississippi never change?

Not long after the "darkies" conversation, I went to a Greenville bar and dance club with a white Mississippi Delta farmer, Burns, an acquaintance of a friend from Ole Miss. We got a drink, and Burns introduced me to a few people. I noticed someone at the bar staring and smiling at me. I returned the stare and the smile, and he nodded as if he had known me my entire life, all twenty-six years. It was Quinn, the plantation lobbyist who had called me at my old job at the *Jackson Daily News* two years earlier, asking me out for a date.

The smile and nod lingered, prompting Burns to walk me over and re-introduce us. Quinn seemed *very* happy to see me. His date noticed the attention he gave me, but didn't seem to mind. Everyone in the bar had either dated, was married, or had been married to everyone else in the bar, except me. I was wary of Quinn. He represented the families who still ran the agricultural economy of the Mississippi Delta that had been built on the backs of slaves their ancestors owned. Sure enough, as we talked, his angle became clear: he wanted information about the congressional race. I turned the conversation in a different direction and called it a night.

A few days after the short but polite conversation in the bar, Quinn called and invited me out. I agreed, telling myself that it would be a good way to get to know more about Mississippi Delta politics. Before picking me up at the house I was renting in Greenville, he called and said, "Hey, I'm on my way to get you for the dance down at the convention center."

"What dance? I don't want to go to a dance with you. Why don't we just have a drink or something, so we can get to know each other?"

I was panicking. This was altogether too much, too fast.

"Naw, girl. This dance is the way we get to know each other," he said. He had more enthusiasm in his voice than any man who had asked me for a date. It was enough to get me to say yes.

When we arrived, the club was packed with people I didn't know. Quinn, seven years older than me, brought me in as "his" date, introduced me to a few people as such, and then said, "I'll be back. I have to slide over yonder and talk to somebody."

I suddenly had a flash of the frat boy from Ole Miss who bailed on me at the swap when I had that big lip. This night, though, I was looking pretty good, at least I thought so. That didn't stop Quinn from disappearing, and I didn't see him for another two hours. Everyone there was white—not one Black person was there, except for service workers. The music was a throwback to the fifties and sixties. Topping the music list at the dance were The Coasters, The Temptations and The Isley Brothers. When the Isley's song "Shout!" blasted from the speakers, everyone went nuts, dancing fast and furious. Plenty of booze kept them shouting.

I sat down in a cheap folding chair and just watched. One woman, who was hands-down the most beautiful woman in the place, sat next to me, and we chatted for a few minutes. She wasn't from Greenville and had only a few friends there, except for the man she was with. She had a few beers in her when some of the man's friends pulled her up to dance. They were gyrating to the music as more and more of the partiers turned to watch her dance. Suddenly, the crowd — and her man — parted ways to create space for her to perform, like a *Soul Train* line dance.

Looking at her face, I could tell she was horrified, but she knew she couldn't run for the exit. She had to perform. She had large breasts underneath a tight top. She danced. The tits flopped. She was a huge hit. I, however, didn't hesitate to find the exit. Two hours was enough of a wait for me. I wouldn't be abandoned by an Ole Miss frat boy again. I was so disappointed in having been suckered into something like this again that I was almost more let down than mad.

Despite his hours of absence, Quinn spied me leaving and grabbed me before I darted out the front door. "Hey, girl," he said, "sorry I wasn't able to get back to you."

Turns out I remembered how to be mad, after all. "I'm leaving," I said, curtly. "Goodbye."

"How're you gettin' back? You came with me."

"I can figure it out," I said.

"No, wait. I'll drive you home. Don't leave."

I stood there looking at him, thinking why in the hell should I care. I didn't know him. No one at the party knew me or bothered to know me, even when I tried to introduce myself. This was not a group interested in electing a Black for their House representative. Most of them had never heard of Robert Clark. On the other hand, I didn't want to find a phone booth to call someone from the campaign to come get me, or even my first cousin, who lived a half mile from the house I was renting.

Quinn was a bit tipsy, I noticed, when he drove me home, which made me uncomfortable, although I didn't say anything. He wanted to come inside and talk politics. I might still salvage the evening if he was loosened up enough to give me the inside scoop on the Delta political scene, and I let him in. During our talk, Quinn seemed surprisingly supportive of Clark, arguing that a Black would almost certainly be elected to Congress in Mississippi — if not in 1984, then soon after. Then again, I suspected he was capable of saying whatever to calm me down so I wouldn't stay angry. Quinn was the kind of guy who wanted to fix whatever got broken. He was good at it, too.

On the couch, he kissed me, but I wasn't in the mood. He wanted to stay, he said, because he'd had too much to drink to drive back to Leland, about half an hour away.

"I'm a little worried about your car being outside because the people who own this house live right across the way and will wonder why I had someone over all night," I protested. "I'm working for a Black man, so I'm sure my reputation isn't stellar around here as it is."

"I know who owns this house. They know my truck. I'll talk to them."

I was too pissy and too tired to argue, so I stopped the kissing and snuggled up to him a bit on the couch to slow him down. "Let's sleep, Quinn. I'll see you in the morning."

Before too long, he was snoring. I left him alone and slept in my bed. When he woke up, I was at the kitchen breakfast table where my typewriter

148

slept, just like in my momma's kitchen. I was typing a press release for Mr. Clark.

"Miss Hinton, what's your news today?" Quinn asked, striding in.

"Not too newsy for you, I suspect. It's about support for public schools. You know what a public school is, right?" I asked.

"Did you go to public schools?"

"Yes, I did. My daddy and momma didn't join the private academy crowd."

"Why not? Is your dad a liberal, a Democrat?" said Quinn.

"I don't know," I admitted. "It's a complicated question."

"Why don't you ask him?"

"He passed. He had a heart attack when I was fourteen. My momma and daddy said paying for the academy school was too much money and going to school with Blacks was no big deal. I never thought about it one way or the other."

"My daddy died when I was young, too. Heart attack," he said.

"Well, we have one thing in common," I said.

"Do you fish?" Quinn asked.

"Yeah, I fish. Or, I did. Why?"

"Want to go check my trotlines with me tonight?"

I grew up with trotlines, a heavy fishing line you string across a creek and bait to catch, well, catfish and bass swimming around the line. Uncle Roy set out trotlines on the small river that flowed through the Soso farm. Robbie and I would go with him to check the lines. Uncle Roy always had a cigarette in his mouth, rolled with tobacco from a Reynolds tobacco can. His long fingers, stretching out of his wrinkly suntanned hands, would tremble as he placed the tobacco into the rolling paper. Uncle Roy was tall and skinny and always said very little when we went off with him. I always wondered what he thought about when we were fishing.

After a few rather normal dates later, I accepted Quinn's trotline invite and wondered about his thoughts, too, as the lightning bugs lit up the riverbank like the fireworks at the county fair. I couldn't take my eyes off of them while I sat in Quinn's fishing boat on the Sunflower River. "I've never seen this many lightning bugs," I marveled. "We had lightning bugs in Soso, but not like this. What is it about the river that attracts them?"

"It's the smell of the water, the moisture, the humidity, the dirt. Lightening bugs like the middle of the Earth. Mississippi is close to the middle," he answered.

"Why do they blink?"

"While flying around, male lightning bugs flash their lights to attract the females. The females don't fly but they flash back, and when they finally find each other, the females will eat the males after they have made passionate love."

"Passionate. Do the males know they are about to be eaten?"

"I don't know."

"I guess the males make love anyway. Even if they know they will die," I said.

A few fish hung on the lines. Quinn took them off and placed them in the boat.

"Let me smell your hands," I asked. "Smells like river mud, not fish."

"It's the river. It doesn't run fast, so the fish smell like the mud in water. It's where they live until they're caught."

"I live somewhere until I'm caught. Then I leave. What about you?" I asked.

"Girl, I don't know," he said while wrapping up the catfish.

A mosquito bit me on the ankle, and I tried to kill it with a slap. "Damn, these mosquitos. Back home in Soso, Libby, one of my best girlfriends, always lit a cigarette to keep them away. She had one cigarette and a lighter—not for smoking, but driving away mosquitos."

He looked up at me and smiled. "Let's go for swim," he said.

"Yeah. I swam in ponds all my life. A river is better," I said.

I stripped and jumped in. He followed. Getting naked to swim was never a sign of anything but swimming down South. The water was as warm as the air, and I could see Quinn through the light of the lightning bugs and the full moon. We swam around each other, flashing questions.

"How many white people will vote for Clark?" I asked.

"Hard to say. But if he doesn't win, the court will redraw the lines with more Blacks, and one day a Black will win. In time, whites will support the Black candidate. They won't have a choice. Mississippi farmers accept politics the same way they accept the weather," said Quinn.

"I don't believe that. I think they'll re-elect the white guy and fight to keep him in."

"As long as possible, yes. But eventually a Black will be elected. Whites will play ball because they'll have no choice. They won't sell their land. They won't lose their money."

"Why are you still here? You could go to Washington and be a lobbyist for farmers there, where decisions get made. That's where I want to go," I said.

"I go to Washington sometimes, but my life is here. This is what I know," he said, stretching his arms out to the river and the catfish in his boat.

"Yeah, you know a lot about here. I know so little."

"You know plenty," he said as he moved closer to me and grabbed my waist.

I pulled toward him, too, and he kissed me hard and deep.

"Let's get in the boat," I said.

"Nah. Too many mosquitos."

"I've never made love in water. How does it feel?"

"It feels like the water, warm."

He moved his hand down between my legs and slowly placed his finger inside me. It hurt a little but in seconds I was inside out. I hung onto the side of the boat and wrapped my legs around him to balance. I eased myself down on him, and he pushed back, inside me. It felt incredible until the boat almost toppled over. We fought the mosquitoes while getting dressed and headed to his house and then to his bed. During the drive home, I was glad I got naked.

Many things were wrong with him, in my opinion, from his politics to his music and his way with women, but I liked him. I suspected he was like the lizards on my back porch. His color changed based on where he was and what he wanted. After several evenings together, he held my face, looked into my eyes and said, "The way we make love, I could get you pregnant when you want to be pregnant."

"I don't quite know how to respond to that," I laughed, astonished by the statement.

"You don't have to."

I'm not sure he meant what he said. More often than not, he would say things to me to confirm his feelings for me and then disappear for a week as a way to distance and then return. I always waited for his phone call in between.

Quinn often whispered into my ear "spread your legs" when he was on top, so he could move against me while inside. His verbal tic sounded like something a man would say to a woman he had bought to marry and have children. Like a mail-order wife. I didn't mind, though, for some reason. In all my relationships before him, I always had control, but I had none with him. I disappeared into him with no regret.

I fell in love with him when he told me the only time I ever relaxed was when I painted my nails.

I was never relaxed around Quinn's friends, though. Quinn changed colors when they showed up to drink beer. It was hard to tell which was the false color and which was true. Sitting with him and his friends one evening, I listened to a story about Quinn and his four buddies driving a car around Black neighborhoods in Leland. From the car window, they hung out a large, fake penis to scare Black people.

"We did scare them, didn't we, man. The women were screaming and calling for help. It was hilarious," Quinn explained.

Everyone laughed. I went to the bathroom.

When I returned, one of Quinn's friends tried again to infuriate me. "Karen, I hope Quinn has never done this to you, but in the past, when we've

152

picked up our dates for a double or triple date, we would turn the heat up in the car and keep the windows closed to wait and see if any of the girls would complain. They never would." He hollered, laughing at his own story and swigging his beer.

"Was that a test to see if your dates would take abuse from a man?" I asked calmly.

"Hell naw," said one friend. "What you talkin' about? It was just a joke."

When they finally left, I got in bed first, waiting for Quinn. He crawled into bed as if nothing had happened, but I knew that he knew something had happened.

"Why did you and your friends tell me those stories, and why did you participate? Did you plan it ahead of time?" I asked him.

"You're being ridiculous, Karen. Just let it go. They were testing you to see how you would respond. They know how mad they can make you. They'll be nicer next time they see you, believe me."

"And what about you?" I demanded.

"Girl, I love you. I don't want to make you mad. I shouldn't have told that story and started it all."

I wanted to believe he loved me. Maybe he did, for a while.

Quinn was a believer in results of his personal and professional interactions with individual people, men and women. He would be helpful to the winning candidate because he needed Republicans and Democrats to help farmers. Over time, he expanded his interests beyond the economics of plantations. He worked to improve public education, reduce poverty and find jobs for low-income people in the Mississippi Delta.

I never feared Quinn's politics. I feared him personally.

I knew he would break my heart.

***

A few weeks after the trotlines, Clark's opponent, Webb Franklin, started running a television and print ad. It was a simple ad, with a picture of himself, a very white man, and of Clark, a very Black man. The tagline said, "Franklin:

He's One of Us." It was as blatant an appeal to race as I could imagine. The ad ran on television and in newspapers, a full-page comparison of the two photos.

I called Quinn before he called me. I told him that we needed to talk and asked him to take me for a drive. He picked me up in his truck and we headed down some road away from the highway cotton and soybean fields.

"What the fuck does this ad mean to you, Quinn?" I asked, showing him the newspaper ad as he drove. "Did you know this was coming out?"

"Let me see it." He looked at me, smiling, and said, "Well, yeah, I knew something like that might happen."

"Why didn't you talk to me about it? Why would they use this? It's racist!"

"It's not racist, it's the truth," he said, calmly.

"It's not the truth! Clark *is* one of us, even though he is Black. How does being Black make him not one of us? Where in the ad does it say he's different in what he thinks and supports? Nowhere, that's where. It makes clear the difference is he's Black," I said angrily.

"There's a difference between Blacks and whites in many ways," answered Quinn, looking straight ahead and not at me. It was as if he was being willfully obtuse and naïve.

I was getting infuriated. "The only difference is the result of racism," I snapped.

"You're gettin' upset about something that's already changing," Quinn said.

"Yes, it has been changing. *Slowly*. And only because a federal court has put more Blacks into one district. This ad will help stir up racism and stop what little change we've seen!" I yelled.

"Why you mad at me, girl? I didn't write this. I didn't tell him what to write."

"You should tell Franklin to kill the ad," I demanded.

That got him to look at me. He stopped his truck on the side of the road, putting it in park. "Are you crazy? I'm not going to do that. They'd tell me to shut up."

"If they'd tell you to shut up, then why do you want to be a part of them?" I asked. I was flabbergasted. It didn't make sense.

"I have to be one of them," Quinn explained, voice still even-keeled. "For now. Franklin is the Congressman. If he loses, I'm there for Clark."

I'd always known Quinn was a chameleon. He'd never tried to hide it from me. But this was too much. "Take me home," I said.

"I'm taking you to *my* house," Quinn said, firmly.

I didn't protest. I was mad, but I wanted him to tell me what to do about the ad—which he did. When we finally went to bed that night, Quinn advised us to ignore the ad and keep Clark talking about how to help farmers, both white and Black. We fell asleep back-to-back.

In August, before the November 1984 election, he invited me to a houseboat party on the Mississippi River with a dozen or more of his friends who brought their girlfriends or wives and a few other women, one of whom sat on Quinn's lap for much of the time on the houseboat. Someone asked me if I wanted to water ski, and I did. I left Quinn on his houseboat with his Southern belle. The ski boaters explained to me this was "typical Quinn," and I shouldn't be offended.

"I'm not offended," I said. "He and I are taking a very short ride together. It won't be his or my last."

By that point in my life, I was very good at hiding the hurt that I felt.

***

As Quinn predicted, a federal court in 1984 redrew the congressional district lines, sweeping in more Black votes. But the ruling didn't help Clark win a second time. My friends and I couldn't believe we'd lost, and it took a long while to recover. We went through the five stages of depression—from pissed off to pissed off even more. Franklin was re-elected with about two percent more of the "he's one of us" vote, thanks to the Southern strategy, white-takeover ads.

Not long after the loss, a younger, lighter-skinned Black man, the

155

Assistant State Attorney General Mike Espy, announced that he would run for the seat in 1986. Espy, a sharp dresser and a respected attorney, was less "country" than Clark. I wanted to help Espy win, so I stayed in Greenville to campaign in the Mississippi Delta, but Espy had hired a white man to be his press secretary instead of me. The decision wasn't surprising; he saw it as a way to appeal to more white voters. A white man always was viewed as more dependable, reasonable and loyal than a crazy liberal woman, be she white or Black. I let it go and worked in a volunteer capacity.

Since I wasn't an official, paid member of Espy's team, I needed a job somewhere. I decided to teach, for a whooping, $12,000 a year. I wasn't trained as a teacher but in a rural area where it was difficult to attract teaching staff, I landed a job very easily. Luckily, I'd grown accustomed to low budgets and credit cards once I left Momma's house and the Social Security checks stopped coming. Teaching turned out to be surprisingly harder than reporting, campaigning, *and* waitressing. Not a surprise to anyone who actually has been a teacher.

Riverside School had a mixed-race student population, the only one in Washington County. The rest had majority Black students in the 90 percent range. Being at a mixed-race school was like being at West Jones High School again; about 60 percent white, 40 percent Black. Only this time, I was in front of the classroom. My classes included English for tenth and twelfth graders, a Creative Writing class and Spanish for high school students. I was the only teacher who had eighteen hours of foreign language instruction in college. I became Riverside's most experienced—and only—Spanish teacher who, of course, spoke the language with a Southern accent. Every morning I feared what my students would think about that day's classes. How could I teach a language without speaking it myself? Was I able to communicate the facts as well as the feelings about a book, a play or a song, in a way that would draw their interest? Could I help them with the writing skills they would need for the workplace? And, thinking back on my own high school experiences, what did I know about them, as teenagers not just as students?

Sherene, a young Black girl, was the sweetest student in my tenth grade English class. One morning she walked up to me in apparent distress, crying.

"Sherene, what's wrong? Why are you in tears?" I asked standing with her outside the classroom in the hallway.

"I haven't told you, but I'm pregnant, and I think I am about to have my baby," she said worried more about telling me she was pregnant than being pregnant and expecting birth right then and there.

"You are about to have the baby now? Here?" I asked. I was in a panic, too.

"Uh-huh," she said, nodding her head up and down.

"Can you walk with me? I'm telling the principal. We will get you to the hospital."

Sherene was pregnant but no one at the school knew, including me. She sat right under my nose in the front row. Sherene was well-behaved and respectful. I talked to her everyday about homework or a test, but she was so short and tiny I never noticed her tummy.

The principal and I got her to the hospital, and she gave birth to an equally tiny baby who grew quickly and healthier as each day passed. Sherene never returned to school, and she had another child a year later.

Why didn't I know? What should I have done?

Mrs. Cook, my tenth grade English teacher, told us, "A salesman sells only when a customer buys. A teacher teaches only when a student learns." The way I saw it was, if my students failed, then I failed.

Creative writing was my best class, because we could all be open about what we thought about any particular topic. I only critiqued the writing. Preparing class plans, checking homework and tests and leading the Student Union club and the newspaper team sucked up my entire day and night. When the Espy campaign got underway, my entire life was about my students and my politics. I had little time for Quinn, and he appeared to have little interest in me or time for me, except for infrequent calls to have me drive over and stay at his place in Leland. Such interludes were painful when they ended, but I couldn't turn them down. I wanted him to tell me he loved me again, but he never did. Was it because Clark lost, so he didn't need me as much or at all? Or was it because he knew now, as I did, that we wouldn't make each other happy?

As election day loomed, the school and political work joined hands. A star student of mine, Debra, was among the six other Black girls in my classes who volunteered for Espy's get-out-the-vote effort in Greenville and Avon, because they wanted to help elect a Black man to Congress. I had been part of a team of Espy supporters, preparing a GOTV plan for Washington County. My students implemented a tiny but meaningful part of the plan to convince neighborhoods to turn out for Espy. On election day, we wore "Mike Espy for Congress" t-shirts and walked the neighborhoods, distributing GOTV flyers and urging residents to take buses or cars or walk to their precincts to vote. By the end of the day, we were sweaty and tired. And, most importantly, victorious. Mike pulled it off and became the first Black Mississippi Congressman since after the Civil War.

While not all the teenage girls in my classes were that enthusiastic about reading their history books, the Black girls who helped Espy *knew they* were making history that day. It was one of the happiest days of my life. I felt that all of the disappointment after Clark's loss had been channeled into satisfaction at finally—*finally*—seeing a victory. I felt satisfied, but Black people in Greenville, on Espy's campaign, and across the nation, especially those who had fought the civil rights battles of the 60s, felt some justice, at least for a day or two.

Mike offered me a job in Washington, D.C. I'd always wanted to move there, and if I wanted to remain in politics — which I did — the nation's capital was the obvious next step. This move, though, was different than all of my others: Aspen was a lark. D.C. would be a life.

I struggled with the decision to resign from my teaching job after only a year and a half. A big part of me wanted to stay. I hated the idea of telling my students—Frankie, Sherene, Debra, Curtis and so many others—goodbye. I didn't want to leave them in the middle of a school year. An experienced teacher, like Mrs. Cook, would have done a better job than me. But I also believed I had made a difference in their lives somehow, right from the beginning. It may be that the only thing they learned was that I wanted to be with them, that I needed them, and maybe they needed me. If nothing else, their stories, their lives had been written all over me, not just in my lesson plans.

I lost another person in my life around then, too.

Willie Morris cared about Espy and what he represented. I had visited Willie periodically in Oxford from 1980 through the campaign in 1986, where Willie had remained author-in-residence at Ole Miss.

Increasingly, we argued over his worsening alcohol problem. After one friendly visit to talk politics turned into an explosive feud about why he should stop drinking, I stormed out of a bar and headed back to Greenville. A few days later, four years after he sent me the love letter, he unloaded on me with all of his literary power:

> **I wish to make it rather plain to you that on Thursday night at Syd and Harry's [a local bar] I was not after your body, I wanted your friendship. As a fellow human being, I wished your deepest advice on a book that had agonized me for a month, and that I had finally decided that day to do a two year's commitment. I was soliciting your help. Haven't you ever asked for mine?**
>
> **Last night I asked you three times: 'I need to talk with you, Karen.' As you left the last time, you literally spat out at me, like a cat: a half-insane, crazed cat. This is sick business. Look, I don't need you at all, Karen. I'm a pretty good, serious writer, and I've been your friend, I think, but you at least owed me the minimum courtesy of a friendship, and of a loyalty I've at least minimally given you. Your incredible rudeness and discourtesy to me at Syd and Harry's was absolutely inexcusable, and is the**

sign of a narrow, frivolous, unfeeling little ingrate.

I don't use these words lightly at all. Quite frankly I don't give a fuck, about you or anything you do. If there's anything I know at all, one's writing suffers severely from pettiness and insensibility, and your own private work as a writer must bear the terrible incubus of shitting selfishness.

This is a very sick, sick piece of work. I'm absolutely furious. Sick crap.

I knew that the booze in his body was the author of both the conversation and the letter. Still, I was heartbroken when I read it. How could I not be? One of my greatest mentors and oldest friends was calling me a "sick, sick piece of work." Did that make it true because I so admired and emulated the person saying it? I wanted Willie to stop drinking, and I told him that numerous times in letters, phone calls, and when we saw each other. By 1986, I had given up. After I got his letter, I didn't try to fix it.

I told myself that whatever faults he saw in me, it was the result of my confusion, my uncertainties and my challenges. A young woman, like myself, trying to fashion a professional career and a personal life in the 1980s took a test that all women had to take. Some passed. Many failed. The only question on the test was easy to read but hard to answer: How do women handle the men they liked, loved, hated, or all three at the same time?

I didn't have the answer. What was wrong with telling a man who was expressing love that I couldn't return it, but I wanted to learn from him, laugh with him and help take care of him?

The test wasn't just about Willie.

Should I have ratted on Coach? Maybe Janice, Maggie and Libby would still be in my life in some way?

Should I have been nice and sucked up to the asshole editor who wouldn't give me a raise but gave one to a guy my age with less experience? Should I have quit and told the editor to go to hell? No, I just left for Aspen.

How could I convince an editor that my story about a Black man's murder by a white street cop was solid and that he should publish the piece without getting the permission of the mayor? Clearly, pouting and stomping away from his desk didn't do the trick.

Should I stay in Greenville, teach my students or work for Espy in Mississippi, and then somehow convince Quinn to marry me?

As the move to Washington drew closer, I laid in bed excited and depressed at the same time. A Black man was becoming a U.S. Congressman from Mississippi for the first time. It was an unbelievable moment in the history of not just Mississippi, but the entire country. Yet I could do nothing but think of Quinn. I didn't want to leave him. I didn't want to leave Greenville, my students, or the people I worked with to elect Espy. I started to have second thoughts.

One night, late, only a week before the move, I called Quinn. "I'm sad," I said, "but I have no reason to be. I want to go to D.C. with Espy, but I also want to stay here."

"Then stay," Quinn said. "I thought you would keep teaching."

"I don't know. I don't want to stay here and teach if you and I have nothing between us. I should go work somewhere else, where I don't have memories."

"We have good memories, though."

"I don't want memories, Quinn. I want a future with you, but I don't think you want one with me."

"I don't know what I want. I don't want to marry anyone right now." He paused. "What are you doing right now? Can I come see you?"

"Give me the answer I want and then come over."

"I can't do that, Karen."

"Then don't come."

Why did I call him? I'd made an idiot of myself. He wanted to talk more, but I hung up and cried myself to sleep.

Along with packing up all of my belongings, I also stored my feelings and memories—of Quinn and his truck on the Leland backroads of the Delta, of the journey with Jay in my VW and the Aspen-bound U-Haul, of my daddy leaving the house in his El Camino the last time I saw him, of my momma driving Myrtle up the driveway after she bought it from Preacher Brent, and, of course, of the coterie on Midnight listening to Janice read us a book.

When I arrived in Washington, D.C. and unpacked my moving boxes, I found the one note Quinn had written me during the Clark campaign, on July 10, 1984 — my 26th birthday. Alone in Washington, I read it over and over some nights, 1,400 miles away, searching between the lines for answers to questions that still lingered in my mind:

> **Often, we take for granted those who are closest to us & mean so much to us. Then, we discover one day that this person has moved on to seek another horizon that brings greater reward or satisfaction, and we cherish the friendship and experience of caring & sharing with this person. I know your life will most probably take you away from this area after November, but I will stop and pause on July 10th each year of my life from now on to think of the day I felt so good about giving you a gift—and saying I don't just think if, or when, or because—I think of you for being—That's special to me.**

After the first read, I said out loud to myself, "It sounds like a Hallmark card." The more I read it, though, the more I knew it was his voice. Oddly, he had a beautiful handwriting, something his mother may have taught him. Whether the words came from a Hallmark card or not, his note told me everything I didn't want to hear. I didn't want a birthday gift. I didn't want to simply *be*. I wanted to be *his*.

I was becoming increasingly less interested in falling in love. Willie was right about one thing: I *was* fucking ungrateful at times. And, maybe rightfully so.

Chapter 9
Bird Legs

I started a new life in Washington, D.C., as so many young people with a taste for politics had done before and after me. It was the first time I'd lived in a city—the first time I had really spent any time at all in a large, cosmopolitan city. I loved it right away.

My new home was at the top of a 150-year-old townhouse on Logan Circle, where rent was cheap and the neighborhood still a little sketchy in the late 1980s. My apartment building was full of very attractive and friendly men interested in romancing other men, not me. I made new friends fast.

A favorite pastime of mine and my gay guy friends, as the weather warmed, was standing on the roof of our building and dropping water balloons on the windshields of cars driven by the johns who tried to buy sex from the prostitutes that frequented the Circle. Some of the guys from the building took photos of the car plates to turn them into the police station. It irritated the johns and the prostitutes so much they began to move on to find other neighborhoods for their liaisons. I didn't know the word gentrification or what it meant, but young white men throwing water balloons at johns from the suburbs looking for an urban thrill was probably a sign that it was underway.

Also underway was my figuring out how Capitol Hill worked. As press secretary to the first Black Congressman from Mississippi, I soon started meeting a lot of people, which seemed to be the real job for almost everyone in Washington. Tagging along with our chief of staff or director of legislation to meetings at fundraisers, meetings at bars, meetings at restaurants was almost as valuable as meetings in the office. Everywhere, I walked up and introduced myself to people as if they wanted to meet me. Most didn't until they heard I worked for Mike Espy.

Yet Capitol Hill had many more men than women walking the halls, whether they were members of Congress or congressional and committee staff or lobbyists. The receptionist was usually a woman, and the chief of staff, a man. Sometimes I wondered why anyone in Washington would want to listen to what a girl from Soso, Mississippi, had to say.

As time passed, I became more nervous and unsure of myself. But at least I didn't have to serve drinks, clean up ashtrays, or pour water. I'd had enough of that as a cocktail waitress in Aspen in a prior life. Still, I stuck up for myself as much as I could for a country girl wandering beneath a Capitol dome as white as the men who dominated there.

Once again I thought about how Gloria Steinem, Jane Fonda, Pam Grier or Janis Joplin might handle themselves and tried to carry myself with confidence, even when self-doubt never let go of me.

Fundraisers and receptions attracted many young staffers, not just because they needed to talk business and meet people, but also because the chow and booze were free. We didn't make much money, so we needed anything that was free. At one reception shortly after I arrived in D.C., hosted by Mississippi's Republican Senator Thad Cochran, I chatted with some of the women staff from his office before grabbing a drink and some hors d'oeuvres, a word I couldn't pronounce or spell then.

As we talked and laughed, Trent Lott—the other Republican Senator from

Mississippi—walked into the reception and quickly made his way over to the clique of women staffers. "I don't know you," he said to me in a booming voice. "What's your name?"

"I'm Karen Hinton," I said, as we shook hands.

"Are you with Thad's stable?"

"His what?" I asked.

"His stable. You know, the women who work for him."

For some reason, I was feeling feisty. I wasn't looking to pick a fight with a U.S. Senator my first week on the job, but maybe a glass of wine I'd had helped me channel Gloria or Janice.

"Yes, I know who they work for, Senator," I said to Lott. "Though I'm not sure I'd call them a stable. I know how to ride a horse, but I'm not a horse. I work for Congressman Mike Espy." (At the time, I had no idea that a stable meant a group of whores owned by a pimp.)

"Espy!" Lott cried, bulldozing past my frosty response. "Great. Good to meet you. Tell him hello. And enjoy the nation's capital."

He turned away quickly and I tried to avoid him as long as I was in the nation's capital.

At another Capitol Hill reception, I met Charlie Wilson, a Texas Democratic Congressman, later known as the "best horse trader" in the capital and an "unapologetic sexist, chauvinistic redneck"—descriptions of him that hadn't yet been written when we shook hands in 1987.

One of his best horse trades was grabbing important committee seats, handed out by Speaker Thomas "Tip" O'Neill, on the U.S. House Committee on Ethics and the House Defense Appropriations subcommittee. O'Neill wanted Wilson to protect congressmen from federal ethics investigations, and Wilson wanted to send buckets of dollars to President Anastasio Somoza in Nicaragua and to groups of Afghans, known as the mujahedeens who with U.S. funding kicked the Soviets out of their country in 1989, transformed into the Taliban in 1994, protected Osama bin Laden after 9/11 until he was assassinated in 2011, and took their country back from the U.S. in 2021.

Wilson's battle to drive the Soviets out of Afghanistan won him praise, but his victory empowered the Taliban.

Without knowing much about Wilson and unable to envision his impact on the future of Afghanistan, I introduced myself and told him I had met Somoza's son in Aspen, where I had served him and his cronies drinks over a long night at the *Arya*, the Iranian-owned restaurant where I waitressed. "Do you know him? Nicaraguans have been abused and killed for no reason other than to benefit his family, you know," I said to Wilson. I had traveled to Nicaragua with Witness for Peace to oppose funding for the contra rebels fighting the Marxist Sandinistas.

My question and statement of certitude entertained him, I could tell, but he had little interest in my political view of the world. "You've lived in Aspen, then?" he asked. "Will you go with me to Aspen and ski? Are you a good skier?"

"Yes, I am a good skier, and no, I can't go to Aspen with you. I don't know you, and you don't know me, and Congressman Espy won't let me off work anyway."

"Don't worry about Espy," Wilson crooned. "I'll take care of that. Let's go to Aspen."

"No, really," I laughed. "I can't go with you."

"Well, then, come to my houseboat next week for a party. Will you do that?"

I debated whether or not I should go, but I figured it would definitely be a good place to network.

One thing I discovered: More young women than powerful men found their way to Wilson's parties, which took place on his boat or roomy apartment in Arlington, Virginia, on the top floor of a building overlooking the Iwo Jima monument. Wilson's parties were boozy, lascivious affairs, obvious to anyone who used his gigantic bathroom in his apartment, which featured a spa tub with handcuffs and whips attached to the wall above it. Wilson was a devilish man, yet always charming in his way. I wanted to like him, but I wasn't sure I should. Tom Hanks later captured Wilson's rakish appeal playing the Congressman in the film *Charlie Wilson's War*. You can't resist Tom Hanks but Wilson I could and did.

Attending a Charlie Wilson party wasn't the only time I found myself putting my morals in harm's way to make connections. One day, the chief of staff for Congressman Joe Kolter of Pennsylvania—whose office was next door to Espy's—told me I should date Congressman Bob Carr of Michigan, who was single at the time. This particular chief of staff needed Carr to give his boss an economic project in his congressional district, and I was part of the trade. He also said Carr would help me advance my own career on Capitol Hill. But I already had done that I thought, working for Espy.

Women working on Capitol Hill eventually learned it wasn't *just* about a kiss on the cheek or mouth—it was about the power and control that their bosses and other influential men had over them. Wilson's parties and others like them were risky in D.C. for young women trying to get ahead. It was a Catch-22. A flirty woman sometimes got a job over a woman with more experience but unwilling to play the game. It wasn't unheard of for women to sleep with potential employers on the hill. It wasn't so much consensual as it was transactional. Every woman knew a woman who went to bed to get ahead.

To avoid being backed into the flirt or fuck corner, I generally tried to be polite, meet some people and find the exit quickly. I probably missed out on building relationships in the halls of Congress, but it kept me out of congressional beds and those nasty stables.

***

Doing my actual job in Washington was challenging in a different way than grappling with the sexual politics that permeated the capital. Mike Espy's win was a big deal in the South and nationally, and he was determined to protect his seat against whichever white man the Republicans would run in the next election.

Espy was an intelligent politician who knew how to appeal to both Blacks and whites. He could be a chameleon when necessary, operating as Quinn did to balance interests and achieve victories for the people he represented. He was flexible enough to change ideological shades to motivate lobbyists and power brokers to help him land legislative victories. My official job was working as a legislative assistant at first.

Both Espy and Robert Clark, who ran for Congress before Espy, treated me with respect and often took my advice, unlike so many white men who became my boss before and after them. Perhaps it was a matter of upbringing or culture. Clark once told me, "My momma would whip my butt if I didn't treat a woman with respect. I learned that early in life."

Meanwhile, my unofficial job for Espy was more important than being his legislative assistant or press secretary. It was developing a strategy to increase his white vote.

We started by identifying the white precincts in Mississippi that had elected Ray Mabus, a white Democrat, as Governor in November 1987, the year after Espy won. At thirty-nine, Mabus beat the Republican candidate 53 percent to 47 percent. We took the zip codes from those white pro-Mabus precincts in Espy's congressional district and mailed them letters from Espy on issues they cared about the most: namely, creating jobs. Espy decided that the way to get a good number of these voters to support him could be summarized in one word: catfish.

Espy wanted to promote Mississippi catfish, the ugliest fish in the water, to expand demand for catfish and create jobs for poor people in the Delta and more profits for white and Black farmers. Espy convinced Congress to pass a resolution to establish National Catfish Day. By this time, I had been promoted to press secretary and, after the resolution passed, my job was to sell the big day to the news media.

"Who gives a shit about catfish," I said to other staffers. "Nobody will write about National Catfish Day. There's a day for every fucking thing in America. Why will catfish matter?" I stomped around the crowded office in the Cannon building, much as I did in the newsroom.

I was right about immediate news coverage. Only small newspapers in

Mississippi towns with "catfish ponds" even bothered to mention the big news about National Catfish Day. The *Washington Post* and *New York Times*—the holy grails for Congressional coverage—didn't take the bait of course. But I was wrong about Espy's effort to boost the popularity of Mississippi catfish.

Before they were grown in man-made catfish ponds, most catfish were snagged from the muddy bottom of the Mississippi rivers. It was fun to catch a large, powerful catfish, but it wasn't that big of a business. By 1988, though, the growth of catfish and catfish ponds by small and large farmers near their cotton, rice and soybean fields soared. Espy even convinced the Capitol Hill cafeteria and the U.S. Department of Defense to buy catfish from Mississippi Delta catfish farmers for their menus.

The Mississippi Delta economy benefited, and today Mississippi is the largest producer of catfish in the country. The relentless work by Espy to support the industry contributed hundreds of millions of dollars annually in jobs and economic growth, mostly in the Mississippi Delta.

Our efforts to broaden Espy's base paid off. The white vote soared from 12 percent in his first race to 40 percent in Espy's re-election. With 40 percent of the white vote, Espy could stay the Delta Congressman as long as he wanted—another Quinn prediction that came true.

Espy was well liked by his colleagues and considered an up-and-coming Congressman with a historic rebuke to Mississippi's dark past. In 1988, Michael Dukakis, the Democratic nominee for President, asked Espy to speak at the Democratic National Convention in Atlanta.

Dukakis wanted to show that he wasn't giving up on the New South and also selected Ann Richards, the Treasurer of Texas, to keynote the convention. Espy would introduce Richards to showcase the diversity of having a Black man and white woman from the South open the event. Espy asked me to draft his introductory remarks to introduce Richards. I was excited beyond belief that something I wrote would be spoken on a national stage. I recommended to Espy that we draw parallels between Richards and Fannie Lou Hamer, the Black woman who stunned the 1964 Democratic National Convention when she fought for Blacks to be part of the Mississippi delegation, which was, at the time, all white.

When I got to Atlanta, feminists were everywhere, and I wanted to look like one, talk like one, and *be* one. Abortion was a center stage issue, though it wasn't one Espy had spent much time on, given the anti-abortion position held among many white and Black Christians in Mississippi. But there, in Atlanta, I heard women speak from the podium and on the floor with incredible passion to protect a woman's right to choose. I was hit upside the head with ideas flying faster than I could catch. Press interviews, meetings and informal debates flew around the convention floor on issues like the Equal Rights Amendment and abortion rights. We'd never talked like that in Mississippi.

Before the convention, Irene Natividad, the executive director of the National Women's Political Caucus, said that the 1988 presidential candidates, Democrat and Republican, were ignoring issues that mattered most to women: childcare, Social Security, pay equity, health care, and others. "Why don't they [the presidential candidates] target the largest clump of voters? Why is something so obvious being so intensely ignored?"

The silence was especially evident, she noted, in the twenty (predominantly Southern) states that held primaries or caucuses on Super Tuesday. Candidates in many of those states, she said, were primarily "thinking about Rhett Butler—the white male in the South." But it wasn't Rhett Butler, a movie character who changed his colors to suit his ambitions, who I thought posed the real threat to what Mike Espy and Ann Richards stood for. It was David Duke, a real life modern-day KKK leader who was growing followers and seeking legitimacy as he ran for President on an unrepentant platform of white supremacy.

The night of Espy's convention speech, I waited backstage with him in the sweeping hall of The Omni Coliseum in Atlanta. Espy popped a piece of hard red candy into his mouth to keep from getting dry mouth during his speech. When it was almost time for him to introduce Richards, I scooted out to the floor so I could see how everyone would react to his remarks. Standing there, I looked up at the stage and felt tingles up and down my spine. When you are an ambitious young person in politics, waiting for your guy to give the speech you worked on at the national convention is kind of like the Super Bowl for political geeks.

House Speaker Jim Wright of Texas, the most powerful man in Washington, D.C. at the time, would introduce Espy. Just before Wright began his introduction, a frantic stagehand informed Espy that an anonymous caller from Mississippi had phoned a convention official and said Espy's home "was engulfed in flames" and that his "two children were still in the house," he told me later. Though Espy's first thought was that the call was a hoax, he couldn't take any chances. Torching the home of a prominent Black man about to make a speech on civil rights and women's rights to a national audience could be a credible threat from a racist looking to make news.

Espy told me: "I thought whoever did this evil thing was so clever: They knew the exact time to pull the stunt. They knew how to locate me backstage. They knew I had kids and they used my son and daughter—my innocent children—to get to me. Then I got angry. Whoever did this was looking at TV at that moment and would see someone who was not rattled or nervous, or filled with anxiety, and someone who was not derailed. That night—that someone would then realize—that their mission had failed."

During a time when the South hadn't yet gone completely Republican, and knowing nothing of the threat against Espy, Speaker Wright said, his deep and accented voice booming through the auditorium: "I particularly take pride in introducing a man from the Mississippi Delta country. His roots are sunk deep into the Mississippi Delta soil. He stands as a living symbol of the pulsating tolerance and growth that has come upon that great state of Mississippi. He is the first Black member of Congress to serve from the State of Mississippi since Reconstruction days. He is respected by all of his colleagues ... my colleague, Mike Espy!"

The crowd roared. I roared. The group surrounding me was a bunch of Democratic women, Black and white, from the Mississippi delegation. They

171

listened intently as Espy spoke about two women of the South.

The first woman he spoke about was Fannie Lou Townsend Hamer. Few women had suffered more for the cause of the civil rights movement. She was her parents' twentieth child, sharecroppers in Montgomery County, Mississippi. Born in 1917, she helped her family pick cotton starting at age six and then dropped out of school at age twelve to work full-time. She married and wanted to have children, but a white doctor gave her a hysterectomy without her consent while she was having a uterine tumor removed.

In 1962, she brought seventeen Blacks to register to vote in Indianola, near Itta Bena, where B.B. King was born and raised. The seventeen Blacks were kicked out of the precinct, and that night the owner of the property where she and her husband picked cotton fired her and confiscated their property. They moved to Ruleville, and she began protesting "white only" restaurants. One of her protests was in Charleston, South Carolina, with a group of women beaten by police in 1963. She suffered injuries from a blood clot in her eye, kidney damage and a leg wound. She later co-founded the Mississippi Freedom Democratic Party and made her way to the 1964 convention to protest the fact that there were no Blacks serving on the Mississippi delegation.

When LBJ learned that Hamer would speak at the convention, he got so nervous, he set up a nationwide television speech to talk about literally nothing just to drive TV networks away from Hamer. It didn't matter, though. Hamer became a hero to voting rights activists and Americans who supported civil rights. I, of course, had never heard about her until I found her book in Square Books in Oxford during college. That made me even more determined to connect Hamer's story to Espy's election and the choices in the 1988 election, and I tried to honor her in writing Espy's remarks:

"It was 1964. Another daughter of the South captured the attention of the nation with her stirring story and testimony about the pains and struggles of Blacks in this country. Her name was Fannie Lou Hamer, a sharecropper and a Mississippi Freedom Democrat from the small town of Ruleville, Mississippi.

"There may be some of you here who are too young to remember her. You need to know her. Her words at this convention twenty-four years ago, and her struggle for poor Blacks and poor whites and her vision of a freer, braver, and more prosperous America, gave birth to the reforms that have made it possible for everyone to play a role in this party, and for me to be able to stand here with you tonight.

"With tears streaming down her face, Mrs. Hamer cried out at Atlantic City, 'Is this America? Is this the land of the free? The home of the brave?' My answer for her tonight is yes. Yes, because the hands that once picked cotton and yes, because the hands that baked bread and rocked cradles, and the hands of men and women who run for president and governor and congress and mayor ... these are the hands that create the great patchwork quilt that is our Democratic Party.

"Fannie Lou's appeal to the conscious of this nation is one of the reasons another daughter of the South will keynote this convention tonight. A convention that will bring together in the spirit of unity a son of immigrants and a descendant of slaves ..."

I hung on Espy's every word, especially since I had written most of them. But not long after the beginning of the speech, many people outside our delegation went back to talking to each other. I wasn't disheartened. Espy was a passing moment—but a good one, nonetheless. And besides, the audience's behavior was fairly typical for convention speeches; the only speeches that they hung on that night were by Richards and then Dukakis. Espy's red sucker helped him cool down after the racist threat, even as he built to a strong finish:

"Change is here, Fannie Lou, because it is a new Mississippi. It is a new South, Fannie Lou ... She often said, 'I am all sick and tired of being sick and tired.' Well, Anne, Democrats all across this party are sick and tired of being sick and tired of a Republican Party that has written off the South... with no vision of the common good ... We will be energized and unified and strong, ready to work together to regain the White House in November. Tonight, America is lucky ... We are going to hear a new voice and get to know a rare voice and a new political leader. America, meet Ann Richards!"

Richards' speech was all Texas accent. She said what she wanted to say, and you could picture her standing up to the men back at her ranch with her trademark Southern drawl. I took it all in and laughed with the thousands of delegates and guests at her joke about George Bush being "born with a silver foot in his mouth."

But then she said something that made me feel like she was talking directly to me. The large hall disappeared, and I was back at West Jones as she spoke.

"You know, tonight I feel a little like I did when I played basketball in the eighth grade. I thought I looked real cute in my uniform, and then I heard a boy yell from the bleachers, 'Make that basket, bird legs.' And my greatest fear is that same guy is somewhere out there in the audience tonight, and he's going to cut me down to size."

Ann got me exactly. I was playing politics in the nation's capital on a pair of bird legs, like I was back in the West Jones gym with the coaches, the fathers, and the boys who stood on the sidelines and never missed an opportunity to cut down the girls playing the game. But when Ann said it, I knew that every woman in that arena and every woman watching from her home knew exactly what "cut me down to size" meant.

Chapter 10
As Sure As Cornbread Goes with Greens

Over the next several years, I climbed the Washington political ladder, working for a number of influential and powerful men in the 1990s. I had become something of an expert in developing messaging and generating media coverage. I landed a great job with the Democratic National Committee working for Ron Brown, the first Black Chair of the Democratic National Committee; and Mike McCurry, who headed the DNC communications office and later became White House Press Secretary for President Bill Clinton.

Every morning, I attended a morning strategy meeting led by House Majority Leader Dick Gephardt in one of his conference rooms in the U.S. Capitol. Gephardt, who had run for president in 1988, often led the discussion, along with his advisor George Stephanopolos. House members Barbara Boxer of California, David Obey of Wisconsin, Martin Frost of Texas, Nancy Pelosi of California, and a few others played key roles in the meetings. Deep South

175

members of Congress either weren't invited or didn't want to be seen in the room, given the political changes underway in their districts.

While working for Brown, I had a boyfriend I wanted to marry, a tech geek named Eric. Eric asked questions about my politics but rarely judged them. He talked about technology, and I rarely listened. I talked politics, and he always wanted more information. He also liked the blues—another reason for me to fall quickly and deeply in love with him.

After dating for a year or so, we decided to move in together. The day the rental truck arrived to move my stuff, Eric walked over to my apartment.

"What's goin' on?" I asked with a smile, excited about the move.

He looked pale and nervous as he stammered out his story: He had been seeing another woman at the same time we were going out and planning to live together. Maybe I should have talked more about technology. And there was more: The woman showed up at his apartment the morning of our move and told him she was pregnant with his child.

I was shocked and hurt, but also was in a bind. I had terminated my lease, and I didn't have the money for an apartment by myself. I got depressed and never went out with friends. I would finish a movie, stick my head out the window, see blue sky, and think I should go outside. I wouldn't. Instead, I'd go back to another movie or another page in a book or another album, my three safe spaces. I felt small and alone, insubstantial and slight.

Eventually I got back in gear, but I also resolved to be wary of men infatuated with their power over me, including emotional power.

Washington was full of smart and attractive men and women chasing the scent of power—and each other. I was no exception. After Eric, I played the field without emotional attachments. In 1990, while at the DNC, I dated James Carville, the Louisiana political consultant, before he became famous for getting Bill Clinton elected as president in 1992. James was fourteen years older than me and had grown up even farther south than Soso, in a Louisiana town, Carville, named after his grandfather.

Some people called him the ugliest man in Washington, which was itself mocked as the "Hollywood for ugly people." But I never saw James that way. He was smart, and I liked smart. I was, needless to say, incredibly attracted to him. He was outlandish and argumentative, hilarious and blunt. People in Democratic politics thought Carville always said the first thing that came to his mind and that he told too many Southern jokes during his presentations at political functions. But behind the one-liners and the showmanship was a brain continuously calculating how to win an argument and, most importantly, how to win a campaign.

Carville entertained me with a lot of stories, not all about campaigns. On one of our first dates, he told me of a free-wheeling dinner party he had recently attended on a large yacht owned by a big political donor. The guests, after snorting cocaine, became "indiscriminately intimate," as he put it.

"Did you?" I asked, raising my eyebrows.

"Naw, I was too timid," he answered.

"You? Timid?"

"Honestly, I was scared to death. I walked into a section of the yacht where a woman was lying on the carpet with a vacuum cleaner hose up her, well, pussy, and she told me, 'I'm havin' a great time. Are you?' I turned and got the hell out of there."

"James!" I snorted. "Oh, Lord, that's worse than bad. Did you tell her to stop?"

"I couldn't stop her!" he cackled. "She was havin' fun. I didn't know what to do!"

"I hope the vacuum cleaner wasn't turned on," I responded, making a joke to hide what I was really thinking: He was less worried about the woman and more concerned about bolting to protect himself from being identified. I couldn't shame him too much, though. Self-preservation was paramount in Washington.

One afternoon, as I was heading into the DNC headquarters, Carville showed up on his bicycle, his regular mode of transportation on Capitol Hill. He cycled in circles in the parking lot in front of headquarters telling me he was going to work for Harris Wofford in Pennsylvania. Wofford had been appointed to the Pennsylvania Senate seat after U.S. Senator John Heinz III died in a plane accident. Now he wanted to win the election in his own right, and Carville's job was to make that happen.

"Will you come with me and work for him?" he screamed from his bike as I stood on the steps of the DNC building.

"I don't know anything about Pennsylvania," I said.

James kept circling on the bike. "I don't either."

I shook my head no. I wasn't quite ready to make big changes in my life on a campaign with a man who would likely start dating the next woman he met.

"Come on, Karen! Come with me! We'll figure it out together," he yelled, making one last loop around the parking lot. I didn't go.

Carville's success with Wofford launched him into his role as one of the masterminds behind Bill Clinton's run for the White House. During the summer of the presidential race in 1992, he dropped by my apartment on Capitol Hill. It was July 4th, and Pat, a Marine I had been dating, was away on a tour of duty. James also had a new girlfriend, Mary Matalin, the campaign director for the Bush re-elect. Everyone thought it an odd relationship. Of course, a jarhead Marine whose father was a two-star Marine Corps General and a Mississippi liberal like me was, too, I supposed.

At my apartment, Carville seemed to be interested in rekindling some old history on the couch. I reminded him that we both had new partners, and we ended up walking several blocks to a restaurant for lunch. I tried not to overload him with questions about the presidential race. Still, I had to ask about Gennifer Flowers and her allegation of a long-term affair with Bill Clinton. For the first time since meeting Carville two years earlier and spending time with him, he had nothing to say.

"I think it's true," I said.

He shrugged his shoulders, looked down and shoveled a forkful of food into his mouth.

"Really," I continued. "Clinton has cheated on Hillary for years. I told you the story about the time in Greenville in 1984, when he invited me to his hotel room. That's why I am not volunteering or doing any work for him. He uses women the wrong way."

"You never told me that," said Carville.

"Yes, I did. I'm not surprised you forgot. You often forget what you don't want to know," I said.

"You're right. I don't want to hear it," he said, effectively shutting down the conversation. "Clinton is going to win this race, as sure as cornbread goes with greens."

And, of course, Clinton did win, as sure as a trite Southernism poured forth from James Carville's lips when he wanted to have the last word.

***

Carville said he had forgotten my encounter with Clinton, but I thought about it a lot as Clinton was running for President. During the campaign, a long line of women accused him of a pattern of sexual abuse and harassment. Clinton's people, including Carville, called them liars and bimbos. I believed the women, though. I had seen the man in action.

I met Clinton through Willie Morris in a chance encounter back in Mississippi in 1984 when I was teaching and working on Robert Clark's campaign for Congress. Willie invited me to dinner with Raad Cawthorn, a reporter at the *Atlanta Constitution* who I knew from when we both worked in Jackson. We met at Doe's Eat Place, a well-known steak joint in Greenville, to talk Southern politics. Cawthorn was especially interested in Bill Clinton's positioning as Governor of Arkansas, and Mississippi Governor William Winter's plans for a U.S. Senate race. Willie and Clinton had been Rhodes Scholars at the same time, and Winter, twenty-three years older than Clinton, was a stand-in father for the Arkansas Governor, when they both served as Governors in 1984.

The first time anyone ate at Doe's Eat Place, whether you were of Southern descent or not, it felt like a novelty. The Signa family who owned

Doe's were Italians who made their way to the Mississippi Delta back in the early 1900s. In 1941, Dominick "Big Doe" Signa and his wife, Mamie, opened Big Doe's in the front of their family's grocery store, selling steaks along with hot tamales, which were a staple of the Delta. They started a honky tonk that catered to Black patrons in the front of the store, but whites liked the tamales and steaks so much, they ate them at tables in the back of the store. Eventually, the restaurant overtook the honky-tonk, and today a visitor to Doe's will find it much as it was eighty years ago.

Behind the front door sat a huge stove and oven where five to six cooks, mostly Black, prepared sizzling cow-sized steaks. We passed the cooks on the way to the dining room tables, and I introduced Willie and Raad to them all. Mostly white women prepared the hot tamales, slaw, rolls, apple pies and teas. Three other rooms held large and small tables covered with red-and-white patterned tablecloths. Diners felt at home, family and friends filling a large table and talking football, shopping and the cotton fields. They also sometimes joined in the conversation from other tables; everyone was family at Doe's.

As Raad and I started talking about Clark and his congressional race, we noticed a large gathering of political types coming into the steakhouse. Willie spotted his friend, Bill Clinton; Little Rock is a close neighbor to Greenville, only two hours away.

Clinton marched over to our table. Apparently he had been attending a Greenville fundraiser for Winter's Senate race and brought his entourage to Doe's for dinner. Willie introduced him to Raad and me. For some reason, Clinton stared at me the entire time, even when Willie was talking directly to him. I tried to keep my eyes on Willie, and I darted my eyes back to Clinton only a few times. Clinton's gaze was unbroken and rapt and made me unsettled. At the end of the awkward conversation, Clinton invited us to another gathering at C&G Railway Depot for drinks after dinner. C&G's was an old railroad station converted into a restaurant and bar right next to the railroad tracks, near the levee.

"Let's all sit together and catch up," he said. His voice was like Coach's voice or maybe Elvis'.

Willie took the lead and said, "You'll see us there, Governor."

Clinton walked away, and the three of us tried not to laugh.

"What was that all about?" I demanded.

"Well, if it were me, I'd only be staring at you, too," Willie said, puffing on a cigarette.

I waved my hand. "You're not a governor," I said. "And you're not married."

"He's one of a kind," Willie said, the admiration clear and thick in his voice. "He'll make a great president one day. I love him and his politics."

"And, what else does he love?" Raad asked.

"That's a long night for an off-the-record conversation," Willie laughed.

We talked our own politics while eating our meal and then made our way over to C&G's. We sat down at a large, long table that had been reserved for the group. Clinton sat beside us and began asking me questions about Clark and his campaign. One question led to another, and I proclaimed my views on any number of subjects: racism, poverty, education, jobs, and more. As others around the table began to pick up conversation among themselves, Clinton shifted his focus entirely to me. My earlier discomfort faded; I was thrilled that a governor found my policy ideas so interesting.

After a half-hour's conversation, Clinton finally turned to Raad and Willie, his friend for two decades, and brought them into the discussion. As Clinton turned to join the conversation on the other side of the table, he wrote something down on a napkin and passed it to me. That's nice, I thought: an autograph from the Governor. I unfolded the napkin and saw that he had written the name of his hotel, his room number, and a question mark.

I quickly folded the napkin back up, keeping my eyes off Clinton and the rest of the table. Excusing myself, I went to the restroom and sat myself down in the stall. I felt like a fool, thinking this Governor wanted to hear my ideas about solving poverty. Humiliated, I tossed the napkin in a toilet, gathered my things, and got the hell out of the bar.

Eight years later, I watched a parade of women tell their stories about Clinton as he ran for President. They were roundly ignored, or made fun of, or dismissed as "trailer park trash" by the media and my fellow Democrats. To me, their stories rang true. And I recognized the look in their eyes as they made the rounds to tell their stories on television. It was the look of someone who was deemed inconsequential, who wasn't believed, because they were taking on a powerful man. I had seen that look in Janice's eyes when she made us promise to keep her secret about the bookroom rape by Coach. And I'd felt that way myself, on my bird legs on the basketball court, in the newsroom with my better paid male colleagues, and at a lively Greenville bar with the future President of the United States.

***

When Clinton won the primary in 1992, the DNC liberals gladly jumped into the moderate Southern bandwagon. They didn't like Southerners very much (including me), but who else could get them inside the White House? We wanted to defeat George Bush, a Nixon apologist and a dubious former CIA Director. I didn't think Clinton could win, given his record of womanizing.

The Presidential election was in full swing over the next year. Mike McCurry left the DNC to work for Senator Bob Kerrey's presidential campaign in the primary, and he hired me to work on scheduling and media in Georgia. Kerrey's campaign failed quickly. McCurry made his way into the Clinton camp, but I was uninterested.

My old boss Mike Espy became a big Clinton supporter, stepping up to support Clinton after he criticized Sister Souljah for saying, "If Black people kill Black people every day, why not have a week and kill white people?" Clinton, seeing an opportunity to showcase his centrist credentials, criticized her and distanced himself from Jesse Jackson's decision to include Souljah in the Rainbow Coalition. Jackson, in turn, unloaded on Clinton, and moderate Black Democrats like Espy, stepped in to bolster Clinton. Espy earned Clinton's gratitude and a cabinet position as Secretary of Agriculture after

Clinton was elected.

When he was named to the Cabinet, Espy asked me to be his press secretary at Agriculture, and I wanted the job. But Stephanopoulos, who was the lead spokesperson in Clinton's campaign, blocked it to ensure that Clinton supporters took the top press spots at federal agencies. A woman who worked in the Clinton campaign and got the USDA job offered me a position as a press person for meat inspections. I would have been happy to promote USDA's efforts to fund meals for low-income families and their programs to end rural poverty. But I hadn't uprooted myself from Mississippi and navigated my way through the D.C. political jungle just to be a spokesperson for E. coli.

I was out of work. But I kept busy with my movies, books and albums. What train was I supposed to chase now?

***

"Karen, I have some bad news."

The call from Momma was like a bullet piercing my Washington bubble. Janice had been on short trip with her baby daughter locked safely in a car seat in the back. The baby was fussy and, as Janice reached back to grab her daughter's pacifier that had fallen, another vehicle blindsided Janice's car. She survived it, but her baby girl didn't.

I told Momma I would come home to see Janice. I suddenly realized my problems were so very small.

I'd only seen Janice a handful of times since our high school graduation. Memories of our friendship raced through my mind . . . suddenly I was on a runaway train.

After the 1982 election I'd covered as a reporter for the Jackson Daily News *and before I headed to Aspen, I headed back to Soso to visit my momma. We took a short drive to a popular diner for lunch and, as if it were meant to be, we saw Janice. She walked out of the diner with a man I had never met.*

"Janice!" I hollered from Momma's car. I waved enthusiastically, like I was sixteen again. I darted over to her, leaving Momma behind.

"I can't believe it's you! I'm so glad to see you," she said. She sounded

genuinely happy. "This is my husband, Donny."

"You're married?!" I responded, with much less passion than the wave conveyed. It started to rain.

Donny was a narc who had convinced Janice's sister, Wendy, to be an informer, and that's how they had met. It was the second time Janice had married someone who had been a part of her sister's life.

Without knowing what to say, I remarked, "You look like you are in love. You are as gorgeous as Natalie Woods was in that movie..."

"This Property Is Condemned, right? I remember," Janice said laughing loudly. "Karen, you haven't changed, and I'm glad you haven't."

Standing in the rain, we kissed each other on the cheek and said that we hoped to see each other soon. And goodbye.

I saw Janice again just before I headed to Washington five years later, leaving Quinn, my students and my momma behind. To find a solitary place to cry, I went to see Midnight alone in my old car, Myrtle, which Momma had been taking care of since the VW appeared. Driving down the dirt road, I thought I'd gone to the wrong spot. The ground where Midnight had rested was empty, the railcar hauled away, leaving a space already sprouting weeds. The train, which had never left its tracks while it took the coterie on journeys far from Soso, was gone.

I was furious. I wanted to see it, touch and smell the dusty seats and the wild flowers right outside the windows. It was like home away from home, and I was losing all my homes. It had been raining cats and dogs, and the dirt once protected from the rain by Midnight had turned into mud. I sunk my sneakers into it and let it rise up to my ankles. Closing my eyes, I imagined so many afternoons and nights with Janice, Maggie and Libby. I needed them now more than ever.

The next day, Momma and I drove over to the farm to see Uncle Roy and Aunt LeeAnn, who lived in a small home made with the same concrete as our own home, taken from my daddy's construction sites. On the way, we passed the Soso Post Office and saw Janice and her husband Donny outside. Janice was pregnant. Her belly was round, and she was laughing harder than I had ever seen her laugh.

"Momma, we have to stop! Janice is having a baby!" Momma pulled over, and I ran to Janice as soon as the car stopped. "Janice! You're pregnant!"

"Karen, you are so observant," she said, pooching her tummy out even farther. We hugged. I could tell she was glad to see me. "You remember Donny."

I said my hellos to him as a million burdens lifted from my shoulders. Janice was still the best medicine for me. Her beautiful black hair curled down her back, just like it did in high school.

Momma chimed in about babies but, soon enough, I told Janice about Midnight.

"Aren't you sad it's no longer there?" I asked.

Janice shrugged. "I didn't know it was gone until you told me. Besides, it was your train, not mine."

The words hurt more than I thought they might. "That's not true. We owned it together."

"Things are temporary. So is life. So is owning something. It's yours one day and someone else's the next."

"It will always be ours."

"At some point you have to stop chasing trains," Janice said. "There was nothing wrong with that in high school, but at some point you have to find a place to land."

"You landed, and I'm glad," I said, trying to cut the tension between us. Janice just smiled.

The truth was that Janice and I had become strangers since she almost dropped her favorite novel, Pride and Prejudice, in the bookroom as Coach approached. Libby and Maggie had graduated from community college and married, too. We stayed in touch only occasionally. It felt a long way from when we whispered in each other ears, sharing secrets on the Midnight railcar.

185

It felt a long way from when we told Coach to leave Janice alone.

***

After hearing about the car accident, I flew to Mississippi and drove to Janice's house with no idea what sort of reception I'd be met with. I stood at the door, hesitating for a moment, thinking about what I should say. How do you comfort a friend whose life had taken so many wrong turns? I knocked. And I knocked. Janice didn't answer the door.

I was relieved. I knew I would feel guilty if I didn't knock, if I didn't reach out. But I was glad she didn't answer the door. It was hard for me to face her. I wanted to shake her and tell her that she shouldn't have stayed here in Mississippi. She needed to escape, like me. Maggie and Libby told me that Janice was beyond broken up. She told them she blamed herself. She was depressed and despondent. I had seen it before, in my own family, in Robbie after Daddy died. I didn't want to think about that scene again. I was learning how to forget things I didn't want to know, like James Carville. And I didn't want to know about Janice.

After living in the nation's capital for seven years, I no longer felt connected to Mississippi, to Janice or to Maggie and Libby. In D.C., people moved in and out of my life quickly. I had a job, then I had another job, and then another job. I wasn't good at being a good friend, or making good friends anymore.

I saw Maggie and Libby for a few minutes when I went home. Sitting in Libby's kitchen—after her son threw a fake snake on me, causing me to scream—Libby didn't hesitate to ask, "Why aren't you married? Why are you waiting so long? When are you going to have children? Don't you want them?"

"Libby," I said, "I've fallen in love once then twice. They didn't want me. I can't find my Robert Redford."

"That's your problem, Karen. Stop looking for your Robert Redford. He doesn't exist. Remember when we had all those lists that we needed to check off before making decisions? Throw yours away!" Libby laughed.

Maggie said, "Exactly, girl! This has been going on since we were sixteen."

"What a year that was," I said, thinking I didn't want to throw anything away.

We fell silent for a bit. Driving back home, I told myself that Libby and Maggie were right. That Janice was right. I needed to land back in D.C. and throw my list away. Driving home, empowered by my closest friends, I thought about going over to Janice's house and boldly knocking on the door once more.

I never did.

That night, I looked through my bedroom bookshelves for Flannery O'Connor short stories and her novel, *Wise Blood*. I wanted to read again what Mrs. Cook had told Janice and me about O'Connor's work: "Where you come from is gone, where you thought you were going to never was there, and where you are is no good unless you can get away from it."

As I returned to Washington, those words stayed with me. And, as I thought about Janice losing her child and being taken care of by a man who loved her so much, another thought rang in my head: I was thirty-four.

Shit.

I craved stability.

I wanted a baby, someday, and time was getting shorter.

Not long after, in June 1994, I married my Marine boyfriend and left Washington, thinking it was time to move on from the craziness of the capital and the emptiness I had begun to feel there. We lived at first on Emerald Isle, close to North Carolina's Camp Lejeune, where Pat was stationed. Every morning, I rose early and ran along the Outer Bank beaches, clearing my head from the stress I had left behind. Porpoises swimming at low tide seemed to follow me as my feet slapped the sand. I loved it.

Yet over the next few months I missed having a job with a mission, like Pat had. He was a captain in the Marines, a leader. I wanted to be a leader and get things done for people who didn't have anyone in their corner. Wasn't that why I had gone to D.C. in the first place? I was good at political communications, and I knew it. The challenge was finding someone in Washington to work for who would recognize what I could do and value me for it. When Pat was transferred from Camp Lejeune back to the Marine Barracks in Washington, I was ready to return, determined to land.

***

"I got you the meeting with Andrew Cuomo."

My friend Terry called with the news when I got back to D.C., as I was hunting for my next gig. She had worked with me at the Democratic National Committee and was now working for Cuomo at the U.S. Department of Housing and Urban Development. Cuomo was an Assistant Secretary, looking to staff up his team; Terry recommended me for press secretary. The White House didn't usually allow Assistant Secretaries at small agencies to hire their own flaks, but Terry said Cuomo could swing it.

"He's got balls," Terry said. "And he knows how to swing 'em ... you may have to duck once in a while though!"

Part Three
Penis Politics

C h a p t e r 11
The Push-Up Man

I didn't know much about Andrew Cuomo, except that he was the eldest son of New York Governor Mario Cuomo. And I knew he had married Kerry Kennedy, a daughter of Robert F. Kennedy. The word in D.C. and among journalists was that the Cuomo-Kennedy match was a dynasty in the making, a merger of two political royal families. The *New York Times* D.C. bureau had done a small piece saying that Cuomo's operation at HUD had developed a reputation among insiders as a "hot shop," i.e. an exciting place to work. I smelled a bit of self-promotion, but the scent didn't bother me. It was, after all, what I did for a living.

***

While I had no particular impression of Andrew Cuomo, I had a vivid image of his father, Mario Cuomo. On a steamy July night in 1984, I'd been in Greenwood, Mississippi at Lusco's Restaurant, a popular spot known for its steaks, its white curtain entryways into private dining cubicles, a Black waiter who sang the menu and its bring-your-own-booze brown bag policy. It was a place where mostly white people went for supper, and mostly Black people worked. The original owners of the restaurant, Charlie and Marie Lusco, had immigrated to the Mississippi Delta from Cefalu, in Sicily.

I was there with Quinn that night, dining with a group of friends whose parents had been Democrats but whose offspring were part of a wave of young, white Southern Republicans beginning to dominate Mississippi politics. We were in the midst of the '84 presidential election, and that evening an Italian-American Governor from New York, was to give the keynote address at the Democratic National Convention in San Francisco.

The Lusco family had the TV on, as loud as possible, in the front section of the restaurant where the grocery store was. An elderly woman was sitting in a rocking chair, watching, as other family members gathered in anticipation of hearing a famous Italian American speak on national television.

I was in one of the back cubicles with my friends, the lone Democrat and notorious for my liberal politics, when I heard Mario Cuomo's voice begin to rise from the 30-inch Zenith TV with rabbit ear antennae. I announced that I would be watching out front if anyone wanted to come. No one did. Not even Quinn. They shooed me away.

I joined the Luscos about the time that Cuomo confronted President Reagan's vision of the United States as a "Shining City on a Hill": "Please allow me to skip the stories and the poetry and the temptation to deal in nice but vague rhetoric ... Mr. President, you ought to know that this nation is more a 'Tale of Two Cities' than it is just a 'Shining City on a Hill.'"

As Cuomo's voice moved through the restaurant, a few other patrons joined us. Pretty soon, a crowd gathered, including Quinn and some of our friends. Eventually, most everybody in the place was listening to Cuomo's words cut through the summer heat as we stood near the screen door in the front of the restaurant.

"That struggle to live with dignity is the real story of the shining city. And it's a story, ladies and gentlemen, that I didn't read in a book or learn in a classroom. I saw it and lived it, like many of you. I watched a small man with thick calluses on both his hands work fifteen and sixteen hours a day. I saw him once literally bleed from the bottoms of his feet, a man who came here uneducated, alone, unable to speak the language, who taught me all I needed to know about faith and hard work by the simple eloquence of his example. I learned about our kind of democracy from my father."

Mario Cuomo's father, like the Luscos, had emigrated to the U.S. from Italy and opened a grocery store in Queens, New York. And here was Cuomo, speaking of his father's life as a metaphor for the philosophy that Democrats could believe in as the rebuttal to Reagan's "trickle-down economics."

"We can have a future that provides for all," he said, "by marrying common sense and compassion. We know we can, because we did it for nearly fifty years before 1980. And we can do it again, if we do not forget ... that this entire nation has profited by these progressive principles; that they helped lift up generations to the middle class and higher; that they gave us a chance to work, to go to college, to raise a family, to own a house, to be secure in our old age and, before that, to reach heights that our own parents would not have dared dream of ..."

The Luscos were moved. I was moved. Cuomo, the son of an Italian-born grocer who spoke limited English, had become Governor of New York and embodied the dream of opportunity in America. Everyone agreed it was a great speech, but one of my Republican dinner companions was dismissive: "It's just a speech," he observed. But to me, words mattered. Speeches, like the one Cuomo delivered, mattered because the people who heard them often go and do things that matter. Or, as Cuomo said: speeches should not just "bring people to their feet" but also "bring people to their senses."

The halls of the powerful in Washington and New York seemed a long way from the Mississippi Delta that night. I had no idea that, twn years later, a considerable distance down the train tracks from Lusco's Restaurant, I would be sitting in front of Mario Cuomo's son interviewing for a job in his office.

192

***

Andrew Cuomo was on the phone in his office when I arrived for the meeting. I had met a lot of high-powered people in Washington and, by this point, never worried too much about impressing them. Either they liked me, or they didn't. However, my time with any hard-edged New Yorker clocked in at zero, and I felt some flutters as Cuomo, still on the phone, waved me into his office. I sat down in a chair across from his desk, observing him as I waited for his attention. He punctuated every point in the phone conversation with his hands, jabbing the air and running his fingers through his curly hair. His eyes were intense, his voice strong, occasionally rising and falling in a sing-song fashion. With my hands in my lap, I wondered if my Soso and his New York City styles could mesh.

Cuomo finished up the call, apologized for the delay and threw a few questions at me about my news media experience. He thumbed through the portfolio of things I had written or pitched for various national media outlets over the years. He liked a concept I created for a DNC event at The Museum of Modern Art in New York. I'd named it "The Art of Governing."

"The name of the event is so perfect," he said, hunching over his desk, staring at the invitation with a huge smile on his face. "Karen, you know, governing *is* an art. It is."

He pulled on his bottom lip several times, thinking about the connection between the two, before he said, "It's as much art as science. It's not about just knowledge and experience but also creativity."

"Obviously I agree, or I wouldn't have written it." I put on what I imagined was my best New York schmooze.

Cuomo grinned. He also offered me the job on the spot.

Terry told me to come back the next day to meet with one of Cuomo's senior staffers and work out the details. When I arrived, the staffer, another New Yorker named Howard Glaser, began interviewing me all over again. Clearly, he hadn't gotten the message that Cuomo had offered me the job already.

"You do know, I assume," I said with a bit of irritation, after trying gamely to answer a few rote questions, "that the Assistant Secretary told me I'm hired."

Glaser looked up from his desk with his glasses perched on the end of his nose. "You don't know Andrew Cuomo, do you?"

Despite the detour, which I soon learned was typical of Cuomo's style, I did in fact get the job. Detours were a constant in Andrew Cuomo's world. Just when you thought the road was clear and safe, Andrew decided to blow up the road and everybody on it.

When I became Andrew's press secretary, the Secretary of HUD was Henry Cisneros, a highly regarded Hispanic politician from Texas with real presidential potential. His government career unraveled after accusations that he had failed to tell the whole truth about support payments he was making to his former mistress. He told his wife—and the FBI—about some payments during his background check for his nomination as HUD Secretary.

Turned out he was sending quite a bit more cash to the former flame than he had acknowledged. This made neither his wife nor the FBI happy, and a $20 million special prosecutor investigation ensued. In Washington, scandals create job openings, and Andrew soon found himself, at the age of thirty-nine, sworn in by Bill Clinton as the new HUD Secretary at the end of 1996.

Andrew didn't settle into the role. He devoured it. His art of governing was painted in bold strokes and primary colors. He filled every inch of every canvas. I had never seen anyone push so hard, day, noon, and night. His daily exhortation to us was, "Make something happen."

In a bureaucracy like HUD, though, "something" was rarely simple. We worked hard, and sometimes Andrew pushed us to—and then past—the breaking point. He could be demanding and difficult. In the office, the staff wilted under Andrew's relentless interrogations about the projects we were working on. No detail was too small, from the staging of a photo op to the process for inspecting federally subsidized housing. You didn't have to have the right answer, but you had to show that you had thought it through. If you couldn't explain your thinking, you didn't last long under Andrew's unnaturally intense gaze.

At one Saturday morning meeting, Andrew looked at the glum faces of tired and overworked senior staff who had been working with flow charts of HUD programs with acronyms like CDBG, CPD, PIH, FHA and other government creations designed to make the straightforward as complex as possible.

"I know you're tired," he told us. "I know you want to be home with your families. I know you want to take a couple of days off on the weekend like everyone else in this agency. But I also know this: The people we are supposed to serve, they don't get a weekend off from substandard housing. They don't get a weekend off from being homeless. They don't get a weekend off from poverty. They live it twenty-four hours a day. I know it's hard for you. I do. But we didn't get into public service to move pieces of paper around. We came here to make change happen."

That was the commitment and passion that I wanted to hear, that I wanted to be part of. Our team left his office ready to work, and I admired Andrew Cuomo for his drive to make change, or anything good, happen.

As his press secretary, I traveled with Andrew to cities across the country as he announced grants, programs and policies, drumming up favorable media coverage for himself and building up chits with the governors and mayors he made happy. He loved it when a news clip captured the political art and the science of his message. But any deviation from the message, or mistake by a reporter, large or small, was my fault. I fucked it up, and I had to call reporters or editors immediately and fix what often appeared to be a minor point: The check was $1.5 million for the housing program, not $1.4 million. And so on.

He fretted about media coverage and was as impatient as a child on Christmas morning when he had to wait for the print version of news reports on his events and announcements. One night, on a red-eye from California to Washington, he was frantic to know how the *New York Times* story about our day's event would turn out in the next morning's paper. He couldn't wait until

195

we landed. I reached a HUD staffer in New York from that clunky phone that once had been built into the back of airplane seats. Andrew wanted me to get the guy to run out and buy the midnight edition of the *New York Times* and then read me the article. Which I did, swiftly writing it down as close to word-for-word as I could before reading the long news clip to Andrew, sitting side-by-side. The article turned out to be terrific, and Andrew was so delighted he squeezed my cheek and gave me a big kiss on the red pinch mark. I was just happy to squeeze in an hour's sleep before we hit the ground.

Away from Washington, if a trip was going well, Andrew could be relaxed and informal. He was enormously curious about the personal lives of his staff, deploying a store of rapid-fire questions for staffers in the car or on a plane ride before and after the day's events.

What do you think of HUD? You like your job? What do you want your next job to be? Are you married? Do you have a boyfriend or girlfriend? What was it like growing up in Cleveland, Detroit, Los Angeles, Des Moines, Mississippi? What do you think of Clinton, Gore, Stephanopoulos, Rahm? How am I doing? Do you like my speeches? Should I change anything?

The peculiar Cuomonian version of "casual" conversation grew on the Cuomo team over time. We competed for attention, like siblings over a parent. If you didn't get the interrogation—whether hostile or friendly—you began to worry that you had disappointed him, somehow. Better to be an object of attention, good or bad, than to be dismissed or ignored.

When Andrew discovered on our first airplane trip together that I had married a Marine, he started probing: "Does your husband work out all the time? Can he do push-ups?"

"Yes, he has to work out. He's a grunt."

"Yeah, how many push-ups does he do?

"I have no idea," I said.

"I can do a lot of push-ups," he said.

"Really? Why do you do lots of push-ups?"

"I'm a basketball player. I played with my father. I still play with him.

196

Bring Pat into my office, and we can have a push-up contest. I bet I can beat him. What do you think?"

"He won't compete against you," I said, trying to get him to understand the difference between a highly-disciplined Marine and a politically appointed Assistant Secretary.

"Why not?" he asked with hopes a push-up contest was possible.

"Pat's a Marine. He wouldn't want to beat a high-ranking government official reporting to his Commander-in-Chief."

"Yeah, bring him to the office," Andrew insisted, bulldozing over me. He lowered his voice to a heavy baritone, pumping an arm muscle at me. "I want to beat a Marine in push-ups."

I waved him away.

Then, he laughed. He had one of the loudest, most pronounced and joyous laughs I had ever heard, though it was frequently self-delight at his own cleverness. For the rest of my time at the housing agency in various staff meetings, both large and small, Andrew encouraged me to convince my husband to come to his office for a push-up contest. Each time, I demurred, and he would exclaim, "No? I bet he's scared of me!" Then, the laugh.

When Andrew Cuomo wasn't laughing at his own jokes, he was deadly serious. Specifically, about fighting to persuade skeptical Republicans to provide adequate funding for the housing needs of low-income families. Republicans, under the leadership of Newt Gingrich, had ruthlessly defunded housing subsidies for the poor, and they were not naturally receptive to Cuomo's push for more and better housing.

But it wasn't always the Republicans who needed convincing. The Clinton Administration did, too.

Cuomo's relationship with the White House was complex. His closest ally was Vice President Al Gore, who had been a key voice in convincing Clinton to nominate Andrew as Secretary. The President himself seemed to grow genuinely fond of Andrew, especially when Clinton's sexual and financial troubles grew in his second term with the Whitewater real estate investment scandal and, of course, Monica Lewinsky and her blue dress. The White House welcomed Cuomo's political acumen.

But as often as Andrew cultivated the relationships, he never shied away from a fight over policy decisions. He viewed the role of HUD Secretary as the only position in the federal government whose job it was to advocate for the poorest communities. Particularly after welfare reform, when it appeared that Clinton was willing to trade the safety net for low-income Americans in order to shore up his reputation as a centrist, Andrew saw HUD and himself as the last defense against assaults on the poor.

That message resonated with me. I had grown up in a state with the highest poverty rates in the country. I saw white Mississippians leave the old Democratic Party and plant themselves with the Republican Party of Newt Gingrich, Trent Lott, Haley Barbour, Lee Atwater, and Ronald Reagan, whose members had a different idea about helping the poor. "Pull yourself up by your bootstraps," they often said. And if you don't have any boots, then too fuckin' bad.

Mississippi was the most racist state in the country, but that didn't mean Democratic strongholds like Chicago or New York City or Los Angeles weren't. That became clear as tensions over poverty and race reached a head when a simmering conflict between Andrew and Richard Daley, the Democratic Mayor of Chicago, landed in the President's lap.

Daley was the pugnacious son of the Chicago Mayor of the same name, who concentrated the poorest and Blackest Chicagoans into titanic high-rise complexes far from the white sections of the city during the 1950s. In the late 1990s, as land near the projects became more valuable, the younger Daley wanted to tear down the "notorious" projects, like the Robert Taylor homes and Cabrini-Green, to open them up to private development. And he wanted HUD to pay for the demolition.

In turn, Cuomo wanted proof that Daley would replace housing for the poor. Daley's plan, Cuomo believed, was urban renewal by urban removal. Cuomo said no, he would not sign off on a plan that displaced thousands of

Black families without anywhere for them to go. Andrew, the push-up man, pushed back. Democrat-on-Democrat violence ensued as a series of escalating (and somewhat dirty) fights between the Mayor and HUD played out publicly.

The question on all of our minds was: Where would the White House come out?

HUD was the last place Clinton wanted a headache. He liked Andrew, but he—and, more importantly, Gore—needed Daley. Gore was planning his 2000 run for the White House, and Daley and his machine were critical to Gore's political needs in Illinois.

Daley managed to get himself invited to accompany the President to the World Economic Forum in Davos, Switzerland because he wanted the President's ear to complain about Andrew's intransigence. The next day, a small group of us sat in Cuomo's spacious office on the tenth floor when his assistant, Rita, put through a call from the Vice President. We heard Cuomo's side, and a good bit of Gore's side through the receiver that Andrew held away from his ear.

"Look, Andrew, Daley spoke to the President on Air Force One and in Switzerland about this public housing thing he wants. Daley was quite exercised about it."

Andrew tried to turn it around to Gore's interests: "Al, you don't want to go into next year with the Black community in Chicago up in arms about this."

Gore was unmoved. "I need Daley, Andrew, and Daley needs this."

Andrew tried again, lowering his voice to a heavy baritone, covered by a whisper, again. "Daley's father warehoused these people, segregated them, and now Daley wants to literally blow up their homes with no plan to find housing for them. It's going to create a bigger problem for them. And that's a problem for you."

Gore, hardened his tone: "The President wants it resolved, Andrew."

Andrew paused a moment, then chose his words carefully. "He's the President. If he wants to have Daley's plan approved by HUD, then that's his prerogative. But I'm not going to be the HUD Secretary who approves it."

Our jaws dropped in unison. Andrew had just told the Vice President that he would quit before he would sign onto Daley's plan. We could almost hear Gore calculating on the other end of the phone: A HUD Secretary quitting in protest over a plan to displace Blacks from their homes in America's third largest city would surely produce bad headlines. Or was Andrew bluffing?

Gore decided that he was not and beat a strategic retreat. "You raise some good points," he said. "What if we host negotiations at the White House to see if we can do it your way but give Daley a way out?"

Andrew agreed. When he hung up the phone, I jumped up and down and clapped as the boy brigade looked at the Secretary, stunned. "Boy brigade" was my name for the small, inner circle of young, white Ivy League lawyers and political gurus who surrounded Cuomo. Andrew often brought the brigade into his office for never-ending strategy meetings, while I stood outside his office waiting for my press release or statement to be approved.

This time I was inside, and I liked it.

***

"We're going to Mississippi."

Andrew took me by surprise with his news. I never thought the utterly urban Andrew would step foot in Mississippi with its mostly rural landscape. The thought of my Washington and Mississippi worlds literally colliding had, truly, never occurred to me before. The thought of returning to my home state with my New York boss gave me incredible anxiety. We, though, had a very good reason for the trip.

White supremacy was never far beneath the surface of Mississippi life. An outbreak of fires at Black churches, suspected to be arson, had been rippling through the Deep South. In a sixteen-month period, over 450 arsons, bombings or attempted bombings had hit mostly Black churches. The True Light Missionary Baptist Church, in Ruleville, Mississippi, had burned to the ground in 1995, one of the growing number of churches burned down during this time period. It was hard to verify arson. And, without a finding of arson, the churches weren't eligible for most federal assistance.

200

Andrew thought that we might be able to cobble together some HUD rural development funds to help them rebuild. He'd found a work-around, putting together a program of grants and loan guarantees for church rebuilding. Even when he could find the money, though, many of the congregations didn't know how to put together a building plan, file applications, deal with local zoning or the hundred other things involved in construction. Before HUD, Andrew had built hundreds of units of housing in New York for homeless families. He immediately recognized the problem and put together a series of partnerships to work one-on-one with each church to get the rebuilding rolling.

"The architects are here," he explained as he pushed the idea in front of a U.S. Senate Committee. "Construction and engineering? We have it. Finance? We have it. Lawyers? We have them. We have all the pieces in place to help the churches build better, stronger and bigger than they were before."

Andrew and I flew out of Washington on a commercial flight to Memphis and jumped into a minivan for the two-hour ride to Ruleville, a town of about three thousand people, mostly Black—a former railroad town serving the cotton trade. Over a third of the population lived below the poverty line. It was where civil rights icon Fannie Lou Hamer, the focus of Mike Espy's 1988 convention speech, had grown up and begun her determined fight for the right to vote. Andrew sensed my anxiety and nervousness and tried to put me at ease by asking a series of more rapid-fire questions about growing up in Mississippi, my family and the Mississippi Delta. I was happy to act as local tour guide as we descended into the Delta from Memphis, along Route 61. I talked about the role of blues in the Delta, and the nickname of the road as the Blues Highway.

"You mean like *Highway 61 Revisited*? The Dylan album?" Cuomo asked.

I replied, "Dylan was just another white man cashing in on music created by Black people."

"This is the road where Bessie Smith died and Robert Johnson," I explained, as we crossed through Clarksdale and turned onto Route 49, the crossroads where Johnson had sold his soul to the Devil in exchange for his blues genius.

"Crossroads'—I know that song—Eric Clapton and Cream!" Cuomo said with satisfaction.

Andrew put his Walkman headphones over his ears, as he often did to relax on road trips. I could hear the notes of Billy Joel's maddening "Uptown Girl", a girl I was not, rise above the road noise as we traveled through the heart of downhome blues country.

When we got to Ruleville, I was still nervous, obsessing like the hostess of a dinner party who wants to make sure every little thing goes just right. I worried that the event would be a reflection of me to Andrew, and that Andrew's performance in turn would be a reflection of me to the locals.

I needn't have worried. It turned out that Andrew was more at ease than me, as he spoke to the church members, gathered in a rundown shack not far from their lost church, still smoldering from the hatred and violence of the fire. They warmed to him, Queens accent and all.

He first made clear that despite his obvious New York background, that what happened in Mississippi was everyone's problem: "If we are one society, one America, then burning one church or one mosque or one synagogue burns us all ..."

A few women in the congregation shouted, "That's right!"

Cuomo continued, "The story of church burnings in America over the past few months is a story of two bookends: one, a bookend of discrimination and anger; the other, a bookend of hope and renewal. In between is story of national faith devotion and humanity—the best chapters of which are being written in places like Ruleville."

Now, a chorus of "That's the truth!" and, "All right now!" rose up.

"Every time we come together and rebuild a church," Cuomo said, voice deepening and getting stronger, "we strengthen our abilities and determination to end racism and hatred in this country and make communities better places to life, work and raise our children." Cuomo announced that True Light would be the first church to receive the help under legislation Clinton had signed to implement the HUD program. "Your communities have saved and sacrificed to build places where everyone can come to worship. We cannot allow others to tear down what you have made without consequence and without assistance."

HUD went to the University of Mississippi (Ole Miss) and asked them to loan the local congregation some engineers to help with rebuilding plans. And by Easter 1997, the congregation had moved into their new home. It was a story repeated across the South, thanks to Andrew's determination to create a federal helping hand.

This was the side of Andrew that reminded me why I came to Washington; why I had put up with the invitations to be part of a "stable" on Capitol Hill, and generally not being taken seriously as a dishwater blonde from Mississippi in Washington, D.C. Andrew pushed hard—*really* hard—to get what he wanted. And as long as what he wanted was to lift up poor people, especially poor women, who had been left behind, I was goddamn exhilarated.

But I was soon to learn that, as Andrew pushed up and up, some of us would be pushed aside.

I had done a good job as Cuomo's press secretary, so when the job of Assistant Secretary for Public Affairs opened up, I not only wanted it, I deserved the promotion. I was the right person for the job, at least I thought so, and I put it directly to Andrew one afternoon in a phone call.

Andrew, meanwhile, didn't even extend the courtesy of pretending to think about it. "You're not qualified to be my Assistant Secretary."

"Are you kidding me?" I asked. I should have said something more aggressive, snarkier, but I was completely stunned. "No" wasn't even close to the answer that I was anticipating.

"No, I'm not kidding," he said flatly. "You've only worked for a small-town, Black Congressman from Mississippi."

I sputtered a litany about my background, suddenly feeling defensive about my experience. "I got serious media experience from working for the first Black Congressman since Reconstruction in a state with the largest percentage of Blacks in the country. You may think it's small-time or small-town, or whatever, but Ron Brown and Mike McCurry at the DNC didn't think that. And, by the way, the national coverage I drummed up helped you become HUD Secretary. But I'm not qualified to be your public affairs assistant secretary. How is that even possible?!"

He knew I was pissed off, and he decided not to engage. "Let's talk about this when I see you," he said.

A day later, in his office, he took a poster of some sort, rolled it up, and looked at me through it, his eye framed by the fake telescope.

"I'm saying," he said, slowly, "that you aren't ready to lead that big of a shop. Focus on yourself, and it will happen. One day."

I was on the verge of tears, but I didn't want to show him any weakness. I got up and walked out of his office, feeling Andrew's eye following me through his makeshift paper telescope.

The door shut behind me. I was in the outer circle, not the inner circle, and I knew it. On one level I understood what Andrew really wanted. He had big ambitions and he wanted a "name" for his top press secretary. Someone he could poach from the White House, or a broadcast outlet, someone who was seen as a "get" that burnished Andrew's own reputation. It wasn't really about doing the actual job but what the hire looked like to the Washington world. And that irritated me even more because it meant that no matter how good I was, I would never be good enough. I had served my purpose for Andrew, and now I could be disposed of.

Back in my office, I closed the door and sat in my chair. My mind couldn't process it. Something about the way he dismissed my experience—and me—because I worked for a "small-town Black" hit a nerve that made me crazy, mad and, above all else, sad. He clearly wanted that big-time name to be his press secretary now that he was a Cabinet member. And, after a year of trying to please Andrew and compete, like my daddy told me, to be first—not last, not second, but first—I was exhausted. I just wanted to disappear.

I grabbed a bottle of Wite-Out that was sitting on my desk. I opened the bottle and dipped the brush into the white liquid, used to make typewritten mistakes disappear. I tightened my lips and began to jab the brush roughly on the back of my fingers, my hands, my wrist. Wielding the brush like a knife, I jabbed the white liquid over and over and harder and harder on my hands, as though I were the mistake I was trying to erase.

A few days later, Andrew invited me to a Capitol Hill meeting in the office of Trent Lott, who was now Leader of the Republican conference in the Senate. He likely thought that bringing a fellow Mississippian with him might soften up the powerful Senator. Lott sat close to me and across from Andrew as we discussed some projects that Lott wanted funded in his state.

Afterward, back at the HUD office, Cuomo laughed and told the boy brigade, "I thought Lott was going to lean right over and lick Karen's thigh."

His comment made the rounds in the office and quickly got back to me. I already knew Lott was a shameless flirt, but I felt minimized and slighted by being the brunt of a joke meant to entertain Andrew's inner circle of white men.

Even the boy brigade sometimes found Andrew's increasing sexual banter to be too much. One of them sheepishly related to me that as they were sitting on the HUD roof early one evening, puffing on cigars with the brigade, Andrew told them a story about two of his Kennedy brothers-in-law. The two of them, marveled Andrew, "are fucking the same woman. She likes to get fucked in the ass and some days she goes from one Kennedy house to the other to get it twice in one day." Andrew leaned back and took a puff of the cigar, contemplative. "You know, when you have anal sex with a woman, you own her soul."

Andrew definitely tried to own the souls of the women who worked for him, and I wasn't the only woman at HUD made to feel like she wanted to disappear. A close friend of mine told me she mentally drew down a curtain in front of her face as her day began at HUD to withstand the hours of bullying, unreasonable demands and public humiliation by Andrew. She pulled the

205

curtain back up as she left in the evening. She told me several times over the course of our time together at HUD, "I can't do anything right. It's all wrong. I think I'm doing what he wants, but then he changes his mind and blames me."

On another occasion, Andrew was planning to hire a highly qualified woman I recommended for a position in the Secretary's office based on her impressive resume. Once he met her in person, he changed his mind. Not because she didn't make a hit with her skills and smarts. He told me he found her plain-Jane looks and dress were just "not attractive enough" for him.

Oftentimes a new aide would join the Secretary's staff and for a time be what we called "the flavor of the day." Andrew would shower them with attention and praise for a time, but things would inevitably turn sour if the aide departed in any small way from Andrew's preferred script. He was particularly brutal in tearing down one top female aide, who possessed a well-regarded Washington pedigree, when she began to push back on his way of doing things. He would wait until he knew she was at a lunch workout in the HUD gym and then have his secretary summon her up for a meeting that "could not wait." She was told to return immediately—no time for a shower or changing clothes. She showed up with her gym clothes on, sweating. Then, surrounded by the rest of the senior staff, Andrew ignored the sweating woman completely, saying nothing to her during the meeting, and quickly shutting down any contribution she tried to make. The flavor of the day melted away, and the smart ones got the message and quit rather than endure further evisceration.

I guessed I wasn't too smart because I decided I had no intention of being one of the ones who quit. There were moments I wanted to make myself disappear, but I resolved that I wasn't going to be run out of my job and that I could give as good as I got.

Chapter 12
A Needle in the Ass

"Karen, I want you to go on the record," Michael Isikoff, the former *Washington Post* investigative reporter, begged me—and not for the first time. "Your story about Clinton fits the pattern of his behavior with women that I've been documenting for my book."

Isikoff had heard my story about Clinton's ham-handed pickup attempt in Doe's Eat Place, and by 1998 the scandal over Clinton's relationship with Monica Lewinsky was deepening. Isikoff believed that my episode was a small but telling example of Clinton's pattern of womanizing. After all, I wasn't the only woman Clinton had slipped a napkin or a matchbook to with an invitation to his hotel room in the years since he tried it with me in 1984. A man who had positioned himself as one of the strongest advocates for women's rights was actually someone who exploited women for his own personal needs.

Still, I had consistently refused to go on the record. I didn't want to wreck my career. By the time Isikoff was writing his book *Uncovering Clinton*, I was actually working for the Clinton administration. Heck, I had even accepted a housing award from Clinton and Gore in the Oval Office. And I couldn't imagine Andrew Cuomo reacting well to a story about the time our boss Bill Clinton invited me to be part of his "stable."

Ironically, it was James Carville who changed my mind, inadvertently, about going on the record with Isikoff. Along with George Stephanopoulos and other Clintonites, Carville called the Arkansas women speaking publicly about liaisons with the President of the United States "trailer park trash." Those words infuriated me.

Janice lived in a trailer for several years back in Soso. My brother and his wife in Mississippi did, too, and some of my cousins, including Carol, who lived on the Hinton farm in a trailer. Carol was a young woman with a young son, no husband and an alcohol problem. One winter she had no money to pay the trailer's electric bill and, soon after, she had no heat. She sent her son to stay with our aunt one night because she worried about the cold, and she needed to drink. No one checked on her—not the aunt, not her brothers and not the other kin living on or near the farm. She either froze to death or drank herself dead. Either way, she died alone that night.

Were they all trash just because they lived in trailers in a park or on a farm? Ragin' Cajun James Carville knew as much about trailer parks and the people who lived there as I did.

Men in the Republican Party could care less about women's rights while men in the Democratic Party would often position themselves as progressive, but when push came to shove, it was women who got pushed over and shoved aside, especially when the political life of an ambitious man was in question.

I knew I would pay a price if I spoke up about Clinton. I might be fired and never hired again in Washington. But by then I also had learned that silence had its own price. I'd been silent all those years ago after Coach sexually abused. My silence—the coterie's silence—altered all of our lives. But Janice was the one who suffered the most. I had bit my tongue too many

208

times in Washington at the small humiliations that came with being a woman in the nation's capital. I'd had my work overlooked, and my looks worked over. I was tired of it. But this time, I'd rather pay the cost of speaking up than shutting up.

I gave Isikoff the okay to include the story. It was a small contribution of six pages in his 401-page book. Isikoff wrote, "Hinton couldn't get over it....Hinton told me, 'I was offended. I felt a bit humiliated.' From then [1984] on...[she] never hesitated to tell her friends in the Democratic Party [about the incident]..." Isikoff also noted what I had said to my colleagues at the Democratic National Committee in the early '90s, when Clinton was considering a presidential run. He wrote, "Everybody at the DNC knew about Clinton's womanizing, she told me. It was indiscreet, blatant. 'People were always sort of joking about it,' she said."

Andrew joked about it, too, in 1998 when the Monica Lewinsky sex scandal broke. Andrew was a known cigar guy, and Clinton had given him a very expensive humidor filled with illegal Cuban cigars, with a personal note that read, "Don't ask ... Don't tell," a play on the name of the Administration policy on accepting gays in the military. When it was reported that Clinton used a cigar instead of his penis to have sex with Lewinsky, Andrew wagged his own cigar as he laughed about cigar sex in front of me and other staff. "At least you can't catch AIDS that way," he said to an uncomfortable silence from the staff.

On another occasion, after Clinton famously wagged his finger and said, "I did not have sex with that woman," his political advisors, including Andrew, gathered at the White House to discuss how to manage the snowballing scandal, as Andrew described the scene to us later in his office. At that point, no one was really sure what the extent of Clinton's relationship with Lewinsky might be, but based on the President's parsing of words the suspicion was that there was something else other than vaginal intercourse. Outside the White House after the meeting, Andrew and Bill Richardson, the Energy Secretary, speculated on what that might be. "I think we can probably defend oral sex,"

Andrew opined to Richardson. "But I have to draw the line"—here he paused for effect—"at Presidential ass fucking." Richardson thought this was hilarious, as did Andrew when he related the story to us.

So I had no regrets even when, as I expected, I would have to pay up for going on the record. Shortly before *Uncovering Clinton* was published, Andrew had finally agreed to give me the Assistant Secretary of Public Affairs position in an "Acting" role, with the understanding that Andrew would recommend that the White House submit a nomination to the Senate for confirmation of the appointment. I finally got the job after two high-powered women in Washington either didn't last long or refused the offer. D.C. television anchor Susan King had broken ground for women journalists by winning litigation against a television network in D.C. that had discriminated against her for an anchor position, based on her sex and age. Once she got a taste of Andrew, she was gone within six months.

Andrew continued the hunt for another well-known woman in D.C. political circles, Tammy Haddad, a media maven in the making who created and produced *Larry King Live* on CNN. He begged and pleaded her to consider the position, but she finally turned him down. Tired of the hunt, he gave me the job.

In Washington, a Senate-confirmed position is a big deal in your career. It certainly would be for me. After the book came out, the White House quietly declined to submit my pending nomination to the Senate. Poking around, I learned that Andrew had discreetly let the White House know that they should drop the nomination. He didn't want to be tainted in Clinton's eyes by being associated with a member of his own staff who was now going up against the President. Even the push-up man, it seemed, had a limit to what he would push for. He didn't fire me, though, telling his chief of staff, "Just leave her alone." He was in a box, really. It wouldn't look good if he fired a Clinton appointee because she ratted on the President.

I was angry that my appointment had been pulled, even though I expected it would happen. But when being honest with myself, part of me didn't mind being left alone by Andrew or the boy brigade. Something else was weighing on my mind: Namely, my uterus. At forty, I was increasingly anxious to have a baby. At that age, you learn that science plays a bigger role than sex in making a baby. Meaning: You need to be poked with a needle more than a penis.

I started trying every science experiment known to womankind to get pregnant. Younger eggs arrived from the womb of a woman I had never met, but I couldn't keep them attached to my own womb. For weeks, I injected fertility drugs into my butt. I did get pregnant, but then miscarried. Twice. The fertility drugs made me extremely sensitive and even downright insane at times. I had to inject the drugs on a very specific schedule and was manic about making sure I timed it down to the minute. I was as crazed about getting pregnant as I always had been about getting work done, from cleaning my momma's floors when I was thirteen to cleaning up Andrew's image in the press when I was forty.

Maybe I couldn't get pregnant because of the stress in my political job or because I worked too hard. Maybe I was just too old. I had intentionally delayed pregnancy in my thirties, when my job in Washington politics was the priority. Maggie, Libby and Janice talked about having children in their twenties after finishing college, but I shut down when they talked about babies. I wanted to travel and see the world. "I'm gonna chase the train all the way to New Orleans, like Alva said she would in her movie, and then who knows where. But somewhere else and then somewhere else," I told them.

I didn't want "somewhere else" anymore. I wanted to be a mother. Maybe that's why I was nonchalant about puncturing my career with *Uncovering Clinton*. Not long after the White House and Andrew denied my confirmation, I began puncturing my ass with a needle instead.

One afternoon, in the middle of a long and arduous meeting with Andrew and others in his conference room, it was time for my fertility-drug-butt injection, timed to the minute. I excused myself and scurried off to the bathroom with my needle gear and locked myself into a stall. After a stressful lecture from Andrew that day and after more than a few tries with the needle, I just could not get the damn thing in the cheek of my butt. As I tried sticking myself one more time, I heard the bathroom door creak open.

"Hey, Karen. You here?" a voice asked timidly. It was my friend, Jacquie, who was Andrew's deputy chief of staff and a fellow Southerner. "Andrew wants you back in the meeting. He sent me to tell you."

I could tell from the tone of her voice she didn't want to return to Andrew empty handed. So she waited.

I couldn't respond.

"Are you okay?" Jacquie drawled.

"I'm trying to inject these baby drugs into me, and I'm so nervous I can't get the damn needle in my ass!"

A pause. "What should I tell him?" Jacquie asked nervously.

I couldn't believe it. I was at the end of my rope. "Tell him I'm trying to stick a needle in my butt so I can have a baby, and I don't need another pain in the ass," I blurted.

Jacquie was silent, as she weighed the likely ramifications of delivering this message to the Secretary.

I sighed. "Hold on," I said. "Do you have a piece of paper and a pen?"

She slipped her notebook and a pen to me under the door of the stall. I wrote a message, folded the note, gave it to Jacquie under the stall door and resumed my efforts.

Jacquie went back into the conference room. Andrew, with irritation in his voice, asked her, "Where's Karen?"

She handed him the note.

He read: *I'm trying to get pregnant. If you want to come in here and get this syringe in my ass, I can come back to the meeting. Either that or leave me alone.*

He left me alone. Andrew was getting very good at that.

Soon after the bathroom incident, Pat and I gave up trying to get pregnant and decided to adopt. I didn't care what color. I didn't care what sex. I just knew I wanted to raise a child from infancy until the rest of his or her life.

We filed for the adoption of a thirteen-month-old Russian girl. I filled out all of the forms as quickly as possible, received preliminary approval and started the plan to travel to Russia for the adoption.

While we were making the adoption plans, I left the press office for good and delved into a project that had held Cuomo's attention for several months: the creation of decent housing on the Pine Ridge Indian Reservation in South Dakota, the poorest Native American reservation in the country, which the *New York Times* had described as the "sickest, most hopeless, most squalid corner of America." Our plan was to unveil the housing project at an event with President Clinton on the reservation. It would be the first time a sitting American president had been to an Indian reservation for an official visit.

My husband and I knew we would have to travel to Russia on a moment's notice for our daughter, but we didn't know when the moment would arrive. That was up to the Russians, not us. I was ecstatic the day the news arrived that the adoption had been approved, and we prepared to leave immediately. As devoted as I was to the work on the Pine Ridge housing effort, my priority was the daughter I had yet to meet.

When I broke the news to Andrew, he dismissed me with a wave of his hand. "Why don't you just let Pat go get your daughter?"

I stared at him in disbelief.

He shrugged. "She'll never remember that you weren't there."

I was momentarily shocked into silence. But only for a moment. "You're right," I said to Andrew. He looked relieved and nodded his head that he was right. Then, in a voice, driven by a maternal determination I didn't know I even had, I said, almost drooling with rage, "She won't remember. But I will. I will remember for the rest of my life that I wasn't there to pick up my own daughter!"

I explained that I was leaving in forty-eight hours and would be out for seven days. Bags had been packed for weeks before the call from Russia, and all of the paperwork had been finalized. I had briefed everyone I was working

213

with, above and below me, of my plans, made sure that my part of the execution plan for the tribal conference was under control and arranged for other staff to cover for me while I was in Russia.

"And when I return, I'll come right back to the office. I won't miss a beat," I promised Andrew.

I got nothing but a blank stare from the HUD Secretary. I had witnessed him be incredibly compassionate and forceful when it came to protecting and fighting for people in the abstract. When it came to actual people in his life? Not so much.

Leaving his office, I felt resentful not only towards Andrew, but also at some part of myself for feeling enormous pressure and more than a little bit of guilt about taking a (tiny!) hiatus from a project into which I had poured my heart and soul. Women are constantly trying to find that balance between their obligations to work and their obligations to their family, to be a "good" mother and wife and still bring their "A" game to work every day. You feel guilty no matter which side of the scale you come down on. In Andrew's world there was only one side of the scale that mattered: him

As I looked over the photographs of a little girl named Natalia in the Russian orphanage, I was glad I couldn't get pregnant. I was claiming a daughter who really needed me. And, most importantly, I needed *her*—much more, I was realizing, than I needed Andrew and the job. I headed to Russia and to my new baby.

True to my word, I returned to the office the very next day after our flight back from Russia landed at Dulles Airport, despite the seven-hour time difference and ten-hour flight between Washington, D.C. and Moscow. Natalia—who Pat and I quickly nicknamed Tali — hung around my neck my first day back, sucking her thumb and staring up from my breasts at me. The women in the office surrounded me with attention. Baby gifts poured in, purchased mostly by my female friends at work or staffers' wives. One of them knitted a blue sweater and a multi-colored one for Tali, who weighed only 15.6 pounds at thirteen months old, about five pounds below average.

As I jumped back into my responsibilities that afternoon, a member of Andrew's boy brigade—a lawyer with a degree from Yale—instructed me to review a stack of letters about Pine Ridge drafted for members of Congress, to see if they were written properly.

"You want me to proofread letters?" I asked before a group of about a dozen other people I had worked with for almost five years.

He nodded. "Yes."

"No, I don't think so," I responded.

"What do you want to do, then?" he said.

"I want a quick briefing on what's happened during the seven days I've been gone so I can get up to speed. And then I'll work with the others on what we still need to do."

"No, I don't think so," the Yalie repeated to me. "The Secretary asked me to take over when you left to get your daughter, so that's what I'll be doing."

I felt my blood rise. "You are not taking over from me. Get one of your Ivy League lawyer friends to read the letters." There was no turning back then. I suddenly felt like I was in charge of myself for the first time in my life.

The lawyer who had swooped in to enable Andrew was, as it turned out, Max Stier. He had found his way to HUD after serving as part of the defense team who helped clear Clinton of his Monica Lewinsky problem. In addition to withdrawing the confirmation of my appointment as Assistant Secretary because of my public comments about Clinton's womanizing, Andrew had given my Pine Ridge job to a man who helped ruin the life of a twenty-one-year-old woman who fell under the spell of the most powerful man in the world —the same man who had aimed his seductive efforts at me back when I was just a bit older than Lewinsky.

What a tidy bit of symmetry.

Despite the humiliation, I saw the Pine Ridge project through. I had made several trips to the reservation already and, over the next few weeks, I worked closely with the Indian nation to finalize the complex meeting. U.S. officials would join 25,000 tribal leaders and members from all over the country on the remote plain home of the Oglala Lakota Sioux. From a logistical standpoint, the conference was a success, and it was well covered in the media. But the real challenge wasn't the logistics or the media. It was the poverty. And a conference wasn't going to end poverty.

The New York Times got it. They covered the event on the front page, with a tough but fair story. The article, "Clinton, Amid Despair on a Reservation, Once Again Pledges Help" reported that it was an historic day that produced a lot of symbolism and not a lot of money. While it was nice that Clinton came to visit, tribal leaders, the *Times* wrote, had no belief that we would help all that much.

After we returned from South Dakota, I learned that the American Indians were right not to trust us. They were about to be double-crossed. Again.

I found out from Jackie Johnson, the Native American woman who ran HUD's Indian housing programs. Jackie, of the Tlingit of the Raven Tribe, and of the Lukaax.ádi from the Sockeye house in Haines, Alaska, had become a good friend. She told me, shocked, that the $4 million in federal aid promised to the tribe was going to be cut in half. Without thinking twice, I called Andrew at home to understand what had happened and how we could recover the funding. He explained that South Dakota Senator Tom Daschle refused to give this one tribe that much money, because all the other South Dakota tribes would want the same, and the feds just couldn't afford it.

I felt like we had lied to Pine Ridge. And, fairly or not, I blamed Andrew on the phone. "This isn't right," I said, almost in tears. "You have to go back to Daschle and get their money. Daschle had agreed to it, and now he's backpedaling. You can't let this go."

"Karen, what the fuck do you know?" he said, anger growing in his voice, too.

My own frustration about Pine Ridge, about Max taking my job, about dealing with the long parade of similar condescending men in Washington and Mississippi, bubbled over. I saw myself sitting in a bathroom stall trying to jam a needle in my ass to get pregnant while the boy brigade smirked in

Andrew's conference room. I heard Andrew's voice telling me that my daughter would never remember my traveling to Russia to pick her up, so stay at work. I felt the humiliation of a twenty-six-year-old girl mistaking a governor's sexual flattery for genuine interest in her ideas.

"Well, fuck you, then!" I screamed at Andrew.

"No, fuck you!" he responded, drawing the "u" out to a dozen syllables.

I hung up. And then I grabbed a box, filled it with personal items, and walked out of HUD. Not that long before, I had resolved that I would never be the one to quit, that I wouldn't be broken by Andrew's relentless attempts to tear down the people that built him up. But with Tali's arrival, I found I just didn't give a shit about him anymore.

I did, though, cry freely as I walked to my car in the parking lot, trying to hold onto my box. I looked up at my office window on the tenth floor. And I thought the hulking concrete HUD headquarters had to be the ugliest place I had ever seen.

***

After the HUD debacle, I traded D.C. for dot.com, joining a public relations firm specializing in technology clients in California, when my Marine husband was transferred to Camp Pendleton near San Diego in 2000. When you marry a Marine, you are marrying the Marines, and I knew that moving crosscountry when your husband is ordered to a new tour of duty was inevitable. Despite the sour taste left in my mouth from the Indian double-cross, fuck-you incident with Andrew, I'd miss Washington and the feeling of being in the thick of things in the most powerful city in the world.

The California weather and our little cottage near a bluff overlooking the Pacific made the move easier. For the first time in my adult life, no one around me was obsessed about politics. The talk was of start-ups and dot.coms or military life. Massive technology growth had spurred the birth of countless tech start-ups and was changing the way we communicated. These new companies attracted wads of cash and minted new millionaires daily—at least on paper. California was ground zero.

As for me? I wasn't quite ready for the new online world. I had a pager, but no cell phone. I spent some time on websites, but I still read my newspapers in print. I wanted to feel and smell them, not plug into my computer. But, hey, the motto of the new tech world was "go big or go home," so I figured I would jump on that train and see where it took me. I didn't go far. The dot.com train didn't, either, at least for a brief period of time.

The Gable Group, a PR firm in San Diego, had been making a name for itself as a publicity guru for the tech start-up world, mostly in southern California. The owner hired me to help develop messages and pitch reporters about technology innovations that could be useful for government operations.

I made the rounds to the startup tech companies that dotted the San Diego and Los Angeles area. Invariably housed in contemporary high-cost buildings with open space floor plans, young employees rode from one end of the building to the other end on scooters to speed delivery of important insights and pressing needs to each other. Californians it seemed, not only needed to drive *to* their offices, they need to drive *inside* their offices. Oddly-designed objects littered the quirky decor to accentuate the founders' superior cultural intelligence. For one branding exercise, a twenty-something CEO wanted to pose on a purple suede couch on the ocean beach with two attractive female employees on each side of him which, in his mind, conveyed creativity, brains and sex appeal. What was the product message? He threw up his hands in disgust. "I have no idea," he said smiling.

The tech bros were in love with their image, yet they often had a hard time explaining what their product was or why real people needed it. And it was a mystery as to what the young people, zooming back and forth on their scooters, actually did all day, other than scoot. I didn't worry about their futures. I did worry about my own, and what the likelihood was of my getting paid when they inevitably went bankrupt.

Driven by a desperate desire to feel relevant again, I volunteered to coordinate press opportunities for Andrew at the upcoming Democratic National Convention in Los Angeles. After telling Andrew to go fuck himself, he and I had managed to smooth things out by the summer of 2000. It didn't hurt that he offered me a consulting contract to help promote his HUD events on the West Coast, centered around the upcoming Democratic Convention in Los Angeles.

I bought a fancy mobile phone to use at the convention. It was as big as a brick with the ability to receive and send not only calls but emails and get some rudimentary internet. Of course, I couldn't figure out how to use it beyond the phone feature. I just liked the look of it. I was surrounded by tech gurus, but I never allowed any of them to tutor me on how to actually use the damn thing lest I reveal my utter lack of tech savvy.

I barely needed it anyway to get Andrew hooked up with press interviews at the Staples Center. Wherever he walked on the convention floor or around the upper floors of the hall, he attracted interest from reporters and broadcasters. Andrew was known as a Gore confidant, and if Gore won the White House there were whispers that Andrew would be Chief of Staff. Lots of people wanted to grab him for a private chat or an on the record interview. Landing a *Larry King Live* interview on CNN, with a million viewers every night and even more during the convention, made for a very happy HUD Secretary as we wrapped up the convention with optimism that Gore was on his way to the White House.

Of course, Election Day ended up deciding nothing. While they counted and recounted ballots in Florida, Andrew set up a series of trips to continue to push his agenda and build up support with key constituencies to position himself for an upgrade, if Gore ended up the victor. In December, Andrew came back to Los Angeles, where I helped with a press event where he and Republican Mayor Richard Riordan announced a multi-million-dollar program that would assist more than five hundred low- to moderate-income families to rehab or purchase HUD-owned homes. After the presser with the Mayor, the HUD staff headed back to a conference room at the hotel where we all were staying to review the next day's events. As the meeting broke up, Andrew suddenly proclaimed that I looked "great ... really pretty." This was a switch.

Once, I came to work with no eye makeup on, and he told me, in front of co-workers, "Karen, you're looking rough today." But on that day I had finally passed the Andrew Cuomo beauty test.

Back at my hotel room, around 7 p.m., I received a phone call from Andrew. "Why don't you come up to my room, and let's debrief from today and go over tomorrow's plan. And tell me how things are going with your new job and how Tali's doing."

It wasn't unusual to have these kind of catch-up meetings on the road in his hotel room. Andrew was constantly rethinking, refining and preparing for his announcements at all hours. And he had made an effort to be nice to me since the fight at HUD, so I wasn't surprised he might at least feign interest in my family life and career.

"Sure, I'll come up," I agreed.

As I exited the elevator, Andrew's security guy, Clarence Day, walked right by me and said, "It's great to see you again, Karen. It's been too long."

"It has. Great to see you, too, Clarence," I responded.

Typically, Clarence stood right outside Andrew's room and didn't leave his post. Still, I didn't think too much of it. Maybe they had changed procedures since I left HUD.

Andrew's door was open, and I went in. We greeted each other with a friendly hug. Andrew shut the door and sat on one couch, and I sat on the couch facing him. The lights had been dimmed, and then I began to wonder what exactly was going on.

The thought receded further and further into the back of my mind as we had a good talk about politics and the day's events. Then the questions became more personal about the state of my marriage. My life as a military wife had not been going well, and he had caught wind of that development. Uncomfortable with the turn of the discussion, I stood up to cut it short and signal that I was ready to leave.

Andrew stood, too, and he came closer and put his hands on my shoulders to say goodbye. He softened his voice and asked, "Let's always help each other, yeah?"

"Of course we can," I agreed, hoping to extricate myself.

Under the dim lights, Andrew put his arms around me and held me a bit too long and a bit too hard. I could tell that he was aroused. I pulled away and said I should get some sleep. Andrew pulled me back in, even closer.

I disentangled myself from his arms and made a beeline out the door. It was a move I had made many times in my life.

I understood exactly what was happening. His move was not about sex—at least, not *only* about sex—but about Andrew's ability to assert his power and control over me. I was working for him. I needed the work, and he knew it. That night I called a girlfriend back East and woke her up with the story. We tried to dissect what he was up to and what, if anything, I should do about it. Whether Gore won or lost, we figured, Andrew would remain connected in political circles, and I wanted to keep those connections.

I never spoke about that evening with him or any of my former colleagues.

I had felt pity for William Styron when I left him in his hotel room when I was twenty-one. I was humiliated by Bill Clinton when he invited me to his hotel room when I was twenty-six. By the time I left Andrew's hotel room at the age of forty-two, I was tired of it all.

Chapter 13
One Dick to Rule Them All

The *New York Post* headline leered at me: **GOV-LINKED LOBBYIST THE WIFE OF THE PARTY**. *What the hell did that even mean*, I thought as I scanned a photo of me accompanying a column by a *Post* writer? A tabloid staffer pulled the photo from a social media account that looked like I was indeed ready to party, complete with very blonde hair, toothy white grin, and dangly gold earrings. A classic *New York Post* story with a headline and photo designed to be suggestive and a story flat out wrong. I was back in Cuomoland. Judging by the *New York Post*, I was off to a rocky start.

After walking out of the HUD building back in 1999, I'd had a busy decade. I patched things up with Andrew, both of us pretending nothing had happened in a Los Angeles hotel. I divorced my Marine husband, built up a successful consulting business back in D.C., and married one of Andrew's closest long-time aides, Howard Glaser. Howard had worked for Andrew's father when Mario Cuomo was Governor, then at HUD for Andrew, and then in 2011 as Andrew's most trusted advisor in Albany, New York. After spending twenty-three years in the Washington, D.C. area, I moved up to Katonah, New York with Tali so we could be together with Howard. Katonah was halfway between Albany and New York City, where the Governor had offices.

As I looked at my face staring back at me from the tabloid, I was seriously beginning to regret the New York move. Despite the fact that I had a thirty-year career as a public relations professional, wasn't a lobbyist, and had moved to New York to keep most of the family together, the *Post* made it look like I was in New York to cash in on Howard's position with the state and my own connection to Andrew. In reality, the move hurt my career, forcing me to work for my Washington-based clients from New York.

Word got back that to me that Andrew was unhappy with the story, but I kept my head down and quietly went about my business of flacking, mostly for nonprofits fighting big banks, big oil and other big bullies. The Governor calmed down.

The peace didn't last long, though. Only a few months after the *Post* article, the race for Mayor of New York City was in full swing. My old friend and HUD colleague Bill de Blasio was running, and I helped him out by hosting a fundraiser at the firm where I had decided to take a job in New York City. This time, the *New York Daily News*, the *other* New York tabloid, jumped in with a piece characterizing my activities as an extension of my husband: **WIFE OF TOP AIDE TO GOV. CUOMO RAISING MONEY FOR BILL de BLASIO'S MAYORAL CAMPAIGN**. Apparently, "wife" was my only role of interest to the New York tabloids.

My frustration with the story had less to do with the headline and more with the Governor's reaction. He was officially neutral in the race, notwithstanding his own earlier friendship with Bill de Blasio, and was none too happy with my support for Bill. In the *Daily News* article, he went right for the kill: "Karen Hinton operates without any kind of direction," said an unnamed Cuomo source. "She does what she does, much to the *frustration* of everybody."

I was more than frustrated by the quote. I was livid. There was no question in my mind that the quote came directly from Andrew personally. It was his M.O.. to provide quotes that would go "unnamed" in a story.

I was fifty-six years old, and fourteen years had passed since I'd last worked for Andrew Cuomo. I also was a political media professional with a hell of a lot of experience who had been running her own consulting business for over a decade. If I was somehow indentured to Andrew for the rest of my natural life, I was certainly unaware of it. I didn't need to cut a deal with Andrew or get any sort of permission from him to help Bill. I wasn't working for *either* of them, for Christ's sake. I was working for *myself,* and my kids' college funds. And, yet, because I had worked for him in the past and was married to a top aide, Andrew was sending a message through the media reminding me that he still demanded my undivided loyalty.

This entanglement was the same as so many of my prior entanglements with Andrew. It was about domination. It was about control. The one thing that the entire calamity *wasn't* about was the fundraiser itself. It was what I had joked about and sometimes called "penis politics," and I'd seen it all my life: men in power seeking to assert control over women in particular ways that diminished them, dismissed them, humiliated them. Sex was a tool sometimes, as disconcerting as an unwanted advance by your boss in a hotel room or as violent as an assault by a high school coach on a young girl in the school bookroom. The common thread was the seemingly insatiable need of some men to affirm their own power and their self-esteem by taking away the power and confidence of the women around them.

It didn't seem to work in the opposite direction. Never mind "pussy power" something my girl heroes had, yes, Steinem, Fonda, Grier and Joplin. I had a pussy, just no power whatsoever.

I was angry with Howard for not forcefully confronting Andrew about the *Daily News* story. In the aftermath, I decided to leave the New York firm, not because of the attacks from the tabloids but, in large part, because of Andrew who ostensibly was my friend but was now turning on me. The whole episode left another bitter taste. It would soon turn downright poisonous when I found myself in the middle of the political death match between Andrew and Bill de Blasio in which only one penis could prevail.

***

"Permission to speak freely?" Bill piped up at one of the first staff meetings he attended in Washington, D.C. after then-Secretary Cuomo hired him at HUD in 1995, around the same time as me. Andrew had wooed de Blasio based on his performance as Harlem Congressman Charlie Rangel's campaign manager in 1994. Bill was an "inside player" and a talented operative with ties to the Black community. Andrew routinely operated dozens of chess moves ahead of both his friends and enemies and hired de Blasio to be his eyes and ears in New York, where Cuomo had ambitions to run for elective office after HUD.

In the meeting, Andrew had gone through a lengthy analysis of options for handling one HUD crisis or another, when Bill piped up with his own critique of the Secretary's reasoning.

The twenty or so Cuomo staff members seated around the table and in chairs along the wall in the Secretary's conference room held our collective breath. Top staff tended not to confront the Secretary in front of a roomful of people, even if we thought he was off base. We would raise our concerns later, in private, where he didn't have to dig in to defend his position. But Bill boldly stuck his head right into the lion's mouth. Andrew drilled Bill with his eyes, but motioned for him to continue.

Much to our surprise, for the next hour they engaged in a spirited, friendly, funny and entirely productive discussion about the pros and cons of how to solve some now-obscure housing issue, all while exchanging inside jokes about New York politicians. I remember the laughter but not the topic, mainly because I didn't know anything about New York politics then—the names, the personalities, the history and the relationships.

***

When Bill scored his surprising victory to become Mayor of New York City in 2013, I figured that the long-standing relationship between Governor Cuomo and Mayor de Blasio would mark a new era of partnership between New York State and New York City. It's hard to believe now I was that naïve after having worked so closely with both Andrew and Bill for so long, but you have to hold on to your idealism when you're a progressive from Mississippi. No matter what the reality is.

The first signs of trouble came when Bill pushed for universal pre-K for New York City's schoolchildren as one of his first initiatives. It was the kind of thing that could (and did) make a genuine difference in the lives of children and their parents, saving them around $10,000 a year in day care bills. Bill got crosswise, though, with Andrew right away over how it would be funded. Bill wanted to impose a tax on wealthy New Yorkers; Andrew knew that the Republican-led NY Senate would never agree to it, and he was focused on defending his centrist credentials with the business community and suburban voters. Nonetheless, Bill pushed for the tax publicly every chance he got. The Cuomo/de Blasio partnership was crashing on liftoff. Behind it all, meanwhile, was the brewing battle of who would wear the mantle of progressivism in New York.

Andrew, entering an election year himself in 2014, had governed as a centrist, citing his accomplishment in passing the marriage equality legislation as his main progressive achievement. As long as progressives to the left and people of color in New York City weren't *too* stirred up over him, Andrew was free to keep to the center and focus on running up his electoral support in the suburbs and whatever he could get in the more conservative areas of upstate New York. When Michael Bloomberg had been mayor, Andrew had no real rival from the left in the NYC political market. But now Bill, riding the start of a progressive and liberal wave, presented a genuine challenge to Andrew from the left. And Andrew was determined to make sure Bill didn't upset his finely-tuned calibration between the centrist and progressive forces

226

in New York.

In other words, there was suddenly only room for one dick to rule New York. I didn't understand that until it was too late.

When Bill offered me the job of Press Secretary to the Mayor of New York City in 2015, I jumped at the chance. I didn't know New York well, but I knew a lot about penis politics; it was no different in Mississippi, Washington D.C., or New York. I wasn't scared off by the deepening fight between the Mayor and Governor. I probably should have known better, but I believed in my skills and thought that I could serve as one link in getting the leaders of New York City and New York State to work together. Hilariously wrong, on reflection. The Mayor's progressive agenda was my agenda, as the governor knew. I supported universal Pre-K, raising the minimum wage, passing paid family leave, ending stop and frisk for good, and pushing policies that helped those at the bottom of the economic ladder, especially people of color. And that's what Bill stood for.

Still, I needed to handle the press secretary job announcement the right way with the Governor's office. I still considered Andrew a friend, despite the fights of the past, and respected what he had accomplished as HUD Secretary and as Governor. The plan was for me to let the Governor know about the appointment, then make it public via the Mayor's press office.

That plan went off the rails when a *Wall Street Journal* reporter heard about the appointment and went to print, online, before I had a chance to alert the Governor. Normally, news of a new flak for the Mayor is barely news at all, but word reached the news media that Andrew was furious I had taken the job. His irritation surfaced publicly in a *New York Times* story about conflicts between the two politicians, fueled by what the *Times* called "private resentments, including Mr. Cuomo's pique over the mayor's choice for a new press secretary.

The Governor, who prizes loyalty, was surprised by the appointment, and irritated that a person he had considered part of his inner circle was headed to work for a rival." Andrew's sudden declaration that I was part of his inner circle rang hollow of course. He had rarely let me in the room where it happened when I worked for him or helped on his campaigns.

There was no time to fret over the bumpy launch of my new job, however. The state legislative session was in its final stretch, and the City had a series of important agenda items to wrap up. I was there to get things done, so I rolled up my sleeves and got to work.

Unfortunately, the tense relationship between the Mayor and the Governor meant that the City was less likely to get what it needed from the famously turgid Albany legislative process. The Governor called the shots at the state level, and he seemed to delight in parceling out the barest morsels to the City and then pointing at the Mayor, publicly, for failure to deliver. When the legislative session ended with the City having few benefits to show for its effort, an anonymous Cuomo source (who was, almost certainly, the Governor himself) told the *Daily News* that Bill was clueless in his dealings with Albany.

What Bill did next sent Andrew off the deep end. With one foot out the door on his way to a family vacation in the New Mexico desert, the Mayor told Errol Louis of *NY1*: "… if someone disagrees with [Cuomo] openly, some kind of revenge or vendetta follows … But I think more and more of us are saying we're just not going to be party to that anymore."

I was barely a month into the job, and my two former bosses were talking to each other through the tabloids with all the maturity of schoolyard boys in a brawl.

"The gloves are off!" screamed the tabloids, gleefully. The *New York Post* went with a full-page picture of Cuomo and de Blasio's heads pasted onto the bare-chested bodies of two boxers in the ring, faces bandaged and the headline: **RAGING BILL! SHOCKING ATTACK AT 'VENDETTA' GOV.**

The *Daily News* one-upped the *Post*, picturing the two men as fedora-wearing mobsters spraying machine gun fire under the headline: **VENDETTA! MAYOR UNLEASHES RAPID FIRE TIRADE AT EX-PAL ANDY.**

"Vendetta" may have been a loaded word to use with any Italian-American politician, but especially one whose father battled anti-Italian bigotry. The revenge part was true, though, and it followed swiftly. While I had no part in the "vendetta" verbiage, I did tell Bill that he had to be tougher and less equivocal in his public stances. He often seemed to prefer musing aloud about issues as though he was in a political philosophy class like the ones that he had taken at Columbia University, instead of making a decision and sticking to it as a chief executive of a world-class city should. His job was to fight for policies that were important to New Yorkers, not to coddle the Governor's ego. My counsel to him was to publicly assume that responsibility with his constituents.

Either Andrew or someone on the Cuomo team offered grudging respect for the approach in a *Politico* article: "There's a clear belief that Karen helped de Blasio grow a pair," said one source. I could play penis politics, too, from time to time.

While the Mayor was having his moment of Zen in the desert, my cell phone just about burst into flames with a call from the Governor's top political lieutenant, lambasting Bill and me and placing responsibility for fixing the situation squarely on me. The bullets would halt, the Governor's aide Joe Percoco, told me, but on one condition: The Mayor had to publicly walk back his comments. I knew that would never happen, and I suspected that Andrew knew that, too. I offered up, halfway joking, halfway not, a radical suggestion: "I know this is *really* out of the box, but maybe Andrew and Bill could, you know … talk to each other?" But Andrew wanted the public disavowal before he would agree to even have a quick chat with Bill.

These male politicians… so emotional! Bitchy!

Meanwhile, with the Mayor navel-gazing in New Mexico, we had no follow-up strategy to build support. Everybody in New York politics understood that Bill spoke the truth about Andrew's vindictiveness, but that very fact made them fearful of crossing the Governor by agreeing with Bill. Andrew's team was working the phones, and New York elected officials began to distance themselves from the Mayor.

The press was having a field day with the whole thing, with the *New York*

Daily News running a piece claiming that I "[didn't] hesitate to fire zingers at her former boss... she certainly knows the enemy." *Politico* observed that I "managed to cut a cool figure throughout, notwithstanding her putative Helen of Troy role in the affair."

Sure, I'd fired a few zingers, but I felt anything but cool. Not only had I been dragged into a silly pissing contest, but Howard — who by this time was back in the private sector — began receiving not-so-veiled threats from the Governor's office over the phone in his new workplace. He was told to "get control of Karen" and "fix it," along with a reminder that Howard's employer wouldn't want any trouble with the Governor. I began to worry about the outrageous college bills for four children. Howard told the Cuomo emissaries the same thing I told them: The Mayor and Governor should have an actual conversation and work it out like two adults.

They both continued to refuse. Instead, Joe Percoco, Andrew's right-hand man, asked for a "sit down" with *me*. On a sunny Saturday afternoon in mid-July 2015, we met for lunch at Peppino's, the Italian restaurant at the old train station in Katonah, close to Joe's home and ours in Westchester County. Clearly, he had a message that Andrew wanted conveyed. There was no screaming this time. Andrew was trying a different tack through Joe, dangling a job with the state as a way to get me under control.

Let's get past this, Joe told me. Andrew is hurt by you; he's disappointed. But he loves you. Forget Bill, and come work for the Governor.

It was utterly ridiculous, of course. And obvious. Andrew didn't want me to work for him. He wanted me off the basketball court and onto the bench. I recognized the benching technique all the way back from high school in Soso. If we didn't follow orders from the coach, we got benched. And I didn't even listen to my coach back then, so Coach Andrew was at a double disadvantage.

Though the fight between Andrew and Bill was more like two high school drama queens than state basketball finalists, the consequences from the brawl harmed New Yorkers in serious ways. They couldn't agree on who was responsible for the homeless. They pointed fingers at each other on the decaying subway system. They jockeyed over control of the largest school system in the country while its one million students continued to receive less state education funding than their suburban counterparts.

Andrew was relentless, marshaling his raw power to beat Bill back at every turn. Bill, for his part, was as hapless as Andrew was ruthless, and he didn't hesitate to push me out as his human shield to take Andrew's shots. That was okay, I figured. That was part of being press secretary for any politician.

But after I rebuffed Andrew's clumsy attempt to buy me off with a job, he decided to get much more personal. It wasn't enough for him to emasculate Bill; I was a target now, too. And Andrew dredged up some ancient history to get the job done.

"De Blasio press secretary Karen Hinton reveals Bill Clinton hit on her when he was Arkansas governor," the *Daily News* breathlessly reported that summer. The headline and story made it sound like Bill de Blasio's spokesperson was suddenly mounting an attack on Bill Clinton while Hillary Clinton was gearing up to run for President. The story was, of course, fifteen years old, picked up from Michael Isikoff's 1999 book *Uncovering Clinton* about an event that had happened in 1984. But the *Daily News* headline made it sound like it was new news.

My own source confirmed that Andrew had planted the story at the *Daily News*. A *Politico* story also had mentioned the Clinton incident briefly, in a sentence or two. The stories served as a "two-fer" for Andrew, derailing me by reducing me to an object of sexual attention who was complaining or perhaps lying about the attention, all while driving a wedge between Bill and Hillary Clinton, who Andrew courted assiduously. Very penis politics.

Andrew had sacrificed me once before, when the Clinton story first came out in *Uncovering Clinton*, and he pulled my appointment as Assistant Secretary at HUD to suck up to the President. It was such a small story, really, a bungling pickup attempt that went nowhere. But it was, all the same, evidence of Clinton's pattern of sexual harassment and abuse. Small as it was, it cost me a job in Washington courtesy of Andrew. Now, unbelievably, here he was using it again in New York, brandishing the Clinton story as a weapon to denigrate me.

As hurtful as that all was—and it hurt me more than I expected or wanted to admit—it paled in comparison to what came next, when Andrew's actions put lives at risk in New York City. In what is surely, in retrospect, a predecessor to the callousness and selfishness he displayed in the COVID nursing home scandal of 2020, Andrew behaved just as awfully during the Legionnaires' outbreak of 2015. And in the calamity, Bill didn't just push me out front to take Andrew's bullets. He shot me up himself.

In July 2015, a Legionnaires' disease outbreak began in New York. By the end of the month, thirty people had fallen ill, with two fatalities. The papers and broadcast news jumped on the story. The crisis quickly turned into the worst outbreak of Legionnaires' in the state's history, which seems almost quaint now that the coronavirus has forever changed our views on infectious diseases.

Legionnaires', like COVID-19, is an airborne illness that can lead to death or worsen the health of someone already suffering from an illness. One of the top health experts in the country, Dr. Mary Bassett, ran the city's health department and swiftly formulated an action plan, ordering the inspection and cleaning of water towers throughout the city, where the bacteria grew and then spread through air conditioners, ventilators and water systems.

In a matter of a few days, the fire, police and building departments tested and cleaned every water tower. Andrew, looking once again for a way to fuck over Bill and the city, told the *New York Times* that the Mayor's actions were not good enough. The Governor then dispatched teams of state employees, wearing gas masks and bright yellow jackets, to the city's water towers to conduct their own testing. Many were desk employees who had never done field work before and, according to our health officials, weren't trained for the job. The Governor's people made sure to set up photo ops of these state workers descending on the city.

While Andrew assured New Yorkers that he was riding to their rescue, health professionals struggled to ensure that the competing state and city teams didn't get in the way of doing the actual work of eradicating the disease. It wasn't easy. The Governor's aide Melissa DeRosa tried to shut out a Center for Disease Control health expert working for Dr. Bassett from a public meeting of city, state and county health commissioners. After I demanded that our CDC official join a press conference, Andrew proclaimed to the *New York Times*, "We are taking matters into our own hands."

I shot back to the *Times*, providing them with information about how the number of Legionnaires' cases outside the city was equal to, if not larger, than inside the city. It wasn't just a New York City crisis, it was statewide. And the last time I checked, the Governor was in charge of the state and had allowed this problem to fester without action for months. Andrew's attempt to shift the focus away from the reported cases in the rest of the state was, in fact, intended to hide the number of infected New Yorkers statewide. Five years later, when he ran a similar play to hide the number of COVID nursing home deaths, local and national media pounced, and investigations into a damning scandal over pandemic deaths of nursing home residents ensued. In 2015, it was pretty much just me blowing the whistle. My language to the *Times* was meant to be ballsy. I was pissed. "People have written about the city's performance, but what about the state's performance?" I asked in response to the reporter. "What has the state been doing to prevent this disease? Where are the state standards on this? The state commissioner should've known about this, and the governor is ultimately responsible for the actions of his health commissioner."

Andrew's fury was unrestrained now that his secret about the spread of Legionnaires' cases and deaths around New York State had been revealed. His reaction was classic Andrew. Instead of focusing on saving lives and getting a deadly infectious disease under control, Andrew did what Andrew does best: attack, intimidate, threaten. He called the Mayor's top deputy and fumed, "Karen has to go! And if she doesn't, I'm going to go out there and say that the Mayor is personally responsible for every Legionnaires' death in the City!"

I was at my studio apartment across from City Hall, exhausted and rattled from the day, when Bill called me. Hot steam practically spewed out of my phone, once again.

"Andrew wants me to fire you," Bill yelled. "I'm not going to fire you. But keep your fucking mouth shut about him!" he shouted at the top of his lungs.

Having just gone toe-to-toe with Andrew via the news media, I didn't want to engage in a fight with my boss, too. "Okay," I said, suddenly bone tired. "Got it, Mayor."

A few minutes later, one of the Mayor's close aides emailed me. "You need to tell the *New York Times* that you're walking back the remark about the Governor."

I responded, "I can't walk back the truth. The state's performance needs some light."

I wasn't going to call the *Times* to disavow the facts just because Andrew was having a hissy fit. It was in the damn story already, and the *Times* wouldn't remove my quote. So, the Mayor's aide called the *Times* himself. He told a reporter that my "remarks regarding the state's performance did not reflect the views of the de Blasio administration." The *Times* printed his comment eviscerating me in the morning print edition.

Ninety days into the job, and I had my legs cut out from under me in the *New York Times* by my own team. How could anything I said to the press be taken seriously after that? Bill wanted me in his foxhole only when I had to be the one to run out first and draw fire away from him. I wasn't surprised by the Governor's threat, after knowing Andrew for so long. But Bill's reaction hurt me. He should have stood by his press secretary, who had been standing up for him. I had fought harder for Bill de Blasio than he had fought for himself. He threw me under the bus and then climbed into the driver's seat and drove it over me.

I'd always thought that Bill was a true believer in the issues I cared about: public education, poverty, affordable housing, homelessness. And Andrew had become the one with his finger in the wind to determine which way the polls would blow, left or right. I still think that way today about both of them.

Howard told me that I had to leave, that I should resign after Bill had deserted me. Worse, Bill folded in his very first test since declaring that he wouldn't get pushed around by the Governor anymore. Andrew pounced on Bill's weakness and tortured his longtime friend-turned-enemy at his pleasure.

A fine job I had done of bringing the two together again. I should've listened to the advice I often gave to the young women who worked under me in the press office: "When you get to be my age, you learn that you can't teach men anything. So don't try."

Unpleasant as the job had become, I wasn't going to be threatened into quitting, reminiscent of my time with Andrew at HUD. I threw myself back into my job, determined to set an example for my young, mostly female, staff. After the Legionnaires' crisis, Bill mostly ignored me, but I had my girls (and a few boys) in the press office to focus on. The shit hit the fan every day in New York City, and we had to keep it from splattering all over the Mayor. Sometimes we succeeded. But it would have been easier if the Mayor would at least try to avoid the crappy breeze.

The press team worked together in one room, on the first floor of City Hall near the Mayor's office — an echo of my Mississippi coterie, but in a historic building instead of a dusty old train car. We were a little United Nations in that room. Black, white, brown. Gay and straight, women and men. The one thing we all had in common was progressive liberalism and a high tolerance for the daily chaos of City Hall.

Each deputy press secretary took responsibility for an area of policy and programs. The New York City Police Department, Fire Department, prisons, and criminal justice were one press secretary's fiefdom. Hospitals and health resided in another; finance and budget in another. Occasionally, I looked up from my computer and scanned the room. Everyone would be glued to their computers, too, reading documents or emails and writing responses. It occasionally seemed peaceful, but I knew from experience that all hell could break loose within minutes. On a regular basis, someone in the NYC coterie would yank us out of our little big worlds and into theirs.

"Goddamn it! I knew this would happen! Fuck! Fuck! Fuck! Help me!" cried Natalie Grybauskas, one press secretary.

"Oh no, not fucking again! What should we say?" asked Ishnee Parikh, another press sec.

"Shit! Can you believe what just happened?" laughed Monica Klein.

The rest of the team—Rosemary Boeglin, Jessica Ramos, Aja Worthy-Davis, Angela Banks, Raul Contreras, Austin Finan, Wiley Norvel—were always quick to help their colleagues and accept support from them through thick and thin, the good and the bad.

I smiled and thought of Janice and Libby and Maggie and me, sharing curse words on the Midnight Train; four young girls chasing a train to find a stop or the many stops in life. My NYC coterie was full of energy and idealism, just like we had in Mississippi. I found strength in the young women around me at City Hall, especially now that my own train had been derailed by two men locked in an endless, pointless fight for dominance.

Domination was and is at the heart of penis politics: a man maintaining power over a woman through gender or sex-based control. I'd seen it in the gym where the boys' team got better sports deals than the girls'. I'd seen it as a journalist when my male colleagues were handed the juiciest stories, and I fought to get mine printed. I'd seen it in working in Congress where men treated female staff as their stable. And I'd seen the most extreme end of the spectrum when Janice, at sixteen, was brutalized by a head coach in the high school building. As bad as that was, Janice, Maggie, Libby and I didn't anticipate what we would be battling in some form or fashion for the rest of our lives: gender discrimination, forms of sexual harassment, sexual abuse and violations of basic rights for women.

Andrew was the master of the art of penis politics. In Washington, he'd given me a job and then worked to undermine me in it. He made me feel as if I were no good at my job and, thus, totally dependent on him to keep it. In Andrew's world—and he would never admit this, even to himself—working for him was like a 1950s version of marriage. The husband came first, and everyone and everything else second, your actual spouse, your children, your own career goals. Your focus, twenty-four hours a day, seven days a week, was Andrew Cuomo. If you needed more time with your own family, he treated you like you were cheating on him. If you have your eye on another, better job, he'd try to make that job disappear. Control is an essential characteristic of penis politics, and Andrew was satisfied with nothing less than total control.

Bill practiced a different brand of penis politics. The charming, easy-going way that Bill had about him when we worked together at HUD had given way to a hectoring, inflexible approach that bordered on sanctimony by the time he was Mayor. His signature move at City Hall was to dig in on an untenable position, against the advice of his staff, slowly raising the cost of an inevitable defeat. Discussions with staff were marked by condescension, leaving the female staffers, especially, feeling marginalized. It made for an exceedingly uncomfortable work environment because it encouraged other men to behave the same way.

In one City Hall meeting, staff gathered in Bill's office with the Police Commissioner and his male press aide as they waited for the Mayor to finish a call. I was back at my desk handling the media disaster of the day when I got an email from the Commissioner's press secretary, a man who I outranked. He wrote, "Could you grab a water for the Commissioner?" I heard the unwritten words, "like a good little girl." I'd seen this movie before, and I wasn't buying a ticket.

I shot back, "You get the Commissioner his fucking water. That's your job."

Although Bill preached a philosophy of egalitarianism, his workplace was pretty much like any other. Women were interrupted more often and listened to less, whether they were a commissioner or a scheduler. By the end of his first term, he had lost twice as many senior officials who were women than men. Still, while they had different styles, both Bill and Andrew had one thing in common: Like many powerful men in politics, Bill Clinton included, they created a public image as champions of women's rights and equality. Behind closed doors, they used gender domination as one of many means to assert their power over women.

Silence and penis politics go hand-in-hand. When Janice swore us to silence about the "bookroom kiss," we honored her wishes and went along with what we thought we had to do to help and protect our closest friend. But the only person our silence protected was Coach.

Years later I was told by a Soso friend that Coach had sex with another seventeen-year-old girl after he left West Jones High School. This underage girl got pregnant. I still can't help but wonder if our silence enabled his sexual abuse of not one, but two young girls.

That was penis politics in 1974 in Soso, Mississippi, when Coach locked the bookroom door on Janice. In 1998, at HUD, I put my daughter's adoption ahead of Andrew's agenda—if only for a moment—and it pushed me off a project I owned and out the door of HUD. And penis politics again in 2015 when Andrew threw his bombs at me, and a frightened Bill de Blasio made it impossible for me to do my job by invalidating what I said to the press on his behalf. You're damned if you shut up, you're damned if you speak up.

By June 2016, a year after I started at the Mayor's office, I'd had enough and headed out the door of City Hall. I didn't want to be blamed for the terrible media coverage of the Mayor when he rarely listened to me. My daily life at City Hall had become too meaningless given I had little input on messaging and policy. For my departure, the *WSJ* did a profile of what the reporters called my "whirlwind year" at City Hall.

"You raised hackles with some of your colleagues at City Hall," the reporter told me.

"I suppose I could have been nicer," I said. "But I wasn't running for prom queen."

In fact, I declared, in my best Southern drawl, more women needed to run for king.

238

E p i l o g u e
While I Was Sleeping

I don't remember anything about the accident that changed my life. All I knew was what seemed like an endless, foggy dream.

Over the course of many months, my husband and my doctors patiently explained to me what had happened. They had to repeat the same thing many times until I began to understand. The gist of it was this: In April of 2017, while exercising at the gym where I worked out several times a week, I was thrown from a treadmill, slamming my head onto a concrete floor hidden beneath a thin layer of carpet. The impact knocked me unconscious and caused my brain to begin to swell. At the emergency room, they placed me on a ventilator, my eyes wide open but unseeing. The attending physician did not think I would live.

To relieve the pressure on my brain, a neurosurgeon peeled back my scalp and removed the left side of my skull from the top of my left ear to the middle of my head and then sewed the scalp back on with my swollen brain throbbing beneath. The saucer sized piece of skull was placed underneath the skin of my abdomen for safekeeping. For the next five weeks, I wore a helmet to protect my brain as I emerged from an induced coma.

As the swelling on my brain went down, a sunken cavity was all that remained where the skull had been removed. It looked like I had lost half of my head. At that point, the doctors popped the piece of skull back on and replaced the scalp. The end of the surgery was just the beginning of my recovery.

All I knew and later remembered was this dream:

I was on a NYC subway train. Fog blocked my view of most of the people around me, but they floated in and out of the haze as they approached me. Their faces appeared small, and then suddenly inflated large. I recognized no one. Their mouths opened and closed, but I could barely hear the sounds surrounding me and them. Their voices sounded muffled, like we were underwater. I worried that I might drown, but a loud foghorn sucked their faces back into the fog. Stuck in the subway, I wanted and needed to get out, but I couldn't. A train door shut and opened, and more people walked toward me, pounding me to the floor. I was on my knees.

A young girl walked up to me and placed her white-gloved hands around my face. She looked like how Janice looked in the sixth grade. The noise from the foghorn pulled her away. She waved good-bye.

I spent what seemed like months stuck in the endless loop of that dream or some variation of it, trapped.

To protect my brain while it healed, they made me wear that helmet twenty-four hours a day. Once I regained some control over my left arm and hand, I tried to tear the helmet off. When I wasn't trying to tear the helmet off, I was trying to pull out my feeding and breathing tubes and drag myself out of the bed. I didn't know what I was doing or where I was. I only knew I had to get out of the bed, out of the building, out of the subway, out of the dream. For a while they put me in restraints until Howard made them take them off.

I couldn't walk, talk or think as I began to wake up. I often didn't recognize Howard or Tali, know the year, my birthday or where I was born. Every morning the doctor came in and asked the same questions: "Can you tell me your name? Do you know where you are at the moment? Do you know what the date is today?" Then came the commands: "Lift your thumbs. Wiggle your toe. Stick out your tongue." The doctor would write my responses and reactions down and then leave without uttering another word. I guess there's no point in having a conversation with someone who is not going to talk back.

The rehab therapists tortured me three hours in the morning, three hours in the afternoon.

Physical therapy, occupational therapy, speech therapy. Everything was hard. Two physical therapists held me under the arms as they taught me how to put one foot in front of the other, only to take a couple of steps. My right leg dragged behind me; the injury to the left side of the brain blocked the nerves from sending any instructions to my right-side muscles. We worked every day on trying to catch or toss a basketball.

I hated speech therapy and resisted it as much as possible. In junior high, I was known as a motor mouth, but not now, in the rehab hospital. Identifying little cartoon drawings of everyday objects was the first order of business: a key, a hanger, a carton of milk, a phone. "Say the word when I point to the picture," the therapist commanded over and over again. I didn't know the words for them. Before the accident, words had been my life. From telling secrets to the coterie to fighting with politicians. Now the words were just … gone.

Progress came over time. The goal was to work my way up to holding a cup to my lips or a fork in my hand, in hopes the day would come when they would remove the tube from my stomach and start me on real food. I started speaking spontaneously, not just in response to questions. It was mostly gibberish, a childlike flood of nonsense, but sentences began to take shape. Howard swore my first fully-formed, grammatically-correct sentence was,

"Get me the fuck out of here."

Despite the little daily triumphs of mastering a muscle or a nerve connection, my emotional and mental state was uncontrollable. I was deeply paranoid, believing I was being held against my will. Delirious at times, I tried to catch floating imaginary objects suspended in front of me. I had bouts of pure panic.

I got creative at my attempts to escape. I asked the nurses to lend me forty dollars to pay a taxi to take me to the train station where I could catch Amtrak to New Orleans. That plan failed when I couldn't figure out how to use my iPhone to make the train reservation. Each day I would forget that I had tried the day before and plotted another doomed escape.

What really got me out of the bed was my daughter Tali's high school graduation. I had the accident and brain surgery on April 8th and no skull over my brain until mid-May. Tali's graduation was the first week of June, and I was determined to be there for it. I had been occupied with my work in the Mayor's office during her junior year, with little time for her, and now Tali had gone through the home stretch of her senior year without me.

Eventually, my doctor agreed to discharge me if Howard hired round-the-clock assistance. I always needed someone with me to make sure I didn't fall; Howard installed grab bars and a seat in the shower, where I was not permitted to be alone; he bought a wheelchair.

And with that, I left the hospital on June 2, after fifty-five days in intensive care and rehab. I was wheeled into the gym at my daughter's school and watched Tali, who had begun life in a Russian orphanage, beam as she received her diploma to loud applause from her classmates and surrounded by family, including her father, the Marine, Pat, and her Uncle Robbie.

Once family left, the realities of my new life took hold.

Traumatic Brain Injury victims have different prognoses, but many have common after-effects. I suffered headaches, dizziness and terrible anxiety. I obsessed about little things and couldn't let go. I told my home-care aides to stop following me. I checked my bank account ten times a day, worrying about having no money. I was angry. I was sad. I couldn't remember words. I couldn't think clearly. I forgot what people told me the day before or an hour before. When my friends began to visit, I didn't understand a lot of what they said to me in conversation, but I nodded politely. I don't think I made any sense when I spoke; my friends nodded politely, too. I lost my sense of smell only to have it replaced by a terrible funky odor all the time, one that only I could smell, a result of damage to my olfactory nerve. Losing sense of taste followed. At night, my body went into spasms, my brain sending phantom signals as it worked out the kinks in the circuitry.

After a year or so passed, I tried writing but I couldn't translate the thoughts in my head into coherent points. I was dependent on others for the first time in my life. I asked Howard one night, "What will become of me?" Neither of us had an answer.

By January 2019, almost two years after my brain injury, my physical strength and mental acuity were improving, but my recovery was far from complete. Large swaths of my past life remained unremembered. One late afternoon, looking for things to do around the house, I walked up to the attic on the third floor of our rambling, century-old home. The attic was unkempt, stacked high with boxes, old albums, books and bins of fading photographs collected over the course of a sixty-year life.

In a corner of the dusty attic I found a light brown, antique cedar hope chest, faded from the sun. My momma got it as a wedding gift when she married my father. Chests were common back then, symbolizing the beginning of a marriage and all its possibilities. For Momma, it had been filled mostly with its namesake—hope—and nothing else. But over the years since Momma died, I had filled it with memories of my girlhood in Soso: yearbooks, newspaper clippings, letters from my friends. There were articles from the *Laurel Leader Call* about our high school basketball wins and losses. Ink-penned goodbye notes from friends and enemies explaining the good and bad things I had done to them, and the things they had done to me. And there at the bottom, beneath the letters and the clippings and my old basketball uniform was my diary, the one I'd kept in high school. A teenager's voice with story after story of Janice, Maggie and Libby, of the coterie's plans, triumphs and failures.

I poured through the documents every day for the next few weeks, each relic helping me peel back a layer of the life that had been shrouded in the fog of my injured mind. I began piecing together who I was and how I'd lived.

Primed by a spark of optimism as my synapses began to fire again, Howard suggested that we take a break from New York and spend a few days in New Orleans. We decided to make the trip by train, a thirty-hour trip on the Amtrak *Crescent,* from New York's Penn Station, deep into the heart of the South.

To pass the time on the ride down, I told Howard about the coterie's first trip to New Orleans, when Maggie, Libby and I snuck away to see Bourbon Street during high school, our faces peering into Big Daddy's strip club. I told him more stories about the four girls in Mississippi: about Coach and the bookroom; about Uncle B.F., the Grand Cyclops of the Jones County Klan pledging to "get em at night"; about my thirteen-year-old brother driving to the hospital with our dead father next to him; about the pumping of the oil jack next to Mitch and in my car Myrtle during a steamy Soso night. The more I talked, the more I remembered.

You can tell a lot of stories in thirty hours. Howard said maybe I should write them down. It would be a good mental exercise and might help my writing ability to come back, forcing me to sharpen my memory. I said I would *think* about it.

The *Crescent* rolls most of the length of Mississippi as it nears Louisiana. In fact, the train goes close by Soso and stops at the station in Laurel. But only if Amtrak needs to pick someone up or drop someone off.

In sixty years, I'd never taken a train into Soso. I'd only tried to chase one out.

***

On a Mississippi summer morning as hot, as muggy and as stifling as the morning in the school bookroom thirty-five years earlier, Janice walked into the backyard of the house she shared with her grown son and ended her life with a gunshot to her head, near a pond we once swam in.

I got the call in my kitchen as I listened to the voice of my daughter, then twelve years old, getting ready for bed upstairs.

"Momma, I can't find any clean towels," she said. "Never mind. Found them."

Janice's suicide came after several crushing events in her life, including the death of her toddler daughter in a car accident. I had heard from friends and family that severe illnesses had taken the lives of Donny, her second husband, and then Tim, who she had remarried. Yet I couldn't help but believe that the sexual assault of a sixteen-year-old girl at the hands of her head coach in the bookroom years ago set her on a path that ended in tragedy and loss. Janice, a star student with the charisma and personality that we all envied, left school as a direct result of the rape. How might her life have been different at any one of the crossroads that followed?

In 1974 Mississippi, an adult male having sex with a sixteen-year-old girl was legal. *It still is.* To me the law itself makes what should otherwise be considered sexual assault legal. *Legal* rape. Penis politics at its worst: institutionalizing the sexual power of a male authority figure over a vulnerable girl. A fifteen-year-old girl in Mississippi is allowed to marry today an adult male of any age, with her parent's consent. (Boys cannot marry until seventeen). A judge can allow a girl *under* fifteen to be married. Mississippi is one of only two states that does not consider fondling or groping of a sixteen-year-old girl by an adult to be sexual battery. These are laws written by mostly white male state legislators in Mississippi, enabling Coach and so many other men to subject girls, Black and white, to lifelong trauma.

When I heard Janice was dead, I blamed Coach. Janice's life had been ruined by a man who saw something that he wanted and took it without thought to the consequences or the woman involved. Her vibrant young life had been thrown off course and ruined by his need for power and control...by penis politics.

I poured a glass of wine and wondered what role the coterie's silence might have played in the spiral of Janice's life.

"We can handle this, Janice," we told her all those years ago on our Midnight Train. "We can talk to Coach or tell his wife or even Principal Sawyer."

I remembered Janice bolting up off the seat of the railroad car, her body tensed. "No! Don't tell anyone anything. Only you three can know. No one else."

"Why no one else?" I had asked her.

"Because! They'll think it's my fault! They will blame me," Janice hollered.

"We won't tell a soul," Maggie promised.

What was the cost of keeping Janice's secret? She had carried it with her as she watched us graduate from the back of the gym and for the next thirty-five years. We understood so little about rape in 1974. **We only had heard the word, rape, when a Black man had been accused.** If Janice had told her parents or a counselor, would the telling have helped her? Changed her life?

As I stared out a window at our poorly lit backyard, I knew nothing had changed much since then. Talking about victimization remained just as threatening and as humiliating for women and girls, whether it was about rape or sexual abuse or the other end of the spectrum, sexual harassment and gender discrimination. What would it take to be believed when a woman or a girl spoke up? What responsibility did we bear for keeping her secret?

Janice may have married Donny or Tim if she hadn't been abused by Coach, but I firmly believe to this day that she would have graduated high school and gone to college. Janice would have taken up a profession and built a fortress to strengthen herself for the highs and lows of whatever life had to offer.

I finished my third glass of red wine, turned the kitchen lights off and laid down with my eyes open as I heard Tali, brushing her teeth and climbing into bed, our house silent and dark as a Mississippi night deep in a rare winter freeze.

***

As the silver train rolled near Soso and the Laurel station, I laid my head against the window, looking out on the piney woods.

We passed an area where you could just make out some old tracks, mostly grown over now. Though I knew Midnight Train was long gone, I squinted to look for it anyway, as though the dusty old train car might somehow be there, sheltering four girls promising to protect their secrets.

Janice died. I almost died, yet somehow I survived. Over the years I had grown from the highs and pushed through the lows. I was far from perfect, but I was here, damn it, on the train track still chasing life.

The clickety-clack of the Amtrak's wheels rang loudly in my ears as we passed, like the sounds Maggie told us to make inside our heads when we ran to catch the 3:14....

Faster.

Don't stop.

Keep runnin'.

After the chase we all piled into Vanilla, Maggie's car, and took off. It was a few weeks after my sixteenth birthday, and the bookroom kiss. Janice suddenly looked the rest of us in the eyes, solemnly, one by one.

"Y'all are my best friends," she said. "No, I really mean it. No one else is on my best friend list."

Maggie, who was driving, took a sudden right turn and slammed the brakes on Vanilla on a dirty, rocky road in the woods near the railroad tracks. She reached over to the passenger seat and grabbed Janice's hand, before reaching back and grabbing mine. I clasped hers, warm and sweaty in the summer heat, and grabbed Libby's, next to me.

"Let's just sit here for a minute and think about what it means to be us, together, right now," Maggie said. "Just one minute." She took a deep breath

and smiled at us before closing her eyes.

Like always, the day was hot and sticky. As we closed our eyes and breathed in the damp air, a cool breeze whispered through the open car windows. We could hear the leaves on the trees swish back and forth as the wind rustled along the branches. A storm was rising, as if the electricity that we felt between us inside of the car had jumped outside and was affecting the small world around us. It was a rare moment, to be silent together. We listened to the crickets outside the car, the frogs from a nearby pond.

A minute passed, and I felt uncomfortable.

"Turn on the radio! I need some noise!"

Maggie smiled and clicked the radio on. It was a song from the Carpenters, who we didn't like, but we listened this time: "And when the evening comes," they sang, "we smile. So much of life ahead."

"I hate this song," said Janice. "Let's go get a fuckin' cherry snowball."

"Hell yes!" Libby cheered.

"Fuck yeah!" I yelled.

Maggie grinned and put Vanilla in drive as we screamed and screamed and screamed, whooping through the open windows loud enough for our voices to reach the Mississippi state line.

THE END

Author's Note

A memoir is about a person's memories, and this book reflects mine. There really was a "Janice" and a coterie of girls who pledged to keep the secret of what happened in the bookroom. Their names and others have been changed to protect the identities of people in my life who are not public figures. In Mississippi, some characters reflect the combined personalities and experiences of several people I knew growing up there. Part One, the coterie section, draws from the diaries I kept and treasured for almost fifty years.

I completed the book before the sexual harassment scandal that brought about Andrew Cuomo's resignation. While I had planned to tell my story before the eleven women recounted their encounters with the former Governor, I hope my memoir supports their voices and that of other women who choose to speak up about the damage that practitioners of penis politics can inflict on women, especially young women.

Writing the book was a way to help me recover from a severe traumatic brain injury I suffered in 2017. Initially unable to speak, much less read and write, my work on the memoir was a form of therapy. It was an important part of my therapy not only to attempt to improve my skills, which had been damaged, but also to reflect on and connect the episodes of my life that revolved around men and power. I am far from fully recovered and the things that once came easy to me are a struggle now. Thinking, organizing and writing remain difficult. I grope for words and still often find the wrong one, and I cannot work in a regular job with my deficits. Retrieving my memories and writing them down was a slow and arduous process. But I hope I have conveyed something of what I intended and badly wanted to communicate to the reader.

Karen Hinton
September 2021
New Orleans

Acknowledgements

Writing this book after the accident was something I could not have done without the help and support of many people. I could not have arrived at my destination without my husband Howard Glaser who helped bring me back to life after my brain injury. He was my best editor and second brain when I needed one. My daughter Tali kept a diary about the first month of my stay at Westchester Medical Center, giving back to me so much that I never would have remembered: what she said to me during my medical coma moments, how I looked, how she felt and, most importantly, how she as a teenager processed the near-death experience of her mother. My step-children, Sarah, Erica and Zach, and my brother Robbie and his friend Tamme were at my hospital bed and by my side through difficult ordeals.

Alessandra Lusardi was the first editor to give me guidance on how to refine my initial drafts into a workable manuscript and was my muse on how to navigate the publishing industry. Jen Schuster edited the working draft in an incredibly short timeframe and contributed significantly to the final product. James L. Dickerson of Sartoris Publishing was a godsend to me. James, a former colleague of mine at the *Jackson Daily News* in the early 80s, has championed Southern writing at Sartoris and was a patient and understanding mentor when I was an aspiring journalist and again when I became an aspiring author. Alessandra, Jen and Jim all helped me in different ways to focus on what was interesting to the reader (I hope!) instead of what was only interesting to me. I'm a Southerner and, as a result, I think readers need to know everything about everything in a story. The trio helped me elevate my stories to a broader perspective.

Nothing would have been possible without the medical teams to whom I owe more than I can express. Dr. Virany Hillard and the surgeons, residents, and nurses at Westchester Medical Center who put me back together again. Dr. Herberth Balsell's fast, initial decisions when I was delivered unconscious to the emergency room at Northern Westchester Hospital gave me a chance to live. Without Dr. Balsell and Dr. Hillard, there would be no book and no Karen. I am beyond thankful.

My rehabilitation at Helen Hayes Hospital was hard on me but harder on the staff and my friends who stood by me while I tried every way I could to escape what I truly believed, in my semi-hallucinatory state, was a prison where I was being held against my will. Rhoda Glickman, a good and lasting friend I bonded with during my Washington, D.C. days, and Mara Gay, a friend from my New York City days have my everlasting gratitude for helping me get through to the other side.

Several good friends generously gave me their thoughtful comments on the pages and pages of initial writing that inundated them as I sent drafts and asked for feedback. They helped me improve the narrative immeasurably. Linda Monk, my close friend from our days studying political science at Ole Miss, is a constitutional scholar and author of *The Bill of Rights: A User's Guide*, which won the American Bar Association's Silver Gavel Award, its highest honor for books about the law. Linda was my personal "users guide" to the initial approach to the book. Her insights helped shape my emerging ideas about penis politics: the role of power, women, men, racism, sexism, love and hate.

Jan Rothschild is my soul sister from the South, a lover of art who worked for the Corcoran and Whitney museums and others, with a deep appreciation for storytelling who is herself one of the best I know. Jan was another constant companion during my recovery and helped me be me again.

I met Ross Garber after we both traded the stresses of the Northeast for the languid heat of New Orleans. Ross, who teaches law at Tulane when he is not advising the nation's leading political figures on their legal exposures or explaining the law on CNN (he stays busy), told me to decide who the reader is to sharpen the narrative. Find your inner journalist again, suggested Ross, and focus on the lede. Thank you all.

I've found strength and companionship from several coteries of women in Mississippi, Washington, D.C., and New York. Like my high school coterie, we joined together to cry, laugh, pout, fuss and brag and live. Laura

Hamilton, Myriam Kane, Marie-Thérèse Rancourt, Mary Smith, Mary Cassidy, Neetu Venkatraman and Argelia Iracema Gonzalez (Ida) were my workout coterie. They empowered me to not only be stronger and faster before and after the accident but also be as emotionally stable as possible. My coterie of City Hall press secretaries cited in the book, younger and more energetic than me, will always sit in my pocket of memories, along with Sara Stroup from my DNC days and Betty Jo Hines, now Boyd, Renee Rappaport and Lynn Jenkins from my Capitol Hill and Mississippi political days. And, of course, my coterie of girlfriends deep down South, Janice, Maggie and Libby.